MILITARY LODGES.

THE APRON AND THE SWORD,

OR

FREEMASONRY UNDER ARMS;

BEING AN ACCOUNT OF

LODGES IN REGIMENTS AND SHIPS OF WAR,

AND OF

FAMOUS SOLDIERS AND SAILORS

(OF ALL COUNTRIES),

WHO HAVE BELONGED TO THE SOCIETY.

TOGETHER WITH

*Biographies of Distinguished Military and Naval Brethren, and Anecdotes
showing the Influence of Masonry in Warfare.*

BY

ROBERT FREKE GOULD,

(LATE 31ST FOOT, BARRISTER-AT-LAW),

PAST SENIOR GRAND DEACON OF ENGLAND,

P.M. NOS. 92 AND 2,076, LONDON; 153, GIBRALTAR; 570, SHANGHAI;
AND 743, 1ST BATT. EAST SURREY REGIMENT, &C.

Author of "The History of Freemasonry," and other Works.

London

Military Lodges: The Apron and the Sword
Robert Freke Gould

A Cornerstone Book
Published by Cornerstone Book Publishers

Cornerstone Book Publishers
New Orleans, LA
www.cornerstonepublishers.com

First Cornerstone Edition - 2014

ISBN: 161342177X
ISBN-13: 978-1-61342-177-2

MADE IN THE USA

PREFACE.

Like, or find fault ; do as your pleasures are :
Now good, or bad, 'tis but the chance of war.

—Troilus & Cressida.

A short account of Sea and Field Lodges has been given in a previous work (*History of Freemasonry*, Chapter XXX.) ; and in the present one, the curious and interesting subject of " Masonry under Arms" has been dealt with on an enlarged scale.

In the preparation of this volume I have received valuable assistance from W. H. Rylands, who has kindly perused the proof sheets, and to whose judicious counsel I owe much : Lieutenant-General Sir Charles Warren : Vice-Admiral A. H. Markham ; G. W. Speth ; W. J. Hughan ; John Lane ; W. J. Chetwode Crawley ; E. Conder ; Rev. C. H. Malden ; L. de Malczovich ; and C. Kupferschmidt, all of whom are members of my own Lodge (*Quatuor Coronati*, No. 2,076).

Particular acknowledgments are also due to Admiral of the Fleet the Hon. Sir Henry Keppel : D. Murray Lyon, Grand Secretary, Scotland : H. E. Flavelle, Deputy Grand Secretary, Ireland ; H. Sadler, Sub-Librarian, Grand Lodge of England : G. W. Bain ; William Officer ; D. C. Wills ; F. C. Crossle ; T. J. Mitchell ; and Major R. H. Murdoch.

For German facts I am largely indebted to Grand Master Carl Wiebe, of Hamburg ; Mathias Hildebrandt ; and Dr. W. Begemann.

In the New World the friends who have chiefly assisted me are E. T. Schultz, the Historian of Maryland ; Past Grand Masters J. H. Graham (Quebec) ; Sereno D. Nickerson (Massachusetts) ; T. S. Parvin (Iowa) ; and last, though by no means least, General John Corson Smith (Illinois).

THE AUTHOR.

WOKING,
October 1, 1899.

CONTENTS.

CHAPTER I.

CHAPTER II.

CHAPTER III.

CHAPTER IV.

CHAPTER VIII.

INDEX.

ERRATA.

Page 37. line 21, *to read*, author of *L'Esprit des Lois*.

" 47. lines 27. 28, Lodge No. 52 was attached to the 37th
(and *not* to the 22nd) Foot.

" 89. line 20, *to read*. John A. Rawlings.

.. 108. line 23, *after* " who were Masons," *to read*. and at the
recommendation of the Deputy Grand Master, the money
was sent to Major-General Kingsley, etc.

" 113. line 19, *for* when, *read* where.

" 132. line 7. the indication is to p. 108, *not* p. 26.

ADDENDA.

Pages 101—108—The name of Lieutenant-General Sir James
Outram. " The Bayard of India," should be added to the
roll of " British Freemasons who have commanded armies
in the field."

.. 201. 205—French Military Lodges in America :—At a meeting
of Solomon's Lodge, No. I., Poughkeepsie (New York),
held January 13th, 1783, " Brother Tachen, Master of St.
John's of Jerusalem Lodge, in the French Army. attended
as a visitor." A similar entry occurs in the minutes of a
subsequent meeting on January 15th.

MILITARY LODGES.

CHAPTER I.

History, in every age, is only popular among a few thoughtful men. It was scarcely known or understood in the early ages of the world, but the place of History was everywhere supplied by Myths and Legends.

—DE GROOT.

ACCORDING to a learned divine of the last century, who is justly esteemed as the Father of Masonic History, "the Free-Masons had always a book in Manuscript called the Book of Constitutions, containing not only the Charges and regulations, but also the History of Architecture from the Beginning of Time."

Of these Manuscript Constitutions many ancient copies are still in existence, and as a written tradition, the Legend of the Craft, or Story of the Guild, is coeval with the early part of the fifteenth century.

The Legend recites that Masonry (or Geometry) had its origin before "Noah's Flood," after which it came into great prominence at the building of the Tower of Babel. Nimrod, the mighty hunter and warrior King, was himself a Mason, and at the foundation of the city of Nineveh sent sixty craftsmen to assist in its construction.

The next military commander who took the Masons under his protection was David, to whom succeeded the "Wise King," who finished the Temple which his father had begun.

At the building of King Solomon's Temple there was a "curious man" called Naymus Graecus, whose days were

B

indeed long in the land, as the adventurous Greek, having completed his studies at Jerusalem, afterwards abandoned the Orient and passed into France, where he taught the Science of Masonry to Charles Martel.

The name of this patriarch, which is supposed by some authorities to be a corruption of "Marcus Grecus," whose writings in the ninth (or thirteenth) century disclose the secret of manufacturing gunpowder, appears under every variety of spelling in the written traditions or Manuscript Constitutions of the Freemasons, and is always allied with that of Charles Martel. But the instructor of the Hammer Bearer in Masonic lore must ever remain a very mythical personage, and it will be difficult to extend our belief beyond the supposition that some one skilled in the Greek or Jewish learning may have taught the art of fortification, in a rudimentary form, to the conqueror in the extraordinary series of obstinate conflicts which are collectively denominated the battle of Tours.

The first English Mason is said to have been St. Alban, after whose death came great wars, so that the good Rule of Masonry was destroyed until the time of King Athelstan, who brought the land into rest and peace, and built many great works.

The mightiest warrior who ever sat upon the throne of Saxon England, like the Saviour of Christendom, Charles Martel, and other military patrons of the Craft of earlier date, loved Masons well. But his son Edwin loved them better still, and procured for them from the King, his father, a charter or commission to hold every year an Assembly, and to correct within themselves Defaults and Trespasses that were done in the Craft. Edwin himself held an Assembly at York, and from that day to this the manners of Masons have been kept and observed.

So far the History of Masonry, as recorded in the old Manuscript Constitutions of many centuries ago, and without looking too far back into the mists of antiquity, certain reasons may be assigned why the names of those valiant soldiers, the stout-hearted Charles Martel, and our own "Glorious Athelstan," have been accorded such prominence in the traditions of the Freemasons.

About the year 1260, Etienne Boileau, Provost of Paris during the reign of St. Louis, codified in his *Livre des Métiers*, the customs of a hundred Craft Guilds in that Capital. Among the rules for the building trades there was the following :—

"The mortarers are free of Watch duty, and all stone-masons since the time of Charles Martel, as the wardens (*preudomes*) have heard say, from father to son."

We thus see that, as early as the thirteenth century, a tradition was current in France that Charles Martel had conferred special favours upon the stonemasons. It is, therefore, not a little singular that the English Manuscript Constitutions should also pointedly allude to the conquerer at Tours as a great patron and protector of Masonry. This community of tradition, which pervaded the minds of the mediæval Masons in Gaul and Britain, is a remarkable fact, and it confirms the opinion of those writers by whom it is affirmed that, at the request of certain Anglo-Saxon Kings, stonemasons were sent to England by Charles Martel.

With regard to the British tradition, the circumstance of Athelstan having been the first King of all England, may perhaps be considered as the most natural fountain-head from which a legendary belief in the grant of a Royal Charter to the Masons can be supposed to have arisen. It is, moreover, a well-established fact that the name of Athelstan, by virtue of his laws and charters, became a favourite one as a legendary guild patron.

No period of Anglo-Saxon history was more glorious or is less known than the reign of Athelstan, but that the great King had no son, at least in the Royal line, is satisfactorily attested by the general agreement on this point of the early chroniclers.

We should, however, do well to recollect, that the chief heroes of romance are not in general ideal beings, but moral heroes, formed of various real persons whose deeds have been combined, and attributed to one single individual.

Thus, by many of the Frankish romancers, the exploits of all the Charleses of the race, from the time of the Hammer Bearer, were ascribed to Charlemagne, who was naturally supposed to be the most famous of the name.

They also sometimes mistook one Charles for another, Charles Martel, in this way, often being confused with Charles the Bald, and thereby made to figure as the grandson, instead of the grandfather of the great Emperor of the West.

Whenever stories or romances passed out of the localities where they originated, but still continued to be handed down by song and recitation, there must have been transformation of the same kind.

The minstrel or gleeman of the Anglo-Saxons sometimes forgot a few lines, or a long passage ; sometimes he lost a line or word, and was obliged to make one to supply its place, or to borrow one which his memory might supply, and at other times he changed particular passages to suit the occasion or to please his own fancy.

The "Old Constitutions" are very strikingly in accord with regard to Edwin being the patron, and York the traditional centre of early British Masonry.

That the Edwin of Masonic tradition was the first Christian King of Northumberland cannot be positively affirmed, but the balance of probability inclines strongly in that direction.

St. Edwin, King and Martyr, for the zeal and tragic fate of the great Bretwalder have inshrined his name in the Calendar, was an undoubted patron of Operative Masonry, and the cathedral of St. Peter's at York, was begun by his directions A.D. 627.

After many years, when Athelstan was on his march against the Scots, he halted at York A.D. 936, and there besought of the ministers of St. Peter's Church, who were then called *Colidei*, to offer up their prayers on behalf of himself and his expedition, promising them that, if he returned victorious, he would confer suitable honour upon the church and its ministers. Accordingly, after a successful campaign, he revisited this church, and observing that the *Colidei*, who maintained a number of poor people, had but little whereon to live, he granted to them and their successors for ever, a thrave of corn from every ploughland in the diocese of York, a donation which continued to be enjoyed until a late period.

It will be seen that two leading incidents in the Legend of the Craft are here brought into a common centre. York Minster, which Edwin founded and whose ministers Athelstan endowed.

If, indeed, in the skein of fable of which the Masonic Legend is composed, there should be a solitary thread of fact, it appears to me that we must look for it among those of our traditions which can be associated in any way with the city of York and the cathedral there.

It may be safely assumed that the foundation of the Minster Church by St. Edwin, and the victorious march of Athelstan, must have been long preserved in the memory of the people; also that these historical events would be handed down from one generation to another by song and recitation, thus leaving in the present instance hardly any room for doubt that the name and fame of each of those great soldiers continues to be commemorated in the legendary history of our Society.

But there is a still older document of the Craft than the "Constitutions" which I have just passed under review. This is best known as the Masonic Poem, or Regius MS. and dates from the early part of the fifteenth century.

It also contains a legend, but of a more fragmentary character, than is met with in the Manuscript Constitutions.

"Noah's Flood" is incidentally referred to, and the "Tower of Babylon," though, in the place of Nimrod, who is ordinarily associated with this edifice, we meet with Nebuchadnezzar. No mention is made of David, Solomon, Naymus Grecus, Charles Martel, St. Alban, the city of York, or even of Prince Edwin, but the introduction of Masonry into England is stated to have taken place in the time of "Good King Athelstan," whose Statutes and Assembly are noticed at some length.

A distinctive feature of the Poem, however, is the passage headed *Ars Quatuor Coronatorum*, which is an invocation of the "Holy Martyres Fowre," the tutelary saints of the building trades, an outline of whose story may be given in a few words.

During the reign of the Emperor Diocletian, five masons, or stone-squarers (*mirificos in arte quadrataria*) refused to

execute the statue of a pagan god (*Æsculapius*), and in consequence were put to death. Other artists were found who
performed the work for the Emperor. On the return of
Diocletian to Rome, he commanded that all the soldiers in
that city should march past and throw incense over the
altar of Æsculapius. Four officers, however, who were
Cornicularii, declined, as being contrary to their principles,
having embraced the Christian faith, and they also suffered
death. The martyrdom of the five is supposed to have
taken place on the 8th of November, A.D., 298, and of the
four on the same day in 300, though by some authorities these
dates are brought down to A.D. 302 and 304 respectively.

The nine were eventually interred in the same spot, a
single festival, November 8th, being set apart for the five
whose names had been preserved, and for the four who were
only known by their military rank. Upon the latter, Pope
Melchiades — A.D. 310 — bestowed the title of *Quatuor
Coronati*, or Four Crowned Ones, by which they are
described in the ancient Missals and other formularies of
public devotions, though in conjunction with the Five, who
are referred to by name, and as Holy Martyrs.

In the seventh century, Pope Honorius I. erected a
handsome church, in the form of a basilica, to the memory
of the Four, out of the ruins of a temple of Diana, on the
Coelian Hill. Into this, the church of the *Quatuor Coronati*,
were removed, A.D. 848, the remains of the Nine Martyrs.
They were interred in an oratory beneath the altar. The
relics of the Four Soldiers were placed in two sarcophagi on
either side, and in two others the remains of the Five
Masons. Hence has arisen a certain amount of confusion,
and the Four officers instead of the Five Masons have become
the patron saints of the building trades, while the occupation of the Five has survived under the name of the Four.

The church, which still exists, now bears the name of the
Quattro Incoronati; according to some authorities *Incoronati*
in modern Italian being identical with the *Coronati* of
mediæval Latin; while by others the word is supposed to
be a corrupt form of the military term *Cornicularii*, which
has been brought back into the Latin from the Italian as
Coronati.

It has also been suggested that as there were two classes of decorated soldiers in the Roman Army, the higher being known as *Coronati* and the lower as *Cornicularii*, so it may very probably have happened that the Four received a posthumous brevet at the hands of the faithful, a supposition which gains further strength if we bear in mind that crowns of martyrdom are also implied by the word *Coronati*.

However this may be, it is at least certain that when associations of workmen were formed in the Middle Ages, according to the fashion of the times they chose patron saints, and that the building trades selected the *Quatuor Coronati*, or Four Crowned Martyrs, as presenting the nearest approach to men of their own calling.

Thus, in the ordinances of the Strasburg Fraternity of Stonemasons, 1459, will be found the following invocation:—"In the name of the Father, and of the Son, and of the Holy Ghost, and of our gracious Mother Mary, and also of her blessed servants, the Holy Four Crowned Martyrs of everlasting memory"

A similar and almost identical invocation is prefixed to the Torgau Ordinances of 1462, and in both instances it will be apparent that the military calling of the Four has been forgotten, while they have had ascribed to them the trade of the Five, who are not mentioned at all.

That the legend of the Four Crowned Martyrs must have penetrated into Britain at a very early date is quite clear, as we find it recorded by Bede, in his *Historia Ecclesiastica*, that there was a church in existence at Canterbury dedicated to the *Quatuor Coronati*, A.D. 619.

They are also mentioned, as already observed, and inferentially as the Patron Saints of the Masons, in the oldest document of the English Craft, the Regius MS. or Masonic Poem, dating from the early part of the fifteenth century.

After this they disappear from British Masonic history or tradition. though as we have seen, their memory continued to be cherished until a much later date by the Stonemasons of Germany.

But as a period of more than a century-and-a-half separates the Manuscript Constitutions (as written documents) from the Poem, the omission of any allusion in the former, either to the Blessed Virgin or the Four Saints, is easily understood when we consider that such invocations in a Protestant country during the last quarter of the sixteenth century—and no dated form of the old Constitutions can claim a higher antiquity than A.D. 1583—would have been inconsistent with the principles of the Reformation.

The fact, however, remains, that during the splendour of Mediæval Operative Masonry, and until the period of its decay, the legendary Patron Saints of the building trades, were those soldiers and martyrs—the *Quatuor Coronati.*

In passing from legend to history, the Collegia which we know from inscriptions to have existed in Britain during its occupation by the Roman legions, are said to have been the progenitors of the Saxon Guilds ; and from the latter, it is further stated that the Mediæval Operative Masons, and subsequently the modern Freemasons, can trace a direct descent.

But in the first place it is very doubtful whether the Saxon Guilds were descended from, or were even imitations of the Roman Collegia. Nor do organised bodies of Masons seem to have arisen until long after the appearance of guilds among the other trades.

The reason is obvious, the necessity of moving from place to place as work called them, would long preclude their having associations such as those by which the other trades were strengthened and controlled, and the essence of which was (as in the case of the Collegia) a local habitation. Hence, I am obliged to pronounce, however reluctantly, against the popular theory that the germs of our present Freemasonry were introduced into this country by the legions of Imperial Rome.

The architectural achievements of great soldiers in most nations of Europe and Asia, though presenting a tempting theme, is one upon which I can do no more than bestow a passing glance. There is documentary evidence which proves beyond dispute, that in the eighth century Charlemagne (grandson of Charles Martel) invited Masons and other Craftsmen from every country of Europe in which they were established, to erect his magnificent church at Aix la Chapelle.

Other examples might be freely cited, but a selection has to be made, and I shall therefore next instance David I. of Scotland, in whose reign many bishoprics were founded and enlarged, and to the same time, also, belong the religious houses of Holyrood, Melrose, Jedburgh, Kelso, Dryburgh, Newbattle, and Kinross. Of this King, we are told that the Scottish Masons " worshipped him as their beneficent Grand Master," a tradition which I shall do no more than relate ; but it is certain, at all events, that the munificence, or rather the prodigality of David in rearing ecclesiastical edifices, seriously impoverished the royal revenue. An old chronicler observes :—" King James the First, quhen he com to Davidis sepulture at Dunfermeling, said, ' he was ane soir sanct for the crown,' as he wald mene, that King David left the Kirk ouir riche, and the Crown ouir pure." As a military commander, David appears to have shown great ability and resource, though the glory of his earlier campaigns has been somewhat obscured by the signal defeat which he sustained at the famous " Battle of the Standard," near Northallerton, in 1138.

Passing to our own Richard " Cœur de Lion," if we may believe the historian of the Holy War, the conqueror of Saladin, built the walls of Acre, Porphyra, Ascalon, and Joppa.

A later English King, Edward I., who also took the cross, built many towers and castles on his return, which in form and strength were imitations of what he had actually seen in the Levant and the Holy Land.

This brings in the Crusaders, whose influence, both on Eastern and Western art, was great and lasting. Seven hundred years ago Palestine must have been as thickly covered with churches as England is now.

In 1187 Jerusalem was captured by Saladin, and the Christians were soon after expelled from the greater part of the Holy Land, though Antioch was not taken until 1268, nor Acre until 1291. Thus there were driven back into Germany, France, and Britain, thousands of skilled men accustomed to work under the guidance of the Crusaders.

It may be next observed, that most of the characteristic signs now called Masons' Marks were originally developed at a very early period in the East, and have been used as distinguishing signs, of some kind, from the middle ages down to the present time. They appear to have been introduced into this country in the first quarter of the twelfth century, or many years after the conquest of Jerusalem by the Crusaders.

A peculiar kind of toolmarking was, however, used in the East from very ancient times, and this was not introduced into England until the end of the twelfth century, the opening period of our beautiful Early English Architecture, when it quickly superseded another style, whose origin had been in the West.

As so well summed up by my friend, Professor Hayter Lewis :—" There was a distinct style of Masonry as well as of Architecture both in England and Palestine at about the middle of the twelfth century. Also, there was another peculiar type of Masonry and toolmarks of an earlier date which was scarcely known in this country until about the time when the Crusaders were driven out of Palestine, that is in 1187. The architecture of the Crusaders in Palestine was mainly designed and carried out under the superintendence of Western architects and masons, and there was a strong Eastern influence in the English Masonry of the thirteenth century after the return of the Crusaders."

Before that time, and during the early period of the Norman Style of architecture, France and England went hand in hand in its progress, but after the expulsion from Palestine, French and English art went quite different ways and from different centres.

After this we have a school of art distinctly English, and in the opinion of the eminent authority whose remarks I am transcribing, it must have been ruled by some such central body as the Freemasons.

Restricting, however, the field of inquiry, and passing to Military Architecture, it may be observed that what has been appropriately termed the style of the Crusaders, was introduced by Edward I. in 1272, and the style of Windsor, by Edward III. in 1350.

Many of the Barons who had acquired wealth by the ransom of prisoners taken at Poictiers and Cressy, were proud to apply it to the decoration and enlargement of their castles, as the example the King had shown at Windsor, excited in them a rivalry of imitation.

Nor was the construction of a castle a matter of mere ordinary skill. These edifices both in England and abroad were erected on scientific principles well known and regularly applied. We may suppose a mediæval castle, fully garrisoned, to resemble a modern man-of-war, in the arrangement of the different parts, the complete occupation of space, and the perfect command of every division of it.

The splendid reign of Edward III. was an era very favourable to architectural improvement; works were commenced by him at Windsor about 1350, and a few years afterwards, at the suggestion, it is said, of the Kings of France and Scotland, who were detained there as prisoners of war, he was induced to extend the castle, and in a manner that could scarcely have been foreseen by his advisers, if we may credit Stow, who relates that our English Soldier-King approved the sayings of his captives, "adding pleasantly, 'that he would enlarge the castle, and the charges thereof should be borne with their two ransoms.' as after it came to pass."

The works were afterwards proceeded with under William of Wykeham, and artisans were summoned from several counties by writs of Edward III. At this period, it has been affirmed, the Masons entered into a combination not to work without increased wages, and agreed upon certain signs and tokens by which they might know one another, and render mutual assistance against being impressed.

They further agreed not to work at all, unless as Freemen, and on their own terms, in consequence of which they were called *Free Masons*. There is probability about much of this, but so far as I am aware, no authority, beyond the circumstance that writs of impressment in connection with the re-building of Windsor Castle, are mentioned by Ashmole, in his *History of the Order of the Garter*.

But while Operative Masonry certainly flourished under

the House of Plantagenet, the closing years of this dynasty witnessed the setting in of its decay.

In 1337, the Hundred Years' War with France began, and in 1349 occurred the first visitation of the Black Death. About half the labourers in England were swept away.

The population before the mortality was four millions, a total which was not again reached until the reign of Elizabeth. Then followed the peasant revolt of 1381, and early in the next century, under the successors of the Plantagenets, commenced the long and savage contest for supremacy, between the respective adherents of the Red Rose of Lancaster and the White Rose of York.

During the continuance of the struggle the nation went back in many ways from the refinement of the fourteenth century. The population still further dwindled. The arts lost their vigour and beauty.

Finally, in the sixteenth century, the Reformation struck the death-blow of mediæval architecture, which, with the monasteries, had long been decaying, and both, perhaps would soon have expired in a natural way, had they not been prematurely extinguished.

It is reasonable to suppose that Masonry, as a speculative science, declined or fell into decay, *pari passu*, with Masonry as an operative art, or to put it in another way, let me state for the benefit of those readers who are not of our fraternity, that while the symbolism of the Craft is of great and undoubted antiquity, only a very fragmentary portion of what must have formerly existed has come down to us.

After the Reformation, no more churches were built, at least for a long period of time. The builders almost died out, and the unions of these men, having lost their *raison d'être*, naturally dissolved.

A few, however, from causes we cannot trace, contrived to escape the great cataclysm of the Reformation, and these Unions or Lodges we find taking a new departure about the year 1717. But by this time the Masonic bodies appear under a new guise. While still retaining many forms and ceremonies, which they had derived from their direct ancestors, the working Masons, we find that the connection with Operative Masonry had almost come to an end, and that Speculative (or Symbolical) Masonry, with a remnant of the old forms, had been substituted in its place.

Evidence, if indeed not entirely wanting, is nevertheless wholly insufficient to supply more than an occasional glimpse of the way in which the old system was gradually succeeded, and ultimately supplanted by the new. The earliest authentic record of a non-operative being a member of a Masonic Lodge is contained in a Minute of the Lodge of Edinburgh, under the date of June the 8th, 1600. John Boswell, the Laird of Auchinleck (ancestor of the well-known biographer of Dr. Johnson) was present at the meeting, and like his operative brethren, he attested the minute by his mark. But that Speculative or Symbolic, flourished side by side with Operative Masonry, at a much earlier period, may be safely inferred from the solemn declaration of a Presbyterian synod in 1652, that ministers of that persuasion had been Freemasons "in the purest tymes of this Kirke," the reference probably being to the years immediately following the Reformation of 1560, and without doubt considerably antedating the introduction of Episcopacy in 1610.

In the South of England, it is only in connection with the Mason's Company of the City of London, that we meet with any actual proof of the existence of any form of Symbolical or Speculative Masonry in the early part of the seventeenth century.

About the year 1530, this Company ceased to use their old title of "Fellowship of Masons," and became known as the "Company of ffree-masons," a title which was retained until 1653. Most of the records are unfortunately missing, but from an old book of accounts, which has fortuitously been preserved, it is made clear that previously to 1620, and inferentially from a more remote past, certain brethren who were members of the Company in conjunction, it is supposed, with others who were not, met in Lodge at Masons' Hall, London, and were known to the Company as the "Accepted Masons."

Seven persons were received into the "Acception" or Lodge, in 1620-21, all of whom were already members of

the Company, which is sufficient to prove that the two
bodies were distinct associations, although, as the accounts
show, the latter had entire control over the former and its
finances.

Of this, indeed, there is a more conspicuous example in
the case of Nicholas Stone, the King's Master Mason, who,
though Master of the Company in 1633, and again in 1634,
was not enrolled among the "Accepted Masons" of the
Lodge, until 1639.

In Scotland, the holder of a similar, if not identical
office, had become a member of the Speculative wing of the
Society at a slightly earlier date Sir Anthony Alexander,
second son of the first Earl of Stirling, Master of Work to
the King, together with his elder brother, Viscount Canada,
and Sir Alexander Strachan, was admitted into the Lodge
of Edinburgh as a fellow of Craft, on the 3rd of July, 1634.

Lord Canada, then Sir William Alexander, had been
constituted some years previously, Knight Admiral of Nova
Scotia, and sailed for that country in May, 1628, in command of a squadron of four vessels carrying upwards of
seventy colonists, who were safely landed at Port Royal.
The admiral and his officers were regularly commissioned
"to make prize of all French or Spanish Ships, and to
displant the French."

The third son of the first Earl of Stirling, Henrie Alexander, who succeeded Sir Anthony as General Warden and
Master of Work to the King, became a member of the Lodge
of Edinburgh, in 1638.   He was subsequently, for a time at
least, like his eldest brother, an officer in the Royal Navy,
and served as such under Lord Aboyne, in 1639, when that
nobleman, in the interest of Charles I., sailed into the roads
of Aberdeen with three ships of war to resist the upholders
of the Covenant.

Among the members of the other branch of the profession of arms who were received into Masonry in the
Lodge of Edinburgh, the first appears to have been David
Ramsay, whose admission is recorded in a minute of August,
1637.

This soldier of fortune, who was equerry to the elder son
of James I., seems to have obtained, after the death of

Prince Henry, a commission as captain of a company in the Low Countries, and in 1624 the colonelcy of one of the Scots Regiments which served under Count Mansfield, in Holland. Two years later he figures in an entirely new role, as we find him the bearer of a letter to the English King from the ambassador to the President of the Rosy Cross, of which an amusing account is given by Dr. Birch in his *Court and Times of Charles I.*

It was by the advice of the same "ambassador" that Frederick, the unfortunate Elector-Palatine, is said to have accepted the Crown of Bohemia, which, if true, may tend to explain why Ramsay was selected as an envoy by the Rosicrucians, since we have it on the authority of Bishop Burnet, that he was strongly recommended to Charles I. by the King of Bohemia, "as one who had served him faithfully in Germany." After this, however, he fell into disgrace, and is referred to in the description by Sir Walter Scott of the last trial that took place in the old Court of Chivalry.

Whether, indeed, the British officers who served on the Continent during the Thirty Years' War, were indoctrinated to any considerable extent with the mystical tenets of the Rosicrucians, must remain a mystery, but there is evidence to show that a secret, or at least an oath-bound society, with customs approximating to those which are severally ascribed to the Hermetical Philosophers and the Freemasons, was established in an English Regiment serving abroad, and by it introduced into this country. In a letter from John Chamberlain, a gentleman and scholar, who was very well informed of what was going on in the world around him, to his intimate friend Sir Dudley Carleton, the writer, December 6th, 1623, observes :—

There is a crew or knot of people discovered. who, under colour of good fellowship, have made an association, and taken certain oaths and orders devised among themselves : specially to be true and faithful to the Society, and conceal one another's secrets, but mixed with a number of other ridiculous toys, to disguise the matter; as having a Prince whom they called Ottoman ; wearing of blue or yellow ribbons in their hats or elsewhere ; having certain nicknames, as *Tityre-tu*, or such like, for their several fraternities : and many other odd conceits. the bottom whereof is not yet discovered, though divers of them

have been examined. and some committed. as one of the
Windsor's. and a few others. Most of them are young gentlemen
who used to flock to taverns. thirty or forty in a company. This
combination began first in the Low Countries. in the Lord Vaux s
Regiment. and hath since spread itself here to the number of
eight score already known. What mischief may lurk under the
mask. God knows. But sure they are confident. and presumed
much of themselves to carry it so openly.

To return, however, to the Lodge of Edinburgh, Alexander
Hamilton, General of the Artillery and Master of the
Ordnance and Ammunition. was admitted as " Fellow and
Master of the Craft " May 20th, 1640. This officer held a
high command in the expeditionary force sent from Scotland
in 1631 to serve under Gustavus Adolphus, King of Sweden,
during the Thirty Years' War.

General Hamilton was present with the Scottish Army at
Newcastle in 1641, and together with other members of the
Lodge of Edinburgh, he took part in the *first initiation on
English soil.* of which any of the surrounding circumstances
have come down to us.

The Scottish troops having crossed the Tweed and
defeated the Royalists at Newburn, had occupied Newcastle,
where they remained during the negotiations that were
proceeding. A minute of the Lodge—" At Neucastell the
20th day off May, 1641," records the admission of " Mr.
the Right Honerabell Mr. Robert Moray, General Quarter-
master to the Armie off Scotlan."

From this we may conclude that there were members of
the Lodge of Edinburgh who accompanied the forces of the
Covenanters in 1641, and that it was at the hands of these
militant craftsmen that the then Quartermaster-General of
the Army of Scotland was made a Mason. Two months
later Newcastle was evacuated by the Scottish forces, and
on returning to Edinburgh it is supposed that the brethren
by whom Moray was admitted (at a distance from the
Lodge) must have reported the proceeding, which being
approved was recorded in the minute-book and attested by
the signatures of General Hamilton and the others who
took part in it, as well as by that of the newly-received
member.

Both Hamilton and Moray—the former having in the
interim commanded the artillery on the winning side at the

battle of Marston Moor—were again present in the Lodge
of Edinburgh in 1647, and signed the proceedings on the
occasion of the admission of "William Maxwell, Doctor
of Fisik," an officer in the King's service, whose name takes
the first place of all on the bead-roll of eminent medical
brethren who have shed a lustre on our Society.

Before holding the appointment of Quartermaster-General
in the Army of the Covenanters, Sir Robert Moray (or
Murray) served with distinction in France under Richelieu.
He was with the Scottish Army when Charles I. sought
shelter in the camp of his fellow-countrymen, in May, 1646,
and planned a scheme for his escape, which, but for the
King's want of resolution, must have been crowned with
success.   After the Restoration he was Secretary of State
for Scotland and one of the founders, and the first President
of the Royal Society.

He was greatly esteemed by men of all shades of opinion,
but I shall pass over the encomiums of his friends in order
to find room for what was said of him by Anthony Wood
with reference to his love for the occult sciences.   According
to this diligent, though somewhat splenetic writer, " He
was a single man, an abhorrer of women, a most renowned
chymist, a great patron of the Rosicrucians, and an
excellent mathematician."

It may be here conveniently referred to, that according
to a rather popular theory, the mystical knowledge or
symbolism of the Masonic Craft is supposed to have been
introduced into the Lodges by the Hermetical Philosophers
or Rosicrucian adepts, whose studies appear to have
embraced the same objects, and between whom the only
difference seems to have been one of title, the former
appellation being the earlier of the two, but the latter
(owing to the alleged existence of a Society of Rosicrucians)
becoming the more common term by which the votaries of
the "Chymical Art," or "Sons of the Fire," were
alluded to.

It is well known that women were the aversion of the
older school of Hermeticists and Rosicrucians, and we may,
therefore, conclude that the abhorrence which Sir Robert
Moray is said to have entertained for the fair sex must have

C

been an unfortunate result arising out of his studies as an alchemistical philosopher. No such characteristic could possibly have been the effect of his training in the profession of arms, nor can we credit for an instant that he acquired it through participation in the fellowship of the Craft. On this point, indeed, the words of the old song, which have come down to us with a very respectable flavour of antiquity, will be regarded by all true believers in Masonic tradition as being absolutely conclusive—

> " No mortal can more
> The ladies adore
> Than a Free and an Accepted Mason."

It is greatly to be regretted that while the minutes and records of several Scottish Lodges, dating from the seventeenth (and in a solitary instance, the sixteenth) century, have been preserved, we meet with none whatever which relate to or illustrate the proceedings of English Lodges until a much later period.

Of the existence, indeed, of an actual living Freemasonry in the South, possessing at the very least an equal antiquity with that prevailing in the North, there cannot be a doubt.

But the evidence upon which we depend is meagre in the extreme.

That there were Accepted or Speculative Masons in London in the opening years of the seventeenth century is amply proved by the records of the Company to which I have previously referred ; but there is only a bare mention of a few names, and the minutes of the Lodge or " Acception " have wholly disappeared. The next evidence in point of date is supplied by the " Diary of Elias Ashmole," from which I extract the following :—

1646. Oct. 16. 4.30 p.m.—I was made a Free Mason at Warrington. in Lancashire. with Coll. Henry Mainwaring, of Karincham. in Cheshire.

At this time Ashmole was a Captain in Lord Ashley's Regiment, and also Comptroller of the Ordnance on the King's side : while Mainwaring, of whom there is frequent mention in the bulletins of the Civil War, was a staunch Parliamentarian.

The Diary also gives " the names of those that were then of the Lodge," which may perhaps amply justify the conclusion that the members of it had been in the habit of associating in Masonic Fellowship for some time ; but even if we suppose that the Lodge was really formed or created for the purpose of admitting Ashmole and Mainwaring into the fraternity, the attendance of other gentlemen on the occasion, for it is a very noteworthy fact that not a single Operative Mason appears to have been present on the afternoon of the 16th of October, 1646, shows with the utmost clearness that English Symbolical Masonry must have had a much earlier existence, and points in the direction of a Speculative ascendency (over the Operative element) having become well established, at least at Warrington, in that year.

It is singular, nevertheless, that although many years before the events at Newcastle and Warrington in 1641 and 1646, there must have been gentlemen Freemasons in the Southern Kingdom, the first three of whose admission to the Craft any particulars are forthcoming, were members of the military profession.

Of Ashmole, Anthony Wood, who seldom errs on the side of panegyric, says :—" He was the greatest *virtuoso* and *curioso* that ever was known or read of in England before his time. *Uxor Solis* took up its habitation in his breast, and in his bosom the great God did abundantly store up the treasures of all sorts of wisdom and knowledge. Much of his time, when he was in the prime of his years, was spent in Chymistry, in which faculty being accounted famous did worthily receive the title of *Mercuriophilus Anglicus.*"

The inducements which led Ashmole, Mainwaring, and other men of their class to become Freemasons have been the subject of much curious speculation, and more than a century ago, Nicolai, a learned bookseller of Berlin, advanced a singular hypothesis. It was, that English Masonry had its origin in the " New Atlantis " of Lord Bacon, and was the actual product of an Hermetical and Rosicrucian fraternity, of which Elias Ashmole and others were leading members. " It was established at Warrington

c 2

in 1646, and afterwards, in order to conceal their mysterious designs, the members were admitted into the Masons' Company of London, and took the name of Freemasons."

The theory survives, though in a modified form, and at the present day there are many who believe that because the Alchemists, Hermeticists, and Rosicrucians had no association (or organization) of their own in England or Scotland, they joined the Masonic Lodges in order to meet one another without giving rise to suspicion.

It is further supposed that to these men, or to others who inherited their opinions, we are indebted for the Third Degree and the introduction of Hermetic and other symbols into Masonry, and that they framed the three degrees of the Craft (as we now have them) for the purpose of communicating their doctrines, veiled by their symbols, to those fitted to receive them, and gave to all others trite moral explanations of them which they could comprehend.

If these views are sustainable, it necessarily follows that a distinction must be drawn between the Morally-Symbolic Masonry of current date and the Philosophically-Symbolic Masonry of more ancient times—the former being, therefore, our "Speculative" Masonry, a system of morality veiled in symbols, and the latter something very different, in which the symbols conceal, and to the adept express, the great philosophic and religious truths of antiquity, or, it may be, the philosophic doctrines of the Hermeticists and Rosicrucians, which, as their books show, are (or were) identical.

It is, indeed, quite true that certain observances and ideas were found to be in existence and prevalent among the Masonic body in the seventeenth century. The fact is also patent (without laying undue stress on the case of David Ramsay) that Sir Robert Moray, Elias Ashmole, and very probably other students of the occult sciences were members of the Society. But evidence is entirely wanting to show that the Hermeticists or Rosicrucians ever practised among themselves any mystic or symbolical ceremonies which they could have passed on to the Freemasons, and what therefore seems incapable of proof, must be pronounced, of course, equally incapable of refutation.

Much weight has been attached to the undoubted fact that Ashmole—like Moray before him—was both an Hermetical Philosopher and a Freemason. Still, conjecture must not be allowed to take the place of evidence, and from this it is only legitimate to infer that the Freemasons had not amalgamated with any of the supposed Rosicrucians or Hermetical fraternities—of the actual existence of which there is no proof—nor that they were their actual descendants, or themselves under another name. A contrary view would, in my own opinion, be ridiculous, though in order to appease the wrath of our modern Rosicrucians, I freely admit that the subject of the Hermetic learning has lain outside my course of study, and is, perhaps, beyond my sphere of comprehension.

Before, however, passing away from Moray, Ashmole, and the associate of the latter at Warrington, Colonel Mainwaring, a few words remain to be expressed.

That these three men—Covenanter, Royalist, and Parliamentarian—were the earliest Freemasons of whose initiation on English soil any details are forthcoming, I have already shown ; but it is also worthy of being recollected that all the admissions occurred in the heat of the great Civil War, and that each Military Brother, so received, belonged to a separate and distinct section of the forces which took part in it.

Returning to Scottish Masonry, we find that of forty-nine fellow crafts (or master masons) who belonged to the Lodge of Aberdeen in 1670, less than a quarter were of the Masons' trade. The Master was of gentle birth, and among the members were clergymen, surgeons, merchants, and three noblemen, one of whom (Lord Errol) was then an old man, and presumably, therefore, must have joined the Society at a much earlier date.

Gilbert, tenth Earl of Errol, who succeeded to the title in 1638, was Colonel of Horse in the army raised for the rescue of Charles I. from the hands of the Parliamentary party, known by the name of the " Unhappie Engagement;" and subsequently raised a regiment for the service of Charles II. James, fourth and last Earl of Dunfermline, who became a member of the same Lodge in 1679, served in his younger days under the Prince of Orange in several memorable expeditions. He joined Viscount Dundee with a troop of Horse in 1689, and fought at their head at the battle of Killiecrankie in that year.

John, seventh Earl of Cassilis, afterwards a prominent figure in the Revolution of 1688, was deacon or head, of the Lodge of Kilwinning in 1672. The same position was filled by Alexander, eighth Earl of Eglinton, in 1678, himself a staunch supporter of the Covenanters, but whose father and grandfather, in accordance with the astute policy of hedging, so well known in Scotland, had fought on opposite sides at the battle of Marston Moor. The former served with the Royalist Army, and the latter, who was surnamed " Grey-steel," for his intrepid courage, commanded the Lancers of Ayrshire, one of the Scots Cavalry Regiments in the " right wing of Horse " under Sir Thomas Fairfax.

John, eldest son of Sir Ewen Cameron of Locheil, chief of the Clan Cameron, was a member of the Lodge of Dunblane in 1696. This " theoretical " Craftsman and other leading brethren of the Lodge were prominent actors on the Stuart side in the rising of 1715.

Before leaving the seventeenth century some of the Scottish Masonic customs of that era demand a passing notice. We find that while the Lodge of Kilwinning was content to meet in the upper chamber of an ordinary dwelling-house, the Masons of Aberdeen held their Lodge in the open fields, except when it was "ill weather," on which occasions they met under shelter, but only in some house or building that was not used as a place of residence. Of what are now termed Masonic degrees, there was at this period, and for long after, only one known to the Scottish Lodges.

It comprised a form of reception in which, under an oath, apprentices received " the benefit of the Mason word, together with all that was implied in the expression."

But what the old Scottish MASON WORD was, remains unknown. It has not yet been discovered either what it was or to what extent it was in general use. Neither can it be determined whether at any given date prior to 1736 it was the same in England as in Scotland.

In both countries, during the seventeent hcentury, there was Operative as well as Speculative Membership in the Lodges, yet a difference is found which should be noted. In Scotland the Lodges existed for trade purposes, and to fulfil apparently certain Operative functions, of which the necessity may have passed away, or at least has been unrecorded in the South.

The Scottish Lodges, therefore, when we meet with them at this early period, were of an essentially Operative character, while the English Lodges of corresponding date, to the extent that there is evidence upon which we can rely, were as essentially Speculative both in their character and composition.

At the Union of the two countries in 1707 there was a marked difference between the ceremonial observances of the English and Scottish Lodges. In the Northern Kingdom the ancient symbolism of Masonry had descended to the level of the ordinary artisan, while in South Britain more of the old frame-work still existed.

A passing glance at the Freemasonry of the South, two years after the Union between the two Kingdoms, has been afforded us by a military officer (and distinguished man of letters) of the period, Captain (afterwards Sir Richard) Steele, in an essay, from which I extract the following :—

June 9. 1709.—My reason for troubling you at this present is to put a stop. if it may be. to an insinuating set of People who assume the name of Pretty Fellows. and even get new Names. They have their Signs and Tokens like Freemasons; they rail at Womankind."

Upon this evidence it will be quite clear that a Society known as the Freemasons, having certain distinct modes of recognition, must have existed in London in 1709, and there is scarcely room for doubt, from a much earlier date. It should be recollected also that, besides being a close observer of what was transpiring in London, Steele must have been fully conversant with the military customs prevailing in his day. Hence, the practice of acquiring "new Names"—referred to in the essay—may be usefully compared with a similar habit which, as already related (on the authority of a letter from John Chamberlain to Sir

Dudley Carleton), was a marked feature of the "Combina tion" that sprang up in Lord Vaux's Regiment while serving in the Low Countries. The final words of the quotation would seem to indicate that the class of persons whom Steele had in his mind, when writing his essay, must have shared the peculiar sensibility of the Rosicrucians with regard to the gentler sex, and, like the members of that shadowy fraternity, were, in theory at least, great "abhorrers of women."

The first naval officer of the "United Kingdom" who can be identified as a member of the Craft, is Admiral Robert Fairfax, who was "admitted and sworn into the honourable Society and Fraternity of Freemasons" at the city of York on the 7th of August, 1713.

This distinguished officer, who was the grandson of Sir William Fairfax, the cousin and companion in arms of the great General of the Parliamentary forces, entered the Navy in 1688, and became a post-captain in 1690. He was present in many battles and fought several gallant actions, particularly distinguishing himself during the operations off Granville, and at the taking of Gibraltar, receiving for his services in the former instance a gold medal, and in the latter a silver cup, which was presented to him by Queen Anne. He attained the rank of Vice (afterwards altered to that of Rear) Admiral, and was appointed a member of the Board of Admiralty in 1708. The next year he fixed his residence at York, and in the month following his reception into the Masonic Fraternity, he was elected as Parliamentary representative for that city.

The Admiral had become the head of the family and possessor of Steeton and Newton Kyme (in Yorkshire), in 1694, when in command of the *Ruby*, chasing privateers in the Irish Sea.

He died at Newton Kyme in 1725, being then in his sixtieth year. A good portrait of him was painted in the last years of his life. The left hand rests on a globe, and in the right he holds a pair of compasses.

Many prominent Freemasons rashly took up arms in the Jacobite risings of 1715 16. Some were executed, and others embarked for the Continent.

Among the latter were George, tenth and last of the Earls Marischals of Scotland, captain of the Scottish troop of Horse Grenadier Guards, who had served with distinction in the campaigns of Marlborough, and ended his career in the service of Frederick the Great; James Keith, his brother—as a soldier, beyond question, by far the greatest of all "Scots abroad"; John Cameron, of Locheil: and George Seton, Earl of Winton, who escaped from the Tower after sentence of death had been pronounced upon him, and was in later life Master of the famous "Roman Lodge" (founded by Scottish brethren in Rome) at the time of its suppression in 1737. It will be seen on a later page that Masonry in Russia, if not actually introduced, was established on a firm footing by the younger Keith; and if we may believe the French historians, it was by another of these exiles, James Ratcliffe, who, after his elder brother was beheaded, assumed the title of Earl of Derwentwater, that the first Lodge in France was founded at Paris in 1725.

CHAPTER II.

*Neither in ancient nor in modern times, has the schoolmaster
made a single step of progress, except by holding on to the
skirts of the soldier's coat. Regular armies gave the
first check to the barbarism of the Middle Ages, and it
was under their protection alone that arts, sciences, commerce and industry, grew up and extended in Europe.*

—MAJOR-GEN. J. MITCHELL.

ALTHOUGH of legendary Grand Masters—many of whom
were great warriors—there is no stint, the prosaic facts of
history assure us that the earliest of Grand Lodges was
established on the 24th of June, 1717. The foundation of
the Grand Lodge of England was a great event, but the
Society of Freemasons organised on a new basis made very
slow progress in public favour. Anthony Sayer, "gentleman," was the first Grand Master, while Jacob Lamball,
"carpenter," and "Captain" Joseph Elliot, were the Grand
Wardens. Sayer was succeeded by George Payne, of the
Civil Service, and the latter (in 1719) by Dr. John
Theophilus Desaguliers, an ingenious natural philosopher,
and after Elliot, the next of the Grand officers that can be
associated with the military profession, as he received,
though in later life, a commission as Chaplain in what is
now the 12th Lancers, but was then (1738) Colonel Phineas
Bowles's Regiment of Dragoons. In 1720, George Payne was
elected for a second term, after whom came the first of a
long and unbroken series of noble Grand Masters—John,
Duke of Montagu, who was installed on June 24th, 1721, when
the Society rose at a single bound into notice and esteem.

The Duke, who was then a colonel in the Army, died of
a violent fever, in July, 1749, aged fifty-nine, and at the
time of his death was Master-General of the Ordnance,
General of Horse, colonel of the 2nd Dragoon Guards,
Grand Master of the Order of the Bath, K.G., F.R.S., and a
Privy Councillor.

Of the first Noble Grand Master of Speculative Free masons, it may indeed be said that he was also the First Grand Master of Speculative Artillerists, having consolidated by Royal Charter in 1741 (when he was Master-General), the Royal Military Academy, which had been established in 1719, as a school of theoretical instruction at Woolwich. From 1741, therefore, Artillery (like Freemasonry at an earlier date) merged into a speculative science founded upon an operative art.

The Duke of Montagu was one of the most remarkable men of the period, and of the generous assistance which he rendered in time of need, both to his brethren in the Craft and his brethren in arms, many anecdotes have been related. The following, from the pen of Dr. Stukeley, appeared in one of the London journals, shortly after the death of his benefactor and friend :—

After a war concluded, when many officers were reduced to half-pay, the Duke, walking in the park, he, as he was an excellent physiognomist, saw a captain, a brave man, whom he had some knowledge of, sitting on a bench, with deep marks of sorrow and dejection on his countenance.

The Duke accosted him, and soon became acquainted with his hard case. He had a wife and four children in the country, who could not possibly be maintained on the allowance. He ordered him, on that day fortnight, to come and dine with him.

In the meantime, the Duke sent for his wife and children to town, and had them at his house at dinner on the day appointed. The captain was prodigiously surprised at the sight of them. The joy, mixed with the concern of the difficulty he had to maintain them, caused an inexplicable tumult in his breast, but the Duke dispelled the cloud, by telling him that he had been soliciting a better commission for him. He presented him with it, and with a bank note of £500, and then put on his grave air, and sat down to dinner as composedly as if he had done nothing.

This nobleman was succeeded in 1722, by Philip, Duke of Wharton, an outline of whose meteoric career will be found on a later page, and the younger peer, in the following year by James, Earl of Dalkeith,—a grandson of the unfortunate Duke of Monmouth, who, in turn, gave place to the Duke of Richmond, in 1724.

The Grand Lodge of 1717 was founded by four lodges, two of which, the "Lodge of Antiquity," and the "Royal

Somerset House and Inverness" (Nos. 1 and 4 respectively below), still exist. These bodies met in 1724 :

1. At the GOOSE AND GRIDIRON, in St Paul's Churchyard.
2. At the QUEEN's HEAD, Turnstile ; *formerly* the CROWN, in Parker's Lane.
3. At the QUEEN's HEAD, in Knave's Acre ; *formerly* the APPLE TREE, in Covent Garden.
4. At the HORNE, in Westminster ; *formerly* the RUMMER AND GRAPES, in Channel Row.

With the exception of Anthony Sayer, the Premier Grand Master, who is cited on the roll of No. 3, all the eminent persons who took any leading part in the early history of Freemasonry, immediately after the formation of a Grand Lodge, were members of No. 4. In 1724, No. 1 had twenty-two members ; No. 2, twenty-one ; No. 3, fourteen ; and No. 4, seventy-one. The three senior Lodges possessed among them no member of sufficient rank to be described as " Esquire," while in No. 4, there were ten noblemen, three honourables, four baronets or knights, two general officers, ten colonels, four officers below field rank, and twenty-four esquires. Payne and Desaguliers—former Grand Masters—together with the Rev. James Anderson—the "Father of Masonic History"—were members of this Lodge. Also Charles, second Duke of Richmond, Lennox, and Aubigny, Master of the Lodge in 1723, and Grand Master of the Society in 1724, who became a captain in the Royal Regiment of Horse Guards in 1722, Major-General in 1742, and Lieutenant-General in 1745. In 1743, he attended George II. to the scene of the war, and was present at the battle of Dettingen in that year. He afterwards accompanied the Duke of Cumberland on his expedition against the Jacobite rebels in 1745.

Henry Scott, created Earl of Deloraine in 1706, a younger son of the Duke of Monmouth and Buccleuch, was appointed to the command of a Regiment of Foot in 1707, promoted Colonel of the second troop of Horse Grenadier Guards (in succession to a more unfortunate Craftsman, George Keith, 10th and last of the Earls Marischal of Scotland) in 1715, and died a Major-General in 1730.

Lord Carmichael, captain in the Foot Guards, who succeeded his father as 3rd Earl of Hyndford in 1737, was sent on a special mission to Germany in 1741, to mediate between Frederick the Great and the Empress Maria Theresa; and also to Russia in 1744, when his skilful negotiations greatly conduced to the peace of Aix-la-Chapelle.

Sir Adolphus Oughton, who was Captain and Lieutenant in the 1st Foot Guards in 1706, and A.D.C. to the Duke of Marlborough during his retirement on the Continent in 1712, afterwards became a Brigadier-General and Colonel of the 8th Dragoons.

Sir Robert Rich, fourth Baronet, who entered the Grenadier Guards in 1700, and saw service under the Duke of Marlborough. Colonel of the 13th Light Dragoons, 1722; Lieutenant-General, 1739. Embarked for Flanders to join the Earl of Stair's Army in 1742, and fought at Dettingen in 1743. Promoted General in 1747 and Field-Marshal, November 20th, 1757.

Count La Lippe, a distinguished officer in the service of the Low Countries, who was actively employed as a Lieutenant-General at the battle of Dettingen in 1743; and Baron Dieskau, a brave military officer, afterwards Commander-in-Chief of the French troops in America during the period anterior to Montcalm, and famous for the active part he took in the wars between the English and French during that period. In his last campaign he commanded the expedition sent to defeat that of the English which was advancing to invade Canada in 1755. But though he achieved a brilliant victory over the Army of Colonel Williams, a second battle on the same day resulted in his sustaining a total defeat at the hands of Sir William Johnson (a brother Freemason), the French commander being himself made a prisoner, and also very seriously wounded.

Count Walzdorf and the Marquis Des Marches, who were also members of the Lodge, may have been, and probably were, like La Lippe and Dieskau, foreign military officers, but further details relating to their biographies have so far eluded my research.

Many other foreign noblemen were initiated in the Lodge during the Mastership of the Duke of Richmond, and among them the Marquis Du Quesne (1730), Captain in the French Royal Marine Service, who was descended from the greatest Du Quesne, Grand-Admiral of France. He was a brave and judicious Governor of Canada from 1752 to 1755, in which latter year he solicited his recall on the plea that he wished to return to active military duty.

The Duke of Wharton was Master of the Lodge at the King's Arms, St. Paul's Churchyard, and the Duke of St. Alban's of that at the Queen's Head, Bath, in 1725. Charles Beauclerk, first Duke of St. Albans, who was the son of Charles II., by Nell Gwynn, served with the Imperial Army against the Turks, and was present at the taking of Belgrade. He afterwards commanded an English regiment of horse, and in 1693 left for Flanders, where he served under William III., in the campaign of Landen. He was a gallant soldier, and much esteemed by the King.

Viscount Cobham, and the Earl of Lichfield, were also members of the Lodge at the Queen's Head.

Richard Temple—created Baron Cobham in 1714, and a Viscount in 1718—in the first year of Queen Anne's reign was appointed colonel of a regiment of foot; served in Flanders and Germany, and having particularly distinguished himself at the siege of Lisle in 1708, was sent express, by the Duke of Marlborough, to the Queen with an account of the surrender of that fortress. Major-General, 1709; Colonel of the 4th Dragoons, 1710; of the 1st Dragoons, 1715; and of the King's Dragoon Guards, 1721; Envoy Extraordinary and Plenipotentiary to the Emperor Charles VI., 1715; Commander of the Land Forces against Spain, 1719; Constable of Windsor Castle, 1716; and Field Marshal, 1742.

George, second Earl of Lichfield, was the son of Sir Edward Lee, who, on his marriage with Lady Charlotte Fitzroy, natural daughter of Charles II. by Barbara Villiers, was created Earl of Lichfield. It has been asserted that the " Merry Monarch,"

" Who never said a foolish thing. and never did a wise one,"

was himself a Freemason, of which, however, there is no

proof; but the number of his descendants, whose names appear in the Lodge lists for 1724-25, is certainly large, comprising as it does the Dukes of Richmond and St. Albans, and the Earls of Dalkeith, Lichfield, and Deloraine.

The first purely Military Lodge (of which any distinct record is forthcoming) would seem to have been the one originally numbered 51 on the lists, which was established at Gibraltar in 1728. This, however, was of a stationary character, as Ambulatory Lodges were first set on foot in a sister jurisdiction, and the practice becoming a general one under the various Grand Lodges of the British Isles, will necessitate a brief digression, wherein I shall relate the histories of those bodies, so far as may be material to a due comprehension of the general narrative.

The Grand Lodge of York was established in 1725, reconstructed in 1761, and expired about 1792. It issued a solitary Military Warrant to the 6th or Inniskilling Regiment of Dragoons in 1770.

A Grand Lodge, of which the Earl of Rosse was Grand Master, existed at Dublin in 1725. This was followed in 1726 by the Grand Lodge of Munster, Colonel the Hon. James O'Brien, Grand Master; and in 1729-30 by the Grand Lodge of Ireland—which still exists—under James, Viscount Kingston, G.M., who had previously been Grand Master of England in 1728, and Provincial Grand Master of Munster in 1729.

The Grand Lodge of Scotland was founded in 1736, and John, Earl of Crawfurd, the first Colonel of the Black Watch (now the 1st Battalion of the Royal Highlanders), would probably have been elected Grand Master had he not declined the honour. William, Earl of Home, who subsequently saw much active service, rose to the rank of Lieutenant-General, and died as Governor of Gibraltar in 1761, appears after this to have stepped into the place of Lord Crawfurd as the candidate whose election would have been most acceptable to the Lodges. Though in the result, and at the conclusion of a pre-arranged drama (the particulars of which are related at length in my *History of Freemasonry*), William St. Clair, of Roslin, a leading member of the Royal Company of Archers (now the Queen's Body Guard for Scotland), was chosen Grand Master.

This was followed by the election of Captain John Young, of the "Kilwinning Scots Arms," as Depute Grand Master, and among the other members of the Lodge at the same period were the Earls of Crawfurd, Home, Cromarty, and Kilmarnock, the two last mentioned of whom will be again referred to in connection with the Jacobite rising of 1745.

These names by no means exhaust the list of the Scottish nobility who were members of the fraternity in 1736, but a few only need be mentioned.

The Duke of Perth, initiated in the Lodge at Dundee, who, on joining the Pretender in 1745, was created Lieut.-General, and served with the Highland Army until the disaster at Culloden.

The Duke's younger and only brother, Lord John Drummond, was a member of the Lodge at Dunblane.

James, fifth Earl of Balcarres, who, having served in the Navy and obtained the rank of lieutenant, afterwards joined the rebels and was especially complimented by the Earl Marischal, by order of the Earl of Marr, for his gallantry at Sheriffmuir. Receiving a pardon, he re-entered the King's service as Lieutenant in the 2nd, or North British, Dragoons (Scots Greys), and attained high distinction as a military officer, displaying great gallantry at the battles of Dettingen and Fontenoy.

John, fourth Earl of Loudoun, who, in November, 1736, when the Grand Lodge of Scotland was erected, occupied the position of Grand Master of England, in which he had been installed in the beginning of the same year. Lord Loudoun, who was Colonel of the 50th Foot, and Governor of Edinburgh Castle, took an active part in the suppression of the rebellion of 1745; Major-General, 1755; Governor of Virginia, 1756; Commander-in-Chief of all the British Forces in America in the same year; Lieutenant-General, 1758. The title eventually descended to the only daughter of the fifth Earl, Flora, who became Countess of Loudoun in her own right, and in 1804 married the Acting Grand Master of English Freemasons, Francis, Earl of Moira (afterwards Marquess of Hastings), then commanding the Forces in North Britain, and who, in 1806, was elected Acting Grand Master of Scotland.

From 1736 to 1752, although a new Grand Master of Scotland was chosen annually, the Deputy (or *Depute*) Grand Master—John Young—continued to hold office uninterruptedly. This worthy, who was a captain in 1736, became a major in 1745, and Lieutenant-Colonel in the 60th Foot, or "Royal Americans," with which corps he served under Colonel Munroe at the capitulation and massacre at Fort William Henry, in 1757.

In the same year he was appointed Provincial Grand Master over all the (Scottish) Lodges in America and the West Indies.

Young was transferred to the 46th Foot, also in America, but which shortly after sailed for the West Indies, in 1761. His name is given in the Army List for the following year as Lieutenant-Colonel commanding the regiment, but disappears in that for 1763. To what extent he was a sharer in the Masonic history of the gallant 46th Foot must remain unknown, but his association with that distinguished corps, coupled with the terms of his patent as Provincial Grand Master, may at least justify the belief that one of the most prominent Masons of the Old World, must have been much favoured by accidental or fortuitous circumstances in carrying out his mission in the New.

Returning to the Grand Lodge of Scotland, George, 3rd Earl of Cromarty, succeeded William St. Clair as Grand Master in 1737. This nobleman was afterwards engaged in the rebellion of 1745, and, with 400 of his clan, took part in the Battle of Falkirk. He and his son, Lord Macleod, were taken prisoners. Both pleaded guilty, but were pardoned. The son, in 1777, was appointed colonel of the 73rd (afterwards the 71st) Foot.

During the Earl of Cromarty's year of office it was resolved that all the Lodges holding of the Grand Lodge should be enrolled according to their seniority, in consequence of which regulation the first place on the roll was awarded to the Lodge of Edinburgh, and the second to that of Kilwinning. The validity of this decision was not at first openly challenged by the latter body. But many influences were at work, aroused by the brilliant oration of a Scottish soldier of fortune, which afforded the Ayrshire Masons, in

1743, at least a reasonable excuse in claiming a pre-eminence for the Old Court of Operative Masonry at Kilwinning, that was clearly absent from their thoughts—as being in the womb of futurity—in 1737.

Andrew Michael Ramsay, better known as the Chevalier Ramsay, was born at Ayr, and about 1706 he went with the English auxiliaries to the Netherlands, where he fought under Marlborough during the war of the Spanish succession. Converted by Fenelon to the Roman faith, he afterwards became tutor for a short while to the two sons of the (Old) Pretender at Rome. His chief works are the "Travels of Cyrus," "Philosophical Principles of Religion," and the Lives of Fenelon and Turenne. The following is an extract from the famous oration which he delivered as Chancellor of the Grand Lodge at Paris in 1737 :—

" At the times of the last Crusades many Lodges were already erected in Germany, Italy, Spain, France, and from thence in Scotland, because of the close alliance between the French and the Scotch. James. Lord Steward of Scotland, was Grand Master of a Lodge established at Kilwinning, in the West of Scotland, MCCLXXXVI., shortly after the death of Alexander III., King of Scotland, and one year before John Baliol mounted the throne."

This passage has been seized upon by the inventors of alleged Scottish rites, all pretending to hail from Kilwinning, and asserting the superiority in point of antiquity and pure tenets of the Grand Lodge held there, which body, it is almost unnecessary to say, never existed. While Ramsay himself, with an equal disregard of truth, has been described as a Jacobite partisan, a Jesuit Missionary in disguise, the inventor of the Royal Arch, and of many other rites and degrees. It may, however, be safely laid down with respect to this gallant soldier and distinguished man of letters, that all genuine tradition with regard to the birthplace of Scottish Masonry was swept away by his famous oration, which substituted for it a spurious tradition, awarding the palm of priority over all the other Scottish Lodges to the Lodge of Kilwinning.

The so-called "Scottish Masonry" of the Continent, which was unknown before the date of Ramsay's speech, appeared shortly afterwards and had attained a great vogue in 1743.

It was in this year that the Lodge of Kilwinning seems to have awakened to the conviction that it had been improperly relegated to a secondary rank. The Lodge therefore resumed its independence, which in the matter of granting Charters it had in reality never renounced, and for well nigh seventy years continued to exist as an independent Grand Body, dividing with that of Edinburgh the honour of forming branches in Scotland as well as in the British possessions beyond the seas.

Ultimately, a reconciliation was happily effected, and " Mother Kilwinning," having returned to the bosom of the Grand Lodge, was placed at the head of the roll without a number, in 1808.

I shall now pass to a still greater schism, which, for upwards of half-a-century, disturbed the peace of Masonry throughout the world.

The " Grand Lodge of England, according to the Old Institutions," was established in 1751, in opposition to the *parent* Grand Lodge of English Masonry (1717), which it was averred by the junior body had adopted *new* plans and departed from the *old* land-marks.

The schismatics, therefore, in reverting, as they alleged, to the "old forms," arrogated to themselves the title of " Ancient" Masons, bestowing on their rivals the appellation of " Moderns," and by those distinctive epithets they have since been generally described.

The two Grand Lodges of England amalgamated in 1813, but during the continuance of the schism, the junior body was a most important factor in the dissemination of particular ritualistic observances in countries beyond the seas, through the instrumentality of the Army Lodges.

Lodges were established in British Regiments by all of the Grand Lodges mentioned above, as well as by " Mother Kilwinning."

The Irish Lodges, however, always worked according to the system in vogue among the so-called Ancient Masons, and the result in America, where the influence of the Army Lodges made itself chiefly felt, was very marked. The customs of the Scottish Regimental Lodges were in harmony with those of the Irish, and the older Grand Lodge of

c 2

England was too sparsely represented among the Military Forces of the Crown to exercise any counter-influence, if indeed her Field Lodges in foreign parts did not—as I imagine must have generally been the case—acquire the tone and character of the vast majority of these associations. Hence, the predominance in North America of the "Ancients" over their rivals, the titular "Moderns," must be ascribed to the influx of Regimental Lodges from the Old World, and to their dissemination of the principles and the practice of what was then termed "Ancient Masonry" throughout the continent of America.

The first warrant creating a travelling Lodge of Freemasons—to which the number 11 was subsequently assigned—was issued to the 1st Foot—then the "Royal Regiment," now the "Royal Scots"—by the Grand Lodge of Ireland in 1732, and the date will be a convenient one at which to resume the general narrative of events from the point where I left off in order to present a short sketch of the Grand Lodges of the United Kingdom.

Among the prominent military brethren, whose names figure in the English lists, up to and inclusive of the year 1732, were the 1st Earl of Portmore, Colonel of the 2nd Foot 1703, who served under the Duke of Ormonde in the Spanish War of succession as Lieutenant-General 1710, Commanded the Forces in Scotland and became General 1710, and was Governor of Gibraltar, 1713. Lieutenant-General Francis Columbine, Governor of the same fortress in 1738, but who is better known to students of Masonry as holding the rank of "Colonel" in 1725, when occupying the combined offices of premier Provincial Grand Master, and Master of the Lodge held at the Sun, in Chester, in 1725.

Colonel George (afterwards 2nd Lord) Carpenter, 3rd Dragoons, initiated 1724, and Grand Warden, 1730 ; the 2nd. Earl of Dunbarton, Lieutenant-Colonel of Foot, 1715, and Ambassador to Russia, 1716 ; and Francis, Duke of Lorraine, the earliest of Royal Freemasons, who was made an Entered Prentice and Fellow-Craft, at the Hague by Dr. Desaguliers in 1731, and later in the same year a Master Mason, together with the Duke of Newcastle, by Lord Lovel, Grand Master, at Houghton Hall in Norfolk, the residence of Sir Robert Walpole, the Prime Minister.

The Duke of Lorraine, who married Maria Theresa, eldest daughter of the Emperor Charles VI., in 1736, was shortly after appointed Field Marshal of the Empire, and Generalissimo of the Imperial Army. It was in that double quality that he commanded, in 1738, the Austrian Army against the Turks. Francis, who (like so many of the "speculative" Freemasons of a still earlier period) was fond of alchemy, and a searcher for the Philosophers' Stone, became co-regent with his wife in 1740, and five years later was elected Emperor.

Thomas Pelham, Duke of Newcastle (1693—1768), with his brother Henry, raised a troop in 1715 for service against the Pretender, for which he received his dukedom ; Prime Minister, 1754.

The first Lodge in foreign parts which obtained a place on the roll of the Grand Lodge of England, was constituted at Madrid, by the Duke of Wharton—at that time enacting the role of a military adventurer in the Spanish Service, in 1728.

Another former Grand Master of England, and also a gallant soldier, the Duke of Richmond, assisted by the Baron de Montesquieu, the celebrated author of *De l'Esprit des Lois*, and Brigadier Churchill (a member of the Lodge at the Rummer, Charing Cross, 1724, Lieutenant-General 1747), admitted into the Society of Freemasons at the house of the Duchess of Portsmouth in Paris, many persons of distinction in 1734.

A similar meeting in the French capital took place in the following year, at the Hotel Bussy, which was presided over by a still earlier Grand Master of England, the veteran Desaguliers. Several noblemen and gentlemen—including the 2nd Duke of Kingston, General in the Army, 1772—were received into the fraternity, and among those who assisted the learned natural philosopher at the admission of the candidates was Lord Dursley, afterwards 4th Earl of Berkeley, at that time an ensign in the 1st Foot Guards, and who subsequently became a General in the Army, and held a command against the rebels in 1745.

Many supporters of the Old as well as of the Young Pretender were Freemasons, as I have already had occasion to remark, and among them was Sir Duncan Campbell, of

Lochnell, who, on August 28th, 1721, received in the Lodge of Edinburgh the degrees of Entered Apprentice and Fellow-Craft.

On the death of Queen Anne, the sympathies of Sir Duncan Campbell appear, like those of many other eminent Scotsmen, to have been enlisted in the Jacobite cause. At his father's death, January 10th, 1714, he kept the corpse unburied until the 28th in order that the funeral might be turned to account. "Hence it came to pass that the inhumation of Lochnell was attended by two thousand five hundred men, well armed and appointed, five hundred being of Lochnell's own lands, commanded by the famous Rob Roy, carrying with them a pair of colours belonging to the Earl of Breadalbane, and accompanied by the screams of thirteen bagpipes."

Sir Duncan was captain of one of the ten independent companies of the Black Watch—so called from their dress being composed of black, blue and green tartan—raised in 1729. Of these (afterwards the 42nd, and now the Royal Highlanders), John, 17th Earl of Crawfurd, was the first Colonel.

It seems that notwithstanding his apparent loyalty (as an officer in the Army) to George II., Sir Duncan was in concert with Prince Charles Edward in 1745, and first made known his arrival in Scotland to the supporters of the Stuart cause at Edinburgh. He assisted in founding the Lodge of Inverary. now St. John, No. 50. His sister was married to John Cameron, of Locheil, a member of the Lodge of Dunblane, and who served with the Earl of Mar in the rising of 1715.

The Earl of Crawfurd was made a Mason in the Lodge of Edinburgh in 1733, and five months afterwards he was introduced to the English fraternity by the Earl of Strathmore—Captain in Barrel's Foot—whom he succeeded in the office of Grand Master in 1734. Lord Crawfurd was for several years Colonel of a company in the 3rd Regiment of Foot Guards, and subsequently of the 42nd Foot. He served with the Germans against France, and with the Russians against the Turks. Afterwards he greatly distinguished himself at the battles of Dettingen and Fontenoy.

The command of the 2nd Troop of Horse Grenadier Guards was conferred upon him in 1740, and the Colonelcy of the Royal Regiment of North British Dragoons, now the 2nd Dragoons (Royal Scots Greys), at a later period.

A second Scottish peer of military renown, the Earl of Loudoun (of whom a short notice will be found on an earlier page) was placed at the head of the English Craft in 1736. This nobleman served with great distinction on the winning side during the Rising of 1745.

I shall now turn to the more chequered career of another Scottish Earl of equal rank in the hierarchy of the Craft, whose misfortune it was to have been arrayed on the losing side throughout the disastrous struggle which ended at Culloden.

William, 4th Earl of Kilmarnock, the first Master of Kilmarnock Kilwinning (1734), and who held the same office in the Lodge of Falkirk and "Mother Kilwinning" when in November, 1742, he was elected Grand Master Mason of Scotland. It was at the recommendation of this nobleman that, in 1743, the first Military Lodge (under the Grand Lodge) was erected, the petitioners being some sergeants and sentinels belonging to Colonel Lee's (afterwards the 55th) Regiment of Foot. This, however, appears at no time to have had a place accorded to it on the official roll, where, as we shall presently see, a Lodge in another regiment of infantry is shown as the earliest Military or Army Lodge chartered by the Grand Lodge of Scotland.

The Baron von Hund, who was the leading figure at the organisation of the rite or system called the Strict Observance (1764), declared that about the year 1743, he was made a Knight Templar in the presence of Lord Kilmarnock, and that the Grand Master of the Temple at that time, was either his lordship or Prince Charles Edward Stuart. No evidence, however, from any Scottish source has yet been produced of Lord Kilmarnock's connection with Continental Masonry, and none whatever that will justify our believing the young Pretender to have been a member of the fraternity.

The eldest son of the Earl of Kilmarnock, Lord Boyd—

Grand Master of Scotland in 1751—was elected Master of the Lodge of Falkirk, with his brothers, Charles and William Boyd, as Wardens, in 1749.

At the Stuart Rising in 1745, the Earl and his eldest son took different sides. Lord Boyd was an officer in King George's Army, and as such he was present with his regiment, the 21st Foot, at the Battle of Culloden, fighting against the insurgents, in whose ranks his father held a high command. Charles Boyd joined the rebels along with Lord Kilmarnock, and on the defeat of the Young Pretender, he with great difficulty managed to effect his escape. The youngest brother, William, was in the Royal Navy, and on board Commodore Barnett's ship at the period of his father's execution. He was afterwards (1761) a captain in the 114th Foot.

The Earl of Kilmarnock was executed in 1746. Lord Boyd, who, on the death of his aunt, became 13th Earl of Errol, officiated as Constable of Scotland at the Coronation of George III. in 1761 ; and neglecting by accident to pull off his cap when the King entered, he apologised for his negligence in the most respectful manner ; but his Majesty entreated him to be covered, for he looked on his presence at the solemnity as a very particular honour.

A Military Lodge, "The Duke of Norfolk's," in the 12th Foot, was placed on the Scottish roll as No. 58 in 1747. The petition averred, that "The Duke of Norfolk's Mason Lodge" had been "erected into a Mason body, bearing the title aforesaid, as far back as 1685," and, indeed, no higher antiquity could well have been asserted, as the 12th Foot was only raised in that year. The fact, however, remains that at the close of the first half of the eighteenth century a Lodge in an English regiment claimed to have been in existence more than thirty years before the formation of the earliest of Grand Lodges.

About the same time (1747) there was also a Lodge in the 2nd Dragoons (now the Royal Scots Greys), the date of whose constitution is uncertain, which, through the influence of the Earl of Eglinton, had been procured from Kilwinning. It is probable, indeed, that Regimental Lodges, though not of an indigenous character, had penetrated into

Scotland before the petition was favourably considered by the Grand Lodge in 1743, of certain "sergeants and sentinels" belonging to the 55th Foot.

As we have already seen, a Lodge was established in a British regiment (the 1st Foot) by the Grand Lodge of Ireland in 1732. Four other similar Lodges—in regiments then bearing the names of their colonels, but which afterwards became the 33rd, 27th, 21st, and 28th Foot—making a total of five, were at work under the same jurisdiction at the close of 1734, and the number had risen to eight when the first Military Warrant was issued by the Grand Lodge of Scotland in 1743. Two of these, dated 1732 and 1734, and bearing the numbers 11 and 33, were attached to the 1st and 21st Foot respectively, both Scottish regiments. Moreover, we hear of other Military Lodges in Scotland besides those previously noticed as existing under the Grand Lodge and "Mother Kilwinning" as early as 1744, in which year the minutes of "St. John's Old Kilwinning" at Inverness record the visit of "David Holland, Master of the Lodge of Freemasons in Brigadier Guise's Regiment"— afterwards the 6th Foot—then "lying at Fort George." This Lodge seems to have been without any charter or warrant, but it is possible that the lost archives of the Grand Lodge of Ireland would supply a key to the mystery, and for a variety of reasons I am led to the conclusion that there must have been many Irish Lodges in the British Army (and elsewhere) of which all traces have been lost.

The number, however, of Military Lodges on the register of Ireland—according to the evidence at my command—had certainly risen to twenty-nine, and of those claiming a Scottish parentage to at least five, when the earliest Lodges of the kind were established by the rival Grand Bodies in South Britain.

Lodges in the 8th and 57th Foot respectively were constituted in February and September, 1755, the first by the titular "Moderns" (or Regular Grand Lodge), and the second by the so-called "Ancients" (or Schismatics).

From this time Lodges multiplied in the British Army, and Abraham Savage, who was authorized by the Provincial Grand Master of North America, under the "Moderns," to "congregate all Free and Accepted Masons in the Expedition against Canada into one or more Lodges," admitted into Masonry at Crown Point after the surrender of that fortified place, twelve officers of the 1st Foot, in the Lodge he had established there, and of which he was the Master, in 1759. Later in the same year, at Quebec, "the Anniversary of St. John, the Evangelist, was duly observed by the several Lodges of Freemasons in the garrison."

In 1768—October 1—the 14th, 29th, and a part of the 59th Regiments arrived at Boston (U.S.A.), and a little later the 64th and 65th Foot direct from Ireland. In these regiments were three Lodges, all working under what was commonly known as the "Ancient system"—Nos. 58 (A.), 14th Foot; 322 (I.), 29th; and 106 (S.), 64th—holding under the Grand Lodges of England ("Ancients"), Ireland, and Scotland respectively. The presence of these troops created an intense excitement. Nevertheless, the members of St. Andrew's, a Scottish Lodge at Boston, saw the opportunity before them of forming a Grand Lodge under the authority of the Grand Lodge of Scotland, and with this end in view did not scruple to enter into fraternal communion with, and to make use of, their brethren in the obnoxious regiments.

None of these Army Lodges were present at the installation of the Provincial Grand Master under England (Regular Grand Lodge) in November, but all of them joined St. Andrew's in December, 1768, in a petition to the Grand Lodge of Scotland requesting the appointment of "a Grand Master of Ancient Masons in America."

Dr. Joseph Warren was appointed in 1769 "Grand Master of Masons in Boston and within one hundred miles of the same"; but in the interval the 64th Regiment had been removed from the station. The Grand Lodge, however, was formally inaugurated by St. Andrew's, and Lodges 58 (A.) and 322 (I.) in the 14th and 29th Foot. By a further Scottish patent (1772) Joseph Warren (afterwards killed at the battle of Bunker's Hill, where, though holding the commission of Major-General, he fought as a volunteer) was appointed Grand Master for the Continent of America.

The last patent was granted by the 5th Earl of Dumfries, Grand Master of Scotland, 1771-72, a Colonel in the Foot Guards; but it is to his immediate predecessor in that office I shall next turn, Lieutenant-General James Adolphus Oughton, who, at the period of his election—November, 1769—was commanding the forces in Scotland in the absence of Lord Lorne, afterwards 5th Duke of Argyll.

The names of other military brethren (in addition to those already given), who at an earlier date than General Oughton, had become Rulers of the Craft, as British or Irish Grand Masters, are very numerous. The Commander-in-Chief of North Britain in 1769, was the twenty-seventh Grand Master Mason of Scotland, and of his predecessors in office, at least thirteen, or one half, held commissions in the army, among them being the Earls of Leven, Eglinton and Kellie, Lord Erskine, only surviving son of the 11th Earl of Marr (attainted in 1715), and James, afterwards the 16th Baron Forbes.

To these examples, I shall for the present content myself with adding the names of the Marquis of Carnarvon, afterwards 3rd Duke of Chandos (1754-56); the Dukes of Beaufort (1767-71), and Manchester (1777-82), Grand Masters of England ("Moderns"); all of whom were colonels in the army; Lord George (eventually Viscount) Sackville—to be hereafter referred to in connection with the 20th Foot—Grand Master of Ireland, 1751; and Sholto, Lord Aberdour, later 16th Earl of Morton, Grand Master of Scotland, 1755-6, and of England, 1757-61, who (while holding the latter office) raised a corps of Light Dragoons, of which he was made the Commandant in 1759.

It may also be mentioned that General Lord Blayney, Grand Master of England, 1764-66, was supported throughout the whole of that period by another soldier as Deputy—Colonel John Salter, who was promoted to the rank of Major-General in 1770.

James Adolphus Oughton, a natural son of Sir Adolphus Oughton—one of the military members of the Lodge at the Horn, in 1724—served with the 37th Foot at Culloden, and also (in command of that regiment) at the battle of Minden in 1759. He became a Knight of the Bath in 1773,

Commander-in-Chief, Scotland, in 1778, and at the time of his death in 1780, was a Lieutenant-General and Colonel of the 31st Foot. Amidst all his campaigns he cultivated a taste for literature and the fine arts, and in the opinion of Dr. Johnson, there were few men of any profession whose range of general knowledge was more complete.

General (then Lieutenant Colonel) Oughton was Provincial Grand Master of the Island of Minorca under the "Moderns," in 1752, and became a member of Lodge Canongate Kilwinning, at Edinburgh, in 1754.

In 1770, the Lodge "Scots Greys, Kilwinning," in the 2nd or Royal North British Dragoons, having lost their charter, and all their records in the wars, petitioned for a warrant from the Grand Lodge, which was granted, and the Lodge re-constituted by General Oughton—March 12th —as the "St. Andrew's Royal Arch."

The affiliation of a Regimental Lodge by a Grand Master, who was also at the time commanding the King's forces in Scotland, points out to us the estimation in which Military Masonry was then regarded, and the significance of the event is heightened by the circumstance that the Master of "St. Andrew's Royal Arch," Colonel William (afterwards 6th Lord) Napier, was in command of the 2nd Dragoons.

After General Oughton, no soldier of equal rank was placed at the head of the Scottish Craft until 1806, when the Earl of Moira, at that time commanding the troops in North Britain, was elected Acting Grand Master—a position which, as will be presently shown, he had long filled with signal ability in the southern kingdom.

Between the eras, however, of these two Military and Masonic Chiefs, there were several Commanders of the Forces in Scotland who were zealous Freemasons, and many Grand Masters, who were very distinguished members of the military profession. Of the former class, may be named Lieutenant-General Archibald, Earl of Eglinton, a former Master of "Mother Kilwinning," who held the chief command at Edinburgh, in 1783 ; Lord Adam Gordon, his successor in 1789, who, while holding the same high military position, served the office of Master in the Lodge of Aberdeen ; and Sir Ralph Abercrombie (1798), who first saw the light of Masonry in Lodge Canongate Kilwinning, in 1753.

Of the Grand Masters, I shall begin with the names of the 3rd and 4th Dukes of Atholl, elected in 1773 and 1778, respectively ; each of them, at the date of his being chosen to fill the Scottish chair, held the position of Grand Master in the Junior Grand Lodge of England, or "Ancients." Both Dukes served in the Army, and the younger one raised a regiment—the 77th or Atholl Highlanders—for the public service in 1778. William, 10th Baron (afterwards 1st Earl) Cathcart—Commander-in-Chief of the Forces of Ireland, 1803 ; of Scotland, 1806 ; and of the Army against Denmark, 1807—obtaining a company in this corps, vacated the chair of the Alloa Lodge, by which body a bounty was forthwith offered to recruits. This practice—often combined with "the freedom of Masonry," was expressly forbidden by the Grand Lodge, but in the Lodge of Kelso, the spirit of patriotism thus awakened, reached a great height, and in the same year the brethren unanimously resolved to testify their zeal for their sovereign, and their respect for their Noble Grand Master, by marching at the head of the recruiting party, beating up for recruits for the Atholl Highlanders, and by offering a bounty of three guineas to every man enlisting in that corps.

John, 4th Duke of Atholl, was Grand Master of Scotland in 1778 and 1779, and of the Junior Grand Lodge of England, or "Ancients," from 1775 to 1781, and again from 1791 to 1813. He was admitted into the first, second, and third degrees, and became the Master of the Grand Master's Lodge (under the "Ancients") on February 25th, 1775. On March 1st he was elected Grand Master, and on the 25th of the same month, duly installed in the presence of the Duke of Leinster (Colonel, 1st Regiment of Dublin Volunteers, 1777), and Lieutenant-General Sir James Adolphus Oughton, former Grand Masters of Ireland and Scotland, respectively.

As a result of the patronage by the Dukes of Atholl, of

the English Schismatics or "Ancients," that body became widely known as "Atholl" Masons, and to the influence of these two noblemen must be attributed in a great measure the marvellous success of the Great Schism.

Of the succeeding Grand Master Masons of Scotland, the 6th Earl of Balcarres (1780-81), and the 7th Lord Napier (1788-89), accompanied General Burgoyne in his unfortunate expedition from Canada, and were present with the force under the command of that officer which was compelled to surrender to General Gates, in 1777.

George, Marquis of Huntley, afterwards Duke of Gordon, while Grand Master of Scotland (1794) raised the 100th, later the 92nd Foot (Gordon Highlanders), of which he was made Lieutenant-Colonel Commandant, and accompanied it in 1799 to Holland, where he was severely wounded. Lieutenant-General in 1808, and in the following year held a principal command in the expedition to the Scheldt. The Earl of Ancrum, subsequently 5th Marquis of Lothian (Grand Master 1794-5) served for many years in his father's regiment, the 11th Dragoons, in which a Lodge was established by the Grand Lodge of England, "in Captain Bell's troop"—while he held a commission as lieutenant, in 1756. He commanded successively the 12th Foot, the 4th Regiment of Horse, the 1st Life Guards, and finally, his original corps, the 11th Dragoons. He attained the rank of General in the Army in 1796.

Lord Doune, afterwards 9th Earl of Moray, the forty-first Grand Master Mason, and the Earl of Dalkeith, later 7th Duke of Buccleuch, the forty-third, were also soldiers; but of greater note in the military service of the Crown, was the 9th Earl of Dalhousie (Grand Master 1804-5), who, entering the Army in 1788, served with great distinction in Holland, Egypt, and Walcheren, and was Commander-in-Chief in the East Indies from 1829 to 1832.

Through the influence of Francis, Earl of Moira, Commander of the Forces in North Britain, a fraternal union between the Grand Lodge of Scotland, and that of England (under the older sanction) was established, with the result that in 1806, the Prince of Wales and Lord Moira, the Grand and Acting Grand Masters of the latter body were elected to similar positions in the Masonic Jurisdiction of the North.

The sympathies, therefore, of the Scottish Masons, which, following the example set them by a former Commander-in-Chief, General Oughton, and two other military Grand Masters, the Dukes of Atholl, had adhered to the "Ancients," were now diverted into a new channel, at the instance of the Earl of Moira, who stated "that the hearts and arms of the Grand Lodge to which he was attached, had ever been open for their seceding brethren," and from that time may be dated a lasting friendship between the Grand Lodge of Scotland, and the only Constitutional Grand Lodge of England, or "Moderns."

Returning, however, for a short period to those rivals of the latter body, the "Atholl" Masons, or "Ancients."

In 1781 the "Ancients" and Field Lodges in New York met as a Grand Lodge, and elected Grand Officers, January 23rd; a warrant for a Provincial Grand Lodge was granted by the Grand Lodge of England ("Ancients"), September 5th; and the Provincial Grand Lodge was duly inaugurated by three stationary and six ambulatory Lodges in December, 1782. The former were Nos. 169, 210, and 212 on the roll of the "Ancients," of which the first-named was acknowledged as the leading authority by the various Army Lodges, while the last two were also to a great extent military bodies. Of the six travelling lodges, one-half were likewise English (or "Ancient"), namely, Nos. 52, 213, and 215, in the 22nd Foot, the 4th Battalion Royal Artillery, and the Regiment of Anspach-Bayreuth, respectively. The other Regimental Lodges that took part in the proceedings were Nos. 132 (Scottish) and 441 (Irish) in the 22nd and 38th Foot, together with Sion's Lodge in the 57th Regiment, holding under a dispensation granted by Lodge No. 210, "Ancients," with the consent and approval of two Scottish Lodges, Nos. 132, "Moriah," in the 22nd Foot, and 134 Eskdale Kilwinning, at Langholm, in Dumfries-shire.

In the following year a majority of the Grand officers left New York with the British Army, and at that date Lodges had been formed by the Provincial Grand Lodge in the New Jersey Volunteers, the Regiment of Knyphausen, the 57th Foot, and the Loyal American Regiment; while within the same period two Irish Lodges, Nos. 478 in the 17th Dragoons, and 90 in the 33rd Foot, had ranged themselves under its banner. After the war, the body thus established by British Army Lodges abandoned its provincial character and assumed the title of Grand Lodge of New York.

Passing from " Field " to " Sea " Lodges, there was a "Sea Captain's Lodge" at Wapping, Liverpool, Sunderland, Yarmouth, and Bristol. But the first Lodge *afloat* which obtained a position on the lists was held " On Board His Majesty's Ship the *Vanguard* in 1760." Similar Lodges were afterwards established "on board " H.M.S. *Prince* and *Canceaux*, in the former " at Plymouth," in 1762. and in the latter at . Quebec, in1768. No other " Sea Lodges " than these three appear to have been regularly constituted either before or since; and as they all seem to have owed their existence to the exertions of a single individual, their further history, to the extent that it may be proceeded with, will be incorporated with the biography of Thomas Dunckerley, the gunner of H.M.S. *Vanguard*, in 1762.

The first member of the Royal Family holding a commission in the senior service, who joined the Craft, was Edward Augustus, Duke of York, brother of George III. He served as a midshipman at the taking of Cherbourg, and the defeat of St. Cas in 1758. Made captain of the *Phœnix* of 44 guns, 1759, and Vice-Admiral of the Blue, 1762. Three years later he was initiated- at Berlin in a Lodge which, with his permission, then assumed the title of " Royal York of Friendship," and is now the Grand Lodge of that name.

The first Naval Officer of rank who presided over a Grand Lodge was Washington Shirley, Earl Ferrers (Captain 1746, Rear-Admiral 1775), who was Grand Master of England in 1762-63 ; and after an interval the same position was filled by the Duke of Cumberland, Admiral of the White, brother of George III., who continued to hold it from 1782 until his death in 1790.

The remaining brother of George III., William, Duke of Gloucester, who died a Field Marshal, was also a Freemason, having been initiated in 1766, when Colonel of the 13th Foot.

All the sons of the same King were officers in the Army, Navy, or Volunteers, and all except the Duke of Cambridge, namely, the Prince of Wales, the Dukes of York, Clarence, Kent, Cumberland, and Sussex, were members of the Society.

On the occasion of the election of the Duke of Cumberland in 1782, a rule was established that whenever a Prince of the Blood accepted the position of Grand Master he should be at liberty to nominate any Peer of the Realm to be the Acting Grand Master.

The Earl of Effingham, a Lieutenant-Colonel in the Army, who had previously served in the 1st and 2nd regiments of Foot Guards and the 22nd Foot, was appointed to the new office, in which he was succeeded (1790) by Francis, Lord Rawdon, afterwards 2nd Earl of Moira, and 1st Marquess of Hastings—the " Bayard " of the British Craft— who continued to discharge the duties incidental to the appointment until his nomination as Governor-General, Commander-in-Chief, and Acting Grand Master of India, at the close of 1812.

This gallant soldier was greatly assisted throughout nearly the whole of his long tenure of office as Grand Master by an equally gallant sailor, Admiral Sir Peter Parker, who had been appointed by the Duke of Cumberland —a brother flag officer—his Deputy, in 1786.

The Deputy Grand Master, who was a distinguished naval commander, had previously served as Grand Steward and Grand Warden, and then held the office of Provincial Grand Master of Jamaica. He was a member of what are now the Grand Stewards, the Royal Somerset House and Inverness (No. 4) and the British (No. 8) Lodges. He is best remembered as the early patron of Nelson, at whose funeral Parker was chief mourner, but in the capacity of Admiral of the Fleet, the senior officer in the Navy, rather than as a personal friend. Sir Peter died in December, 1811, having held the office of Deputy Grand Master for more than a quarter of a century. No other naval or military brother has ever served for an equally long period as a Grand Officer in either North or South Britain, though the most famous of Scottish " Deputies," Colonel Young, remained at his post for a period of fifteen years, and the Earl of Moira, as Acting Grand Master of England, for nearly twenty-three.

The service of neither of these worthies, however, nor even that of Parker himself, will, in point of duration, compare with the record of a very distinguished Grand Officer of Ireland, John Hely-Hutchinson, who was Senior Grand Warden from 1791 to 18-4. This high military and Masonic dignitary entered the Army in 1774, became Lieutenant Colonel 77th ("Atholl Highland") Regiment in 1783, and Colonel of the 94th (Hutchinson's) Regiment of Foot in 1784. He accompanied the expedition to Egypt in 1801, and on the death of Sir Ralph Abercrombie succeeded to the command. For his services he was created Baron Hutchinson of Alexandria, a title afterwards exchanged for that of 2nd Earl of Donoughmore, which devolved upon him at the death of his elder brother (the 1st Earl) in 1825.

The latter was Grand Master of Ireland from 1789 to 1813, and therefore occupied the chair of the Grand Lodge when his younger and more distinguished brother entered upon his long career as Senior Grand Warden, in 1791. The 1st Earl, then 2nd Baron Donoughmore, who entered the Army somewhat late in life, as cornet in the 9th Dragoons, became on the same day—May 31, 1794— Captain in " Hutchinson's " Regiment of Foot, which he probably raised, as it will tend to explain his rapid advancement to Major in another infantry regiment on July 19th, and to Lieutenant-Colonel in a third on July 21st in the same year. He became a Colonel in 1800 and a Lieutenant-General in 1812.

The Prince of Wales, then a Colonel in the Army, accepted the position of Grand Master of England, on the death of his uncle, the Admiral, in 1790, and a pause will be made in order that some statistics may be laid before the reader.

At the above date, about a hundred Military Lodges are known to have been constituted by the Grand Lodge of Ireland, and many others were doubtless formed, of which no traces are now forthcoming. The Lodges of a similar character, established under the Grand Lodge of Scotland, numbered twenty-one.

About forty-nine had been set on foot *directly* by the "Ancients," but a large number of subsidiary Lodges were chartered by the provincial authorities under this system, particularly in America, Upper and Lower Canada, Nova Scotia, Gibraltar, and Jamaica, which, in the comparative absence of lists, cannot be satisfactorily identified, though various regimental Lodges are traceable among them ; and of the existence of others there is scarcely room for doubt.

To a more restricted extent the same practice of issuing local warrants prevailed in foreign districts which were under the obedience of the "Moderns." In 1790, fourteen regimental Lodges had found places on the lists. About an equal number of Army Lodges were attached to the various Brigades in Bengal, and others of a stationary, though military character, existed in all three of the Indian Presidencies, flourishing, perhaps, with the greatest luxuriance on the Coast of Coromandel. There was a "Royal Navy" Lodge at Deal, Gosport, London, and Halifax (Nova Scotia), and a "Marine Lodge at Plymouth," "in the second division of Marines." The "Royal Military," at Woolwich, and the "Lodge of Mars," at Yassy, in Russia, were established under the same sanction (original Grand Lodge of England) in 1774. The "Carnatic Military Lodge" was constituted at Arcot, in 1784 ; and "St. John's Lodge of Secrecy and Harmony " (in the Order of Knights of St. John) at Malta, in 1789.

The older Grand Lodge of England continued to be ruled by a Military Chief (the Earl of Moira), aided by a Naval " Deputy "(Sir Peter Parker), until the death of the latter in 1811, and the removal of the former, in 1813, to a greater sphere of usefulness in the East. During this period English Masonry was well represented both at home and abroad by members of the two services. Among the Provincial Grand Masters under the older Grand Lodge of England were Ferdinand, Duke of Brunswick, who commanded the British and Hanoverian Forces at the battle of Minden ; Generals Sir Robert Melville, and Sir Adam Williamson, in the West Indies; and Brigadier-General Matthew Horne (who held the chief command of the Coast Army) on the Coast of Coromandel.

Captain Sir John Borlase Warren, while Provincial Grand Master of Derbyshire, gained a signal victory over the French naval force intended for the invasion of Ireland, capturing the whole squadron, consisting of a ship of the line, *La Hoche*, and three frigates (1798), for which on the next promotion he was made Rear-Admiral of the Blue. There were also Generals Sir Samuel Hulse (afterwards Field-Marshal), and Sir John Doyle, who ruled the Craft in Sussex and the Channel Islands, respectively. The former saw much service on the Continent, and was Deputy-Master of the Prince of Wales's Lodge from 1787 to 1820. The latter, then Major John Doyle, was initiated in the same Lodge, in 1792, and in the following year raised the 87th Regiment, "the Prince of Wales's Irish" (later, the "Royal Irish Fusiliers"), in command of which he embarked for the Continent with the expedition under the Acting Grand Master of England—the Earl of Moira—in 1794. He afterwards accompanied the Senior Grand Warden of Ireland, General Hely-Hutchinson, to Egypt, and took part in the campaign of 1801.

Prince Edward, then a Colonel in the Army—at a later period, Duke of Kent, and a Field-Marshal—held office under both Grand Lodges of England, having been appointed Provincial Grand Master of Gibraltar, by the "Moderns," in 1790, and of Lower Canada by the "Ancients," in 1792. At the latter date there were no less than eleven Military Lodges at "The Rock," one Scottish—32nd Foot; Six Irish—1st, 11th, 18th, 46th, 51st, and 68th Foot; three English (*Ancient*)—50th Foot, Royal Artillery, and Garrison; and one Provincial—in the Company of Artificers. The records from which I quote, also mention three Lodges of a similar character as having recently left the Garrison, besides a warrant (*Irish*) "held by the officers of the 32nd Foot, but for neglect erased."

The Earl of Moira embarked for India in 1813, and the Prince of Wales declining a re-election as Grand Master, the Duke of Sussex, Colonel of Volunteers, and at a later period

Captain-General of the Hon. Artillery Company of Tondon was chosen as his successor. In the same year the Duke of Kent, Field-Marshal, and Colonel of the 1st Foot, was installed as Grand Master of the other Grand Lodge of England, and on St. John's day (in winter) 1813, the Union of the two fraternities who had been so long mistermed *Ancient* and *Modern* was accomplished.

The Act of Union was ratified and confirmed. *One* Grand Lodge was constituted. The Duke of Kent then proposed his royal brother for the office of Grand Master of the United Grand Lodge of England. This being put to the vote, was carried unanimously, and the Duke of Sussex received the homage of the fraternity.

At this epoch (1813), without counting the remote pendicles under provincial Grand Lodges in foreign parts, the approximate number of Military—or it will be more correct to say Regimental—Lodges, which had existed under the Irish, English, and Scottish jurisdictions, was as follows:— Irish, 190 ; English, 141 (*Ancients* 116, *Moderns* 25) ; and Scottish, 21 ; showing a grand total of 352. Of these, many of which were dormant, though not yet erased from the lists. there remained in 1813—Irish Lodges, 135 ; English, 65 (*Ancients* 46, *Moderns* 19) ; and Scottish, 19 ; amounting in all to 219. A period of decay, however, had set in ; the following year showing that only 52 English Military Lodges (45 *Ancient*, 7 *Modern*) were really carried forward at the Union. In 1816, the Scottish Regimental Lodges had shrunk to ten, and in the same year the records of the Grand Lodge of Ireland disclose that there were then twenty-five Military Lodges "of which no account had been received for years." In 1822, the latter jurisdiction, which, as already observed, has always included the greater number of (British) Army Lodges, only possessed a military following of 42. About 30 Irish, 25 English, and 2 Scottish—or in all, 57 Regimental Lodges have been chartered since the "Union" of 1813, thus forming a grand total of at least 409 Ambulatory Lodges, which are *known* to have been constituted by the Grand Lodges of the British Isles.

Nor would the record be complete without my adding

that no less than 40 " Regimental," " Military." or " Army "
Lodges, and several others bearing the titles of " Royal
Navy " or " Marine," are shown by Mr. John Lane, in his
valuable work, to have been warranted by the English
provincial authorities abroad, which were never registered
in the books of any Grand Lodge. The last " Travelling "
Lodge on the Scottish roll (in the Turkish Contingent) was
" cut off" in 1860. Fifteen only, under both the remaining
jurisdictions, were at work in 1886, and the number has
still further dwindled, at the present time of writing, to
eight, of which six are Irish and the remainder English—
the latest to disappear being, I regret to say, a Lodge
attached to the 31st Foot (now the 1st Battalion East
Surrey Regiment), of which I had the honour to be a founder
and the first Master, in 1858.

CHAPTER III.

In types we speak : by tokens, secret ways,
We teach the wisdom of primeval days.

— DOUGLAS JERROLD.

OF the assistance rendered by one brother to another in cases of danger or distress, many stories have been related, and a selection from the number, showing the influence of Masonry in warfare, and its beneficial effect in soothing the angry passions of those soldiers and sailors who are ranged under its banner, will be laid before the reader.

As mentioned in another chapter, the statement of Sir Robert Wilson that a French captain owed his life when about to be transfixed by the lance of a Cossack to the fortunate circumstance of giving a Masonic sign, was described by the editor of a leading journal as an incident so incredible that no amount of evidence could induce him to believe it. The story, however, was really very well authenticated, as the narrator and one of the chief performers was Sir Robert Wilson himself, who was always on the alert during his numerous campaigns to recognize a brother in the Craft, and of whom a short memoir appears in another portion of this book.

The same fortunate presence of mind in resorting to the language of Masonry saved the life of a gallant officer, Lieutenant-Colonel Tytler, during the last war in which this country was engaged with America, who, when lying on the ground with a bayonet at his breast, succeeded in interesting a generous American officer in his behalf and saving his life. The truth of this story was vouched for by Sir A. Alison, not only in his "History of Europe," but also in his address to the brethren as Grand Master of the Masonic Province of Glasgow. At one of these meetings shortly after the close of the Crimean War he related the following anecdote in connection with the attack on the Redan :—" During that assault an English officer led a small party of soldiers up to one of the guns placed in a recess of the Redan, and most of the men fell before the fire with which they were received. The others were met by a body of Russians, and the English officer was about to be bayoneted when he chanced to catch the hand of the Russian officer, and had presence of mind enough to give him a Masonic grip. The Russian in a moment struck up the bayonets of his soldiers, led his newly-found brother to the rear, and treated him with the kindness of a Mason."

A similar story is related of the late Captain Herbert Vaughan, 90th Foot, of whom a brother officer (the present Commander-in-Chief, Viscount Wolseley) wrote as follows :— " It is quite true that poor Vaughan was the only English officer removed at once from the Redan to the hospital. And this he owed to the fact that he was a Mason."

An incident, which is well attested, in the career of General James Lindsay, of Balcarres, may also be recorded. While a prisoner in the hands of the Turks in the north of Africa, he made a Masonic sign to an old man who held some employment in the fortress in which he was detained. This man thereupon suggested to him a method of effecting his deliverance from captivity, and on his leaving the fortress provided him with a boat in which he escaped to Gibraltar.

The examples might be greatly multiplied where the accuracy of anecdotes, like the foregoing, has been deposed to by persons of credit and reputation. But it will be sufficient to say, that if the improbability of any of the stories I am about to relate, is the only reason that can be assigned for casting discredit upon them ; then the circumstance that other and similar tales have been (and are) well authenticated, will permit of our reasoning by analogy, which should entirely set at rest the question of probability.

Naval Anecdotes.

It will be seen from the following examples that the influence of Masonry has made itself felt not only in vessels of war, but also in the merchant navy, and among the crews and commanders of privateers and slavers, and has even operated like a charm in the case of actual buccaneers.

On the 27th November, 1812, a very large and valuable fleet sailed from Spithead for the West Indies, under the convoy of the *Queen* man-of-war. A very short time after their sailing a most violent tempest arose, and this valuable convoy was so much dispersed that only forty sail remained under the protection of the *Consort*. At this crisis it happened that the *Gloire*, a French frigate of forty-four guns was cruising betwixt the Western Islands and Ferrol, and fell in with the numerous stragglers of this ill-fated convoy. The frigate made many valuable prizes, and among them the *Princess Royal*, Captain Alexander Foster, a fine ship of 400 tons, laden with plantation stores for the Island of Jamaica. Captain Foster, on being taken on board the *Gloire* to deliver his papers, took the opportunity of making himself known as a Mason to the brave and chivalrous commander of the frigate. The French officer, after some private conversation, said that the duty which he owed to his country was paramount, but that next to it was the duty he owed as a Mason, "To help a Brother in the hour of need." Feeling encumbered by his numerous captives, and wishing to continue a cruise destructive to our commerce, as being strictly compatible with his duty, he thought that he might with honour show his respect for the Craft by making "Brother Captain Foster" a present of his ship the *Princess Royal* and her cargo, as *cartel* to receive from the frigate all the prisoners by whom he was then encumbered—a proposal most gratefully and fraternally accepted.

"During the late war with France," recites an old naval officer, "I was taken, with several others, a prisoner of war. We were carried to the Mauritius, and in that island confined together in one dungeon. Some few months had elapsed, and we had experienced many disagreeable privations, when one of our companions in misfortune requested the use of pens, ink, and paper, and permission to despatch a letter to the Governor. On the day following this event some French gentlemen visited our cell, and paid particular attention to our comrade. Our general condition afterwards was rendered less insupportable ; but what most surprised us all, and myself especially, for 1 was not *then* in the *secret*, was the mysterious change which took place in our fellow-sufferer's lot. The former misery which we had all equally endured was certainly greatly alleviated, but our comrade was soon altogether removed, and, as we subsequently learnt, not only released from prison, but every necessary procured for him, his purse well stocked, and a passage obtained for him to his native country. This man was a Freemason. We, however, remained in confinement, though its former rigour was mitigated, for two years after his departure."

About the year 1824 the ship *Leven*, engaged on a survey, commanded by Captain Bartholomew, having arrived off Cape Bolador, crossed the Bar, and anchored in the river Ouro, on the N.W. coast of Africa. The captain and some of the officers, with two boats' crews, proceeded to examine the river. The shore represented, as far as the eye could discover, one vast desert of sand. The boats proceeded, after rowing for about forty miles, to what appeared to be an island. The crews landed and slept there, but in the morning were awoke by the loud yells of savages, and suddenly surprised also by the appearance of a large number of Arabs, who were armed with Spanish muskets (afterwards found to be loaded with balls and slugs) and long knives. Hostilities seemed to be inevitable, but the captain advanced towards the Arabs and made a Masonic sign, which was answered by their leader, who immediately laid down his musket and embraced the British officer. The captain and party were assisted to regain their ship, and the Arab Chief intimated his intention of visiting them on the following day. Nothing, however, was seen of these natives afterwards.

Within a year or two of the date of the last anecdote an English naval captain was travelling in Egypt. He was accompanied by his servant, an active and intelligent young man. They were attacked in a desert by the Arabs, two of whom they slew, but were ultimately overpowered. It was settled that the captain's life should be forfeited, and he awaited his destiny (the two prisoners having been separated) with what fortitude he could command. In the morning, however, he was agreeably surprised by his servant's approach with the joyful intelligence that the sentence was not only remitted, but that he was at liberty to resume his journey, and this retributive justice was accompanied by the restoration of all the property of which he had previously been despoiled. It is not to be wondered at that his gratitude to his servant ended in his taking early steps to claim a nearer association with him as a Brother in the Craft, for by the exchange of the mysterious secret the robber of the desert kept faith with a Brother Mason.

Captain O'Brien, R.N., in his "Adventures," comprising shipwreck, captivity, and escape from various prisons during the war with France, relates that "after many severe and cruel hardships our route was through Hesden and St. Pol to Arras. Some genteel young men of the town, to whom Tuthill and Essel had contrived, in passing to the gaol, by signs to make known that they were Freemasons, obtained permission for both to accompany them for the night to their houses, where they were most hospitably entertained, whilst Ashworth and I were left upon straw and scanty prison fare in the dungeon." After this experience, as may readily be conjectured, the captain embraced the first opportunity which presented itself of being admitted a member of the Masonic Institution.

The following appeared over the *nom de plume* of "An Old Soldier" in a Masonic Journal of 1839 :—"I was some years in the Foot Guards, from which I was discharged in consequence of ill health, and was induced in 1831 to enter the service of the Queen of Portugal ; and in 1833 returned to England and joined a ship just fitted out for the

Portuguese service, as a non-commissioned officer of marines. We had on board a complement of 120 seamen and 14 marines. When passing Dover, in consequence of some little misunderstanding between the captain and crew, the latter attempted to run the ship aground upon the sands, and but for the prompt and determined spirit of the marines the ship would have been lost. They, however, succeeded (with the most determined assistance of the officers of the ship) in driving the whole crew below, with the exception of one very young man, who was at the helm at the time, and who remained there for *twelve hours*, aiding the captain in the most praiseworthy manner, the officers and marines working the ship all night; and in the morning, after a proper concession from the crew, all was amicably arranged, and we sailed direct for Oporto to join the fleet of Admiral Carlos de Pouza (Napier), where we arrived on the 19th of June, 1833, but he had sailed twelve hours previous. We, however, spent that night in Oporto roads, where we had an opportunity of seeing the constant firing of shell, shot, and small arms, carried on the whole night between the armies of Pedro and Miguel. We sailed next morning for the south, but were, most unfortunately, wrecked on the following morning at Peneche, a strongly fortified place belonging to the enemy, Don Miguel, and lost everything we had except our clothes that we had on at the moment. We had amongst us a petty officer, who spoke very good Portuguese, and who had an opportunity of making *himself known* to the *Provost Marshal*, who, it appeared, was *enlightened* as well as ourselves. From that moment he devoted all in his power to our interest and comfort, always giving us the lightest work to do, and sometimes a little wine, a great luxury at times, and sometimes a little extra food, our allowance being a pound of coarse, black bread per day, with some boiled beans that an English pig would not eat, and were worked very hard, from five in the morning until seven at night, resting about three hours in the middle of the day, our employment burying those who died of the cholera (about fifty or sixty a day). We had to carry naked dead bodies about two miles in the broiling sun, and lost four of our own men

by the same dreadful disease. I had an attack myself
slightly, and attribute my recovery to the indulgence
received as above alluded to. In a country like Portugal,
torn by contending armies, where father was divided against
son, and brother against brother, I consider it as an
unlooked-for mercy, that a man should, from principle,
protect and shelter a *foreigner* fighting against him on his
own native shore ; and it shows at once the full advantage,
as well as sound principle, of Freemasonry."

The late gallant Commander J. A. Pritchard, R.N., when
employed on the coast of Africa in the suppression of the
slave trade, rendered important services to his country by
his daring and successful capture of slavers. On one
occasion, off the dreaded Bight of Benin (where it is said, in
reference to the fearful mortality from fever which prevails
there, "a hundred come out where a thousand go in"),
H.M.S. ———— hove to and lowered two boats, each containing fifteen seamen and marines, for the purpose of
boarding a suspicious-looking barque-rigged vessel, then
under full sail and steering directly out of the Bight.
Commander Pritchard, then a lieutenant, had charge of the
two boats—they neared the dark sides of the rakish craft
and hailed her captain to heave to, but were answered with
a shower of musketry bullets, which wounded three of the
crew of each boat—the wind lulled almost immediately into
a calm (another remarkable scientific mystery of these
climes, perhaps the concussion or report of the firearms
having something to do with it). Amid the unwelcome
salutation the stern, clear voice of the lieutenant was heard
"board her, boys, starboard and port" (which means one
boat to each side). The crews bent to their oars, and ere
they reached the sides a broadside from the slaver commander passed harmlessly over their heads, and cutlass in
hand, with a dash and spontaneous British cheer, both
boats' crews at the same moment were clambering either
side of the fated craft ; the struggle was sharp and severe.
Lieutenant P. had two pistol balls through the collar of his
coat each side of the neck, and his face blackened by
powder; he gained the deck, and was in the act of cutting

down the captain, an American, when the latter made the
M M. sign of distress and cried out "I am your prisoner."
Lieutenant P., being a brother of the mystic tie,
sheathed his sword and spared his victim ; then taking
possession of the slaver, with five hundred slaves on board,
permitted the reckless American to keep his sword and have
as much liberty as he liked. The captain was afterwards tried
for his life, in making armed resistance, but the energetic
appeal of Lieutenant P., in conjunction with others of the
Masonic fraternity, turned the sentence of death passed
upon the inhuman fellow, into one of a term of imprisonment,
thus in a two-fold manner saving the life of a fellow-creature
and illustrating in a noble manner the glorious principles of
our Order when thoroughly acted upon.

At a meeting of the Liverpool Marine Board on September
8th, 1869, a presentation of a splendid telescope was made
to Captain Sharp, of the *Jeff Davis* schooner, of 237 tons,
for rescuing the crew of the water-logged barque *Albert*,
when about 200 miles off Cape Hatteras, at the eastern edge
of the Gulf Stream. A frightful gale prevailed at the time of
the rescue, and the crew of the *Jeff Davis* had for thirty-
four days subsequently to go on half-allowance, till the
schooner reached Bermuda. Captain Sharp said that the
other captain having passed the Freemason's sign, he felt
himself doubly bound to rescue him, if possible.

In 1823 a merchant ship belonging to Sweden was
wrecked upon the coast of Africa, about five hundred miles
from Cape Town. The crew, about seventy in number,
were saved, and afterwards conveyed to the latter place.
Fifty-seven of ship's company, including the captain, were
Freemasons, and immediately made themselves known to
the Dutch Lodges there. They were supplied with food,
clothing, and every necessary for about a month, until an
opportunity occurred of sending them home, passage free.
In consequence of this benevolent act, the inhabitants of
Cape Town opened a subscription and sent home the
remainder of the men, so that the benefits of Masonry were
experienced by the entire crew.

About the year 1742, Captain Preverot, of the French Navy, brother of the celebrated Doctor of Medicine (of the same name) in the Faculty at Paris, was shipwrecked off an island, the governor of which was a Freemason, who hearing of his misfortunes, and learning that he too was a brother, conducted him to his house, where he was furnished with all the comforts of life until a ship bound for France touched at the place. Before his departure, however, his benefactor loaded him with presents, and gave him as much money as was sufficient to carry him to his native country.

In the summer of 1835 (writes an inhabitant of the Shetland Islands), the schooner *Vigilant*, Captain Berguin, from Dunkirk, arrived in Lerwick harbour with loss of sails and other damage. The captain procured an agent with whom he agreed for the necessary repairs, which were soon effected, and the vessel declared ready for sea. A misunderstanding, however, arose between the captain and agent on the charges incurred, which, in the sequel, proved to be excessive. The captain threatened to sail without acknowledging the account, unless corrected, whereupon a *meditatione fugœ* warrant was procured against him. As he understood the English language very imperfectly I proffered my services in his forlorn state. He earnestly requested that a Freemason might be sent him, and to some of these I made his case known. The agent who procured the warrant, the judge who signed it, and the captain who suffered by it were all Freemasons. Instant justice was rendered, and the captain immediately liberated.

In 1762, two French prisoners in Edinburgh Castle, who were Freemasons, were allowed four guineas from the Grand Lodge. In the same year the Earl of Elgin and Kincardine, Grand Master, ordered the several Lodges under his jurisdiction to assume Don Antonio de Pizarro, Governor of Tarragona in Spain, as a nominal member, the reason for this being as follows :—

Mr. Dickson, a Scottish Mason, was sailing from Gibraltar to Italy, and during the voyage a storm compelled him to run his ship ashore under the walls of Tarragona. The captain and crew were seized as prisoners of the Spanish King, and brought before the Governor, Don Antonio de Pizarro, who, however, treated them with the utmost humanity. After conversing for a while, the Governor inquired of the captain concerning some persons at Gibraltar whom he knew to be Freemasons, which made him conjecture that Don Antonio himself was a member of the Society. Mr. Dickson, therefore, made a sign, which was returned by the Governor, who gave orders that nothing should impede the captain's journey, whom, because of his being a brother, he allowed with his crew to return to Gibraltar, and supplied them with all necessaries for the passage. On arriving at Gibraltar, Mr. Dickson informed the Governor of what had occurred, who was so charmed with the story that he forthwith released sixteen Spaniards belonging to the garrison of Tarragona, and the same night he was made a Mason. The captain afterwards sent an account of the whole affair to the Grand Master of Scotland, who, with his own hand wrote a letter of thanks to Don Antonio, and ordered the story to be recorded in the books of the Grand Lodge. Also, as the noble behaviour of Don Antonio de Pizarro had done honour to Masonry, the Earl of Elgin and Kincardine ordered that he should be assumed as a nominal member of all the regular Lodges in Scotland. The Governor of Gibraltar, referred to in this anecdote, would appear to have been Major-General Parslow (1761), who was preceded in that office by the Earl of Home, and followed by Lieut.-General the Hon. Edward Cornwallis, both of whom are known to have been active members of the fraternity at a much earlier date.

During the last war with France, a small coasting vessel, trading between Plymouth and Hampshire, was captured by a French privateer. The officer who boarded the vessel discovered among its papers the certificate of a Master Mason, which belonged to the English captain. The circumstance having been reported to the French Commander, who was a member of the Craft, he came on board the prize and proposed to his captive that if he would pledge his word, as a man of honour and a Mason, to use his best exertions to obtain the release of his (the French captain's) brother, who was then a prisoner of war at Plymouth, he would restore his vessel and allow him to proceed on his voyage. The terms were gladly acceded to, and the grateful Englishman proceeded to his destination, where, on landing, he assembled the Masters of the Plymouth Lodges and communicated to them this remarkable convention. One of the Masters was employed by the government in the management and supply of the prison, and, on reporting the facts to the Head Board in London, received by the next post an order to complete with despatch and fidelity an exchange which the French Brother had commenced with so much confidence and generosity.

On the resumption of the war—after the short "Peace of Amiens"—in 1803, Captain Akerman was returning from Newfoundland to Poole, and his vessel was captured by a French privateer off Portland, nearly in sight of his native place. On nearing the coast of France, as the prize-master was overhauling the ship's papers, he observed a Masonic certificate, dated September 10th, 1783, showing that the captain belonged to the Lodge of Amity at Poole. He then called one of the crew who could speak English, and through him conveyed to Captain Akerman his great regret at not knowing sooner that he was a Mason, or he would have put him on shore at Portland or Albany Head. On landing at Bordeaux the captain was treated very kindly, and regularly billetted at the house of a Freemason when proceeding to Verdun on his parole. At that depot the unfortunate victim of war remained until the peace of 1814, but during his eleven years of imprisonment often experienced the kindness of his captor. While thus detained, Napoleon passed through Verdun, and, hearing that several Masons were among the prisoners, he inquired how they conducted themselves, and, on receiving a favourable report, ordered a dinner to be given them. They were invited accordingly, and, after a due examination by the proper officers, sat down (on Christmas Day) to an excellent repast, the Commandant presiding. At the close of the meeting each Englishman was presented with a five-franc-piece in the Emperor's name, which they gratefully received, though from the hands of their national enemy.

In the year 1807, writes another victim of the war, I became a prisoner in France, and was for a time detained at Verdun. But in the following year, from some caprice of the French Government, several of the *détenus* were ordered to Givet, another depot for English prisoners, and a place at a considerable distance from Verdun. We left, a party five, four naval officers and one civilian, escorted by *gendarmes*. Occasionally we were handcuffed to deserters from the French Army, and otherwise illtreated, particularly at night. This continued until our arrival at Mezieres or Sedan (I forget which), where a rest of three days occurred. This interval was made use of by the civilian already mentioned, who, discovering that there was a Masonic Lodge in the town, contrived to send a note which fell into the hands of the fraternity. Shortly after, a gentleman came to the prison and conversed with the writer, whom he supplied with money and informed him that better food would be furnished during the remainder of our stay there, also that the rest of our journey should be rendered more easy and agreeable. These promises were strictly carried into effect. We were at once supplied with abundant fare, including wine of the best quality, and indulged with a ramble in the town under the escort of a solitary *gendarme*, while the concluding part of our journey was rendered more like a tour of pleasure than the march of prisoners from one depot to another—and all this because one of our party happened to be a Freemason.

During the early part of the present century, on the arrival of a British frigate at Havannah, the captain received a letter urgently soliciting his protection on behalf of some British sailors who were forcibly detained on board a privateer, then at anchor. A lieutenant was immediately despatched with a proper complement of hands to demand the men. He duly executed his task and returned to the frigate with his countrymen, but, on leaving the ship where they had been detained, the master of the vessel swore that before night he would be revenged.

In the evening the lieutenant went on shore and engaged in a game at billiards. While thus occupied he observed a swarthy, ill-looking man watching him most intently. In a corner of the room there was also a slender young man with a pale countenance also regarding him very earnestly. To his surprise a "Sign" was hastily given. It was fortunately exchanged, and a few seconds after a note was put into his hand containing these words,—"Beware! Take caution from a *Brother.*" Two other persons now accosted him and behaved in a manner likely to provoke a quarrel, in which they would probably have succeeded but for the caution he had just received. Prudence, however, came to his aid, and feigning an excuse he left the room, but without his hat, the better to deceive the persons of whose unfriendly intentions he had no longer any doubt. With difficulty he reached the house of the American Consul, four men pursuing him with knives in their hands, but the door opened in time and he was saved.

On the 6th November, 1812, the schooner *United Sisters,* of Poole, Joseph Webb, Master, was captured off the Start Point by *Le Furet,* French privateer, under the command of Captain Louis Mariencourt. Later in the same day, the Irish sloop *Three Friends,* of Youghal, James Campbell, Master, hove in sight, and was also taken possession of by the enemy. Soon, however, the signals of Masonry were exchanged between the three commanders, and instantly, ship, cargo, and liberty were bestowed on each of the prisoners of war, by the captain of the Privateer, Bro. Joseph Webb pledging his word to effect if possible the release, in exchange for the liberation of himself and his ship's company of Bro. J. Gautier of the French Schooner *La Confiance,* who had been captured in the earlier part of the same year, and was at that time detained on board the prison ship *Crown Prince* at Chatham.

Conduct so truly noble was soon reported by Bro. James Campbell to his Lodge, the Union, No. 13, at Limerick, and a silver vase of one hundred guineas value was voted to the generous Frenchman who, in the meantime, with his vessel, had been captured by the British Frigate *Modeste.*

D 2

This votive tribute, which, owing to the speedy liberation and subsequent death of the gallant Mariencourt, could not be presented, has since been reverentially preserved as the brightest ornament of the Lodge, and is the St. John's Box in all appeals to the sympathies of the brethren.

It is gratifying to relate that the efforts of the other Merchant Captain, Bro. Joseph Webb, to shorten the captivity of Bro. J. Gautier, were crowned with success.

The narrator of the following, shipped as a lad on board a vessel called the *Rover*, commanded by James Holley, and bound to the Bay of Honduras, from Kingston in the Island of Jamaica. One night about the middle watch, they were surprised, overpowered, and captured in an incredibly short period, by a French privateer. All hands were taken on board the Frenchman, and the vessel and crew plundered and made prisoners. The moon at this moment burst out in unusual splendour, and they could observe all that was going on upon the quarter-deck ; and it appeared to him and the others that the commander of the privateer was questioning their captain as to what his vessel had on board. When, after a short time, they approached each other, made some signs, and were at last locked hand in hand, the lookers on thought that they had each found in the other some long lost friend. A few hours afterwards everything was returned that had been taken, and the vessel delivered to the English captain, while the two men who had been enemies only such a short time before, now parted with the greatest apparent reluctance. They were Brother Masons.

In April, 1804, Lieut.-Colonel Duncan Campbell, of the Royals, arrived at Barbadoes from Guadaloupe. He had been captured together with Majors Blair and McDonel (of Keppoch), by a French privateer, on his way from England to join his regiment. On its being discovered that Major McDonel was a Freemason, the privateer's captain was particularly kind to him, as well as to his companions, and their baggage was preserved from plunder. He was introduced at a Mason's Lodge in Guadaloupe, where the whole party received great attention. Soon afterwards, having

been supplied with money, they were permitted to leave the
island on their parole until exchanged.

The following inscription is attached to a BISCUIT which
is enclosed in a glass case and preserved by the Lodge of
Amity, No. 137, Poole : —

"THIS BISCUIT

is preserved by the Lodge of Amity as a memorial of their
gratitude and brotherly affection for Jacques de Bon, captain of
the *Junon*, French privateer, of St. Malo, who captured at sea, on
the 13th of December, 1813, at Ham, in lat. 49·50 North—long. 7
West, the brig *Oak*, of Poole. Bro. Stephen Pack, Master,
belonging to Bros. G. W. Ledgard and John Goss, on her passage
from Bilbao to Poole, who, after treating him and his crew with
every mark of kindness, restored him his vessel, and sent on
board a dog, which before had been taken from a brother, with
this Biscuit suspended by a string round his neck, signifying he
would not keep a brother's dog in bondage nor see him want
bread. Thus the man who holds forth his hand for the relief of
his necessitous brethren, is fully repaid by the gratitude of those
whom he obliges, by the approbation of his own mind, and the
favour of that Omnipotent Being who cannot behold such a
bright display of Masonic virtues without asserting his divine and
everlasting approbation."

Then came Captain L. with his five daughters (writes
Harriet Martineau), he looked too old to be their father, and
well he might. When master of a vessel, he was set ashore
by pirates, with his crew, on a desert island, where he was
thirty-six days without food. Almost all his crew were dead,
and he was just dying, when help arrived—by means of
Freemasonry. Among the pirates was a Scotchman, a
Mason, as was Captain L. The two exchanged signs. The
Scotchman could not render aid at the moment, but after
many fruitless attempts he contrived to sail back at the
risk of his life, and landed on the desert island on the thirty-
sixth day from his leaving it. He had no expectation of
finding the party alive, but not to throw away a chance he
went ashore with a kettle full of wine in his hand. He
poured wine down the throats of the few whom he found
still breathing, and treated them so judiciously that they
recovered. At least it was called recovery. Captain L. took
the Scotchman home, and cherished him to the day of his
death.

Of Babastro, a renowned Spanish corsair, who, under the protection of Napoleon, did much injury to British small-craft in the Mediterranean I must (says Mrs. Broughton), in justice and charity, trace one redeeming trait. After the capture of an English prize by this so oft-named corsair, and while his crew were following their usual practice of stripping our unfortunate countrymen— to which they compelled submission by holding over them unsheathed knives—it so occurred that the master of the English vessel while under-going this unceremonious disrobing, made use of one of those mystic gestures invisible to all but the initiated brethren of the trowel and apron. Whatever that sign was, it did not pass unnoticed, for the hand of the giver was immediately clasped in that of Babastro, who at once ordered his satellites to release the English captain from their grasp, and he desired that whatever property was exclusively his own should be held sacred and restored to him. All that I recollect besides of this chieftain of the privateers which so long infested the coast of Algiers is, that the Emperor Napoleon judged him worthy of being named a member of the Legion of Honour.

A vessel of some 250 tons, with a crew of eighteen hands had left the Havannah, and was passing through the Keys, when a sail was descried, and the ship neared them every instant. The merchantman being a heavy sailer, was soon boarded by at least fifty men, the captain and crew ordered below, and the work of pillage commenced. A short time sufficed to secure all the portable valuables, which were put into a boat and conveyed on board the pirate. The captain and supercargo were then ordered on deck and interrogated as to the cargo itself. Concealment or subterfuge being entirely out of the question, they rendered the best account their indifferent knowledge of the Spanish language would permit. Matters were apparently assuming a civil character, when on the pirate's boat boarding for the second time, the captain observed in the bow a man standing upright in "the bloody shirt," with an axe resting on his shoulder. The party soon came on deck, and the captain was ordered to go forward ; the supercargo insisted on accompanying him. They had scarcely proceeded a few paces when the captain felt himself struck a severe blow on the shoulder, and turning quickly round beheld the supercargo struggling. It appeared that the latter, observing the intention to strike off the captain's head, had averted the blow—the other coolly remarked that he thought the chance afforded him of saving time and torture was lost, and that, therefore, the windlass would be a good block for the purpose. Not a moment was allowed for preparation. They reached the windlass, the captain and supercargo embraced. The former knelt down, and was about to place his head on the block, when, in addressing a short prayer to his God, he made a sign—the axe that all but gleamed for its fatal purpose fell at his feet. The pirates swore they saw a ship, and that no time must be lost in clearing the cargo. In two hours they sacked the vessel, left a few days' provisions, gave the captain his ship, and spared the lives of all.

Some three years afterwards the supercargo, on revisiting the Havannah, was accosted by a man who inquired after his captain, and hoped he was well, saying that he, the supercargo, was lucky in having sailed with " one of them " (alluding to the captain being a Freemason), as otherwise they would all have been beheaded. A promise was also made that if the captain should re-visit those parts he should go " free."

In June, 1823, the *Minerva*, a Dutch merchant vessel, returning from Batavia to Europe with several rich passengers, most of whom were Freemasons, including Bro. Engelhard, Deputy Grand Master of the Lodges in India, was attacked off the coast of Brazil, and defeated by a corsair under Spanish colours. Pillage and massacre were about to take place. In this extremity Bro. Engelhard made a Masonic signal, when the commander of the corsair, who the moment before was insensible to prayers and entreaties, became moved even to softness. He was himself a Mason, as well as several of his crew. He acknowledged the Brethren, embraced them, restored their vessel and property, made compensation for the damage inflicted, and only demanded in return the favour of affiliation with a Dutch Lodge

In the year 1830, a Bro. Glen, afterwards a member of the Phœnix Lodge, Sunderland, but who had not then been initiated into Masonry, was mate of a merchant vessel bound for the island of Cuba. The crew, besides the captain and mate, consisted of seven seamen. When approaching their port of destination they discovered a suspicious-looking schooner hovering in their course, which bore down quickly upon them, and the merchantman was boarded by twenty-five desperadoes, all of whom were armed with pistols and cutlasses. The commander of the pirate was a Spaniard, and from the appearance of the lieutenant, who was dressed in a peculiar manner, Bro. Glen conjectured that he must have been a Maltese. The unfortunate crew of the merchantman were bound and secured in the fore part of the vessel. The captain and Bro Glen were also tied to two pillars in the stern cabin. The work of plunder being finished, directions were given for the destruction of the vessel by fire. Gunpowder, tar-barrels, and other combustible materials were brought from the schooner, and the train was actually laid. At this juncture the lieutenant of the pirates went aft and entered the cabin where Bro. Glen and his captain were secured. The latter, fortunately for himself and crew, happened to be a Mason. As a last resource he attracted the pirate's attention, and addressed him (in the language of the Craft) as an apprentice. The other regarded the captain steadfastly for an instant, and replied as a Fellow Craft. Some further communication then passed between them, though neither could understand the speech of the other : but in this short interval they had made themselves understood by the universal medium of Masonry. The lieutenant then returned to the deck, where, as it subsequently appeared, he dissuaded his commander from burning the vessel. After this he went again into the cabin and wrote a short note in the Spanish language, which he carefully folded up and left on the table. Next he cut the cords with which Bro. Glen had been bound, and making a gesture of caution left the ship with the remaining portion of the boarding party. Bro. Glen speedily released his captain, who said that he had made himself known to the pirate as a Mason, and to that circumstance their deliverance must be attributed. After waiting for a while they cautiously proceeded to the deck and released the crew. Nothing particular occurred until the second day following, when to their consternation they again espied the piratical schooner, which bore down upon them as before. They hoisted their English colours, when the pirate recognising the vessel as the same which had been recently pillaged, merely displayed his black flag, the terrible ensign of his dreadful calling, which he immediately lowered, and then altering his course was seen by them no more. The letter which had been left on the cabin table was couched in the following terms :—" Brother,—Having recognized you as a Mason, I have induced the captain to spare the lives of yourself and crew—but for this you would all have perished." It only remains to be stated that Bro. Glen on his return to England lost no time in seeking admission into a Society, which, under Providence, had been instrumental in the preservation of his life.

In the year 1795, the ship *Betsy*, belonging to a Boston merchant, sailed from West Gardner, Maine. It was commanded by Captain Chapin Sampson, who had been received into Masonry, in what is now St. George's Lodge of Harmony, at Liverpool, on the 15th of August, 1793. The vessel was taken off Malaga, by an Xebec from Tripoli, and carried with all on board into that port. There, the captain and crew were stripped of their clothing, except a slight piece of cotton about the waist. Being the first Americans brought into Tripoli, they were driven through the city chained, and were pelted by every offensive missile. The captain was thrown into a dungeon, but after a few days taken out and set at work clearing the cargo from his ship. While thus engaged, an officer named Hassan Bey, occupying a high station in Tripoli, made himself known as a Freemason. Captain Sampson was soon liberated, clothed, and furnished with many comforts. An opportunity of releasing him was found, and when about to leave, Hassan Bey, still mindful of his Masonic duties, made him numerous presents. This worthy native of Tripoli, and faithful brother, had been initiated in France. Captain Sampson, then eighty years of age, was living at West Gardner, Maine, in 1845.

Military Anecdotes.

June 18th, 1815.—A Belgian officer during the engagement, recognised in the opposing army about six in the evening, a former associate and Brother Mason, member of the same Lodge ; they were at such distance apart that he feared the chance of a mutual greeting was impossible, but he dreaded more the possibility of a personal conflict. At length when he saw his friend attacked and wounded—he forgot everything but that they were brothers. The Belgian rushed into the *melee*, and at the risk of being considered a traitor, he protected him—made him prisoner —placed him in safety—and, after the battle, renewed his friendship. On the same evening, about nine o'clock, about fifty men, nearly all wounded, the miserable remains of two French regiments, found themselves encompassed by a considerable party of the enemy ; after performing prodigies of valour, finding retreat impossible, they decided on laying down their arms ; but the enemy, irritated by their obstinate defence and the havoc they had made, continued to fire on them. The lieutenant in command, as well as the men, considered that nothing but a miracle could save them ; a sudden inspiration seized the officer, he advanced to the front in the midst of the firing, and made the sign of distress. Two Hanoverian officers observed him, and by a spontaneous movement, without consulting their commander, ordered the troops to cease firing, and, after securing the prisoners, they placed themselves at the disposal of their General for the breach of military discipline ; he also was a Mason, and instead of punishing he approved of their generous conduct.

A French officer at the battle of Waterloo was so badly wounded as to be unable to keep up with his regiment, and in that situation was discovered by a Scottish Dragoon of the British Army, who put spurs to his horse and galloped up to dispatch him. But just as he was on the point of striking the fatal blow, the officer gave a Masonic sign of distress. This was recognised by the Scotsman, whose arm was immediately unnerved. Love and sympathy were depicted in his countenance, and as he turned his horse to ride away, he was heard to say, "The Lord bless and protect thee, my Brother!"

On the memorable 16th of June, 1815, at the moment when the allied army commenced a retrograde movement, a Scottish field officer, who had been seriously wounded in the affair of Quatre Bras, was left on the field of battle. Trampled on by the French Cavalry, he thought but of death, when he perceived the patrols of the enemy who came to succour the wounded. Rallying the little strength that remained, he cried out in a faint tone, and implored the assistance of his brethren. This attracted the attention of a French surgeon, who, recognising in him a Mason, hastened to his aid. He first dressed those wounds which presented the greatest danger, and then raised and carried the patient to the sick quarters—placed him on his own pallet—watched by his side—and directed him to be conveyed to Valenciennes, where he was warmly recommended to his friends, from whom the officer received the kindest attention, and by whose care he was completely restored to health.

The 17th (French) Chasseurs, entering the town of Genappe, made prisoners of all they found. Some musket shots, fired from the windows of a house, struck several of the soldiers, who instantly attacked the house, vowing revenge, and determining to put to the sword nine wounded enemies that were lying there. The chief of the Chasseurs was at their head. At the critical moment he observed one of these poor wounded fellows, a Brunswick officer, who made the "sign of distress." Vengeance ceased—war lost its vigour—the Masonic appeal conquered. He threw himself between his own soldiers and the wounded men, and then generously saved their lives. This noble action was not unrewarded, for, on the morrow, he was wounded in his turn, and taken prisoner by the Prussians. He was recognised as a Mason by an officer, who took him under his care, attended to his wants, and restored to him the money of which he had been despoiled as a booty.

At the close of the fierce battle of the Moskowa, in the general *melee* which ensued, two members of the Craft, a French officer of Cavalry and a Russian officer of Infantry, engaged in a hand-to-hand combat. The former's sword had shivered that of the latter, and was already uplifted to cut him down, when he made a Masonic sign. The sign was recognised, and although it was made too late to stop the descending blow altogether, yet it was not made too late to weaken its force. The Russian officer was only slightly wounded, and instead of being killed he became a prisoner, and received such succour as in the circumstances it was possible for his captor to afford. This story is related on the authority of an eye-witness of the incident to which it refers, M. de Beaufort, who served as Chef de Bataillon during the Russian campaign, and greatly distinguished himself at the Moskowa, receiving the cross of the Legion of Honour from the Emperor Napoleon on the field of battle.

A French officer, at the battle of Austerlitz, had, with his company, been separated from his regiment at the commencement of the action. After performing prodigies of valour, the devoted band were cut to pieces, and the officer dangerously wounded, but he still refused to give up his sword, until, exhausted by loss of blood, he fell, making the Masonic sign. The Prussian officer in command, who was one of the initiated, on perceiving this, ran forward and drew off his men, who, in their fury, were preparing to strike the death-blow. Faithful to his Masonic principles, he had his brother, no longer his enemy, carried to his own tent, where his kindness and attention was so great that his prisoner was in doubt whether he ought not to bless his glorious defeat. When his health was completely restored, he perceived the necessity of complying with the laws of war, and prepared to depart to the place assigned to the prisoners; but he first demanded an interview with his captor. What was his gratitude and astonishment to learn that he was free! The Prussian officer had managed to get his name placed on the first list of those who were to be exchanged

Again, in the time of the late war, the Prussians invested the frontiers of France, and committed all sorts of outrages. They one day entered a Chateau, and after insulting the inmates and destroying everything they could lay their hands on, seized a box containing a large sum of money. The owner, on trying to prevent their taking his property, would have fared very hardly had he not, on a sudden thought, made the sign. The officer, who was a Mason, was immediately recalled to the duties which he had unknowingly violated. He dismissed his men, and placed a guard at the Chateau to prevent similar outrages.

The following appears in the autobiography of M. Gerard (Master at one time of the Globe Lodge, Vincennes) who for his military services was decorated with the Legion of Honour in the Kremlin, at Moscow, in the year 1812 :—

"On the 2nd of May 1810, during the sanguinary revolt at Madrid. I belonged to a troop of Dragoons ordered to that much-disturbed city. We reached our destination towards the end of April, and were temporarily stationed in a village about three miles distant from the city on the road leading to France.

" A few days after our arrival. I mentioned to a young officer, a nephew of our Colonel, that I desired very much to visit Madrid. of which I had heard a great deal. He expressed also a wish to spend a few hours in a visit to its far-famed churches and other public buildings. and promised me to ask for leave of absence. His request was granted by the Colonel and we obtained a pass for the 1st and 2nd of May.

" As soon as we had obtained our *conge*. we made good use of our time and entered the city early in the morning and spent the whole day in examining the gorgeous churches and half-oriental public places. of which I had heard so much when a boy. Weary and exhausted we spent the night at the house of a French tavern-keeper upon the Square Del Sol. where the officers and employers of our army were in the habit of congregating. The next morning we took our breakfast at an early hour, and were just preparing to resume our sight-seeing, when several officers of the staff abruptly entered the house and requested us to repair immediately to the barracks or to our quarters. They also informed us that the troops had been ordered to remain in their quarters, that everywhere they were beating to arms. and that the streets and squares were swarming with armed Spaniards evidently much excited. No time was to be lost and we resolved to leave instantly. in order to quit the city and repair to our quarters.

" As soon as we had gained the open air. we heard the terrible sound of a general *rappel*—drummers were everywhere beating to arms. We endeavoured to redouble our speed, but perceived very soon that it was impossible to reach our quarters while thus surrounded. A large number of Spaniards, armed with deadly weapons of every conceivable kind, now advanced upon us and obstructed the street through which we had to pass. We knew that attempting a passage through their ranks would be certain death ; we, therefore, looked for an opening through which to escape. but we could perceive only a little street or rather blind alley on our right. My friend seized me by the arm. and. dragging me along. cried. · Come let us enter into ——.' But before he had time to finish the sentence he fell dead at my feet, pierced by several balls. I escaped with only a ball through my hat : but confused by the sudden attack. and wholly at a loss how to attempt any further escape, I already gave myself up for lost, when it happily occurred to me that I had been made a Mason, and I made use of the means which the Craft had placed in my hands to call for help in imminent danger. My appeal was not made in vain. That happy thought saved my life. The door of the house. from which the shots had been fired, was immediately thrown open. and a powerful and tall man with a heavy moustache and a military overcoat rushed out and drew me into the house while he whispered to me in French. · Fear not, and follow me. a brother leads the way.' When he had taken me into an outhouse and fastened the door. he proceeded to test me, and we exchanged those proofs known only to the initiated.

"Having satisfied himself of my claim to his protection, he offered me a goat-skin filled with wine and we fraternized. He then bade me wait for him a little while he went out and locked the door behind him. In less than five minutes he returned with a *sombrero* and a large Spanish cloak in his hand. Disguised in these. he led me from the house and through different streets until we reached the gates of the city. After we had passed them by means of the countersign in his possession, he pointed out to me my quarters, of which I had given him a description. Before he took leave of me, he threw his arms around my neck and said : ' My Brother. I am a Captain in the English infantry, but now on a secret mission in Spain. My name is Henry Sneton. If ever the Great Architect should offer you an opportunity to save the life of any of my countrymen. do for them what I have this day ·done for you. Farewell. God speed you.'

"The name of this dear brother has ever since remained engraven upon my heart and there it will remain until it shall cease to beat.

"Ever since that epoch in my life have I sought to learn more concerning the fate of my noble preserver : but only lately have I been able to ascertain from a Captain of the English army. whom I met in the South of France. that Brother Sueton fell in 1812 at the Cape of Good Hope, after he had attained to the rank of Major.

"May the Great Architect cause the earth to rest lightly upon his grave."

The memorable battle of Mars-le-Tour (the second day's battle at Metz), at about 2 o'clock, p m., the third company of the Ninth Battalion of Prussian Rifles were ordered to dislodge the enemy from a copse of wood about 150 yards in front. The men advanced under a galling fire, which in less than two minutes, cut down about half of them. Notwithstanding, they advanced at a run with a hurrah! and, reaching the wood, charged the French, who were of the Sixty-fourth Regiment of the line, about 200 strong. Many were bayonetted, many taken prisoners, and the remainder fled, save a company of about thirteen, who stood their ground, got behind a large log, refusing to surrender, and unable to get away. They were all shot down except three, one of them a corporal. Half-a-dozen Prussians jumping over the log, were about to bayonet them, when the corporal gave the "sign of distress." Instantly, non-commissioned officer Bertran called out, "Don't harm him! he is my *brother!*" and with his own rifle, parried the blow aimed at him. The Frenchman was disarmed and led away, but his life was saved through the silent language of the Craft.

Captain Laurent Michel, who was initiated in the Lodge, "Disciples of Solomon," Marseilles, in 1811, was distinguished as a good man and brave soldier, and became known as the saviour of the "Holy Battalion," a title earned by his prompt and energetic conduct. He was one of those of whom Dryden says,

> "Oh, but 'tis brave to be admired, to see
> The crowds with heads uncovered cry. that's he."

When the star of the Emperor Napoleon was declining, and the wish for peace had become as unanimous as the previous desire for fame, among the earlier movements were those of the national guards for centralization and union, in opposition to the Emperor. A portion of the imperial troops had fallen into an ambuscade—carefully planned by a large division of the national guards, and many "a good tall fellow" who had escaped the bullets of the enemy, must have met his death at the hands of his countrymen, had it not been for the occurrence which I am about to relate. Marseilles was again to be the theatre of destruction, the scene of blood. The troops of Fort St. Nicholas had already received orders to march, already had the hour arrived for the death of the devoted little band—the line was formed, the command to make ready and present being given—but one word, one minute more, and the souls of the doomed men had been sent before their impartial Judge. Every hand was prepared for destruction, when the Captain of the Artillery, Laurent Michel, crying "stop!" in a voice of thunder, threw himself before the guns of the Artillery under his command. A powerful and pathetic appeal to his companions in arms, soon convinced the national guards of the error they were about to commit, and they yielded to his eloquence by allowing the troops they had encompassed to disperse. It appears that when the unfortunate battalion had arrived at the trap prepared for it, and saw that every avenue for escape had been closed—that not a hope remained—one man, with desperate resolve, appealed by a sign of distress to the sympathy of his opponents. Laurent Michel's eagle eye watched the motion of his brother—and to see, to recognise, and to place his life in the most imminent danger to save others, was the work of a moment.

The following is given on the authority of an American captain of infantry, who took part in the capture of Fort George, during the last war (1812). The British troops were informed that orders had been issued to the American soldiers to give no quarter. This had probably been done for the purpose of inducing them to fight with greater desperation, and to prevent desertion. After Captain Arrowsmith's Company had landed and formed, he led them ·to the charge. The British troops retired as the Americans advanced, leaving a young wounded officer directly in the line of Arrowsmith's Company. As they approached he arose on one leg (the other was broken) and attempted to get out of the way, believing they would bayonet him if he did not. Unable, however, to accomplish his purpose he fell, but turning to them as he sat on the ground, he gave the soul-thrilling appeal of a Mason. Captain Arrowsmith described his feelings at that moment as the most extraordinary he had ever experienced. I felt, said he, as if the hairs of my head stood upright and held off my hat. But he instantly called out to the wounded man, "don't be afraid my brave fellow, you shan't be hurt." Soon after he saw a surgeon, and informed him that a friend of his, with a red coat on, lay wounded in the rear near a certain bush, and requested his attention to him, a wish that was immediately complied with. Arrowsmith, who was wounded in the head during the same battle, was shortly afterwards laid by the side of his friend with the *red coat*, where they had time to cultivate an intimate friendship, which lasted for many years.

About the year 1815, while the 4th Regiment of Foot, commonly known as the " King's Own," was passing through the Bermudas, on its way to take part in the last war with America, both the officers and men experienced the utmost inconvenience and distress, their pay being greatly in arrear, and their rations extremely limited. At this crisis in their affairs the officers were one day invited to the table of a merchant residing in one of the principal towns. In the course of the entertainment the generous host did not fail to discover that among his guests there was one for whom, though a stranger, he felt the warmth of friendship, and with whom, though a foreigner, he felt the ties of brotherhood. In a word they were Masons. To draw the brother aside, to hear the record of sufferings and privations, and to furnish ample means of relief and consolation, was but the work of a few moments. A considerable sum of money was advanced by the merchant for the use of the regiment, and thus—by the existence of a certain principle of action in two individuals—a multitude were raised from a state of suffering and destitution to one of comparative ease and enjoyment.

Captain George Smith. R.A., Inspector of the Royal Military Academy at Woolwich, in his " Use and Abuse of Freemasonry," a work published in 1783, and dedicated to " Mankind in General, and the Ladies in particular," relates that a Scotch officer, in the Prussian service, who unfortu-

nately was taken prisoner at the battle of Lutzen, with four
hundred of his companions was conveyed to Prague. The
Scotchman made himself known as a Mason, was immediately released from confinement, had the honour to dine
daily at the tables of the most distinguished of the Society,
was always requested to assist at their meetings, and
desired to think himself a *Freemason* and not a *prisoner of
war*. On the exchange of prisoners, which happened about
three months after the engagement, the Scotch gentleman
was in the politest manner presented with a purse of sixty
ducats, to defray his expenses to the regiment. This
circumstance, adds Captain Smith, was communicated to
him by the officer himself, in a letter dated May 13th, 1760.

The following was related at a meeting of the Shakespeare
Lodge, No. 99, in 1839 :—A Brother, whose pursuits led
him to that scene of turmoil and strife, the Basque
provinces, saw much of the nature of the intestine war that
was raging, and which was marked by little else than
rapine, murder, and all the effects of faithless depravity.
Upon one occasion he witnessed the capture of four
prisoners, who were little accounted, and ordered for
execution. The fiat went forth, and there was no appeal—
no hope—the *Durango Decree* consigned the captives to an
ignominious and merciless death. On the following morning
the jailor brought three of the prisoners from their
dungeon and delivered them to the fatal guard, by whom
they were shot. But where was the fourth? The answer
was, "Dangerously ill—he would die before night." The
jailor, accustomed to deal with—to obey the orders of a
despot—and to witness the ghastliness of doomed men on
the verge of eternity—himself without feeling, for all
feeling had been blunted by the customs of his horrid
office—indifferent to everything passing around him—such
a man—*this* man was arrested in his course of unholy
occupation on being reminded of his obligation by one
of those unhappy captives, who pleaded for mercy to his
God through the hope—the last hope that was left—the
trial of strength, from the bursting chords of his heart,
to affect that of the executioner with the sign of

sympathy and distress. Mysterious agency! Freemasonry triumphed—the man that was callous to all other humanities blenched at the signal, and saved the Brother. The continued horrors prevented immediate inquiries after the subject of this anecdote. It was at length announced that he had died, and no one cared what had become of his body; indeed, little inquiry was ever made after those whom the *Decree* had denounced. The jailor, however, had secured the Brother until he found means to favour his escape, and thus, in a measure, has made some reparation to society, by showing that if war be declared against society, the feelings of humanity, by the blessed aid of Freemasonry, will triumph over the Demon of Darkness.

Early in 1837 an English gentleman arrived at St. Jean de Luz, and after resting for a night at an inn, rang the bell and asked the servant girl to inquire if there was any boat about to start for St. Sebastian. The girl soon returned with the information that a boat would be ready in an hour. But on arriving at the beach the traveller found to his surprise and vexation, that the craft in which he was about to trust himself was a small sailing lugger of about twelve tons burthen. The passage across the bar was rough in the extreme, but the weather then moderated, and at this juncture the skipper addressed his passenger rather freely, intimating his belief that he was a military man, and declared it would be impossible to make for St. Sebastian, but that he should put into Fontarabia. The traveller's eyes were now clearly opened. The *Durango Decree* rang in his ears—he had heard that the Carlists paid as much as £20 to any boat that landed a Christino officer. He implored in turn all hands to alter their course, but ineffectually, and the dreaded harbour was in sight. Providence, at this awful moment, suggested the attempt to practise the Masonic test. Forlorn hope as it was it succeeded. The skipper came deliberately forward, took the traveller by the hand, called him "Brother," and ordered the mate to "put about." The course was altered, and he was safely landed at Passages, and even escorted to the protection of his friends.

At the battle of Dettingen, in 1743, one of the French Guards, having had his horse killed under him, became so entangled as to be unable to extricate himself. While in this condition an English Dragoon galloped up, and, sabre in hand, was about to deprive him of life. The French soldier, however, made the signs of Masonry, which, the Dragoon recognizing, not only saved his life, but freed him from his perilous situation—making him, of course, a prisoner, as the fraternal ties cannot dissolve those of patriotism.

Not among civilized men only has the universal genius of Masonry extended her purifying and protecting influences. Joseph Brandt, a celebrated Mohawk Indian, chief of the Six Nations, who had received the advantages of an English education, subsequently went to England, where he was initiated into the mysteries of Freemasonry. On his return to America, however, the habits of early life resumed their influence, while the acquired ones of education were abandoned ; and Brandt, throwing off the dress and usages of civilization, assumed once more the blanket and the rifle, and seemed to forget in the wilds of his native forest the lessons he had learned in his transatlantic schools. But the sequel of the story will show that, to whatever extent his memory may have been treacherous in other things, on one subject, at least, it proved to be admirably retentive.

During the Revolutionary War, at the battle of the Cedars, thirty miles above Montreal, on the St. Lawrence, Colonel McKinstry, then a captain in Paterson's regiment of -Continental troops, was twice wounded, and afterwards taken prisoner by the Indians employed in the British service.

The previous bravery and success of Captain McKinstry had excited at once the fears and resentment of his Indian conquerors; and, in accordance with the customs of savage warfare, he was forthwith doomed to die at the stake, accompanied with all those horrid and protracted torments which the Indians know so well how both to inflict and to endure. Already had he been fastened to the fatal tree, and the preparations for the human sacrifice were rapidly proceeding, when, in the strong agony of his despair, and scarcely conscious of a hope, the captive made the great mystic appeal of a Mason in the hour of danger. It was seen, and understood, and felt by the Chief of the Six Nations, also a Colonel unattached in the British Army, who was present on the occasion. Brandt at once interposed, and succeeded, by the influence of his position, in rescuing his American Brother from his impending fate. Having freed him from his bonds, he conducted and guarded him in safety to Quebec, where he placed him in the hands of the English, by whom he was permitted to return to America on his parole.

A pleasing incident—with which is associated another anecdote relating to the same Indian Chief—occurred at the raising to the third degree of the Hon. Thomas S. Wilson, of Iowa :—Upon his admission to the Lodge he saw an Indian present, sitting with the members. After being introduced to him he learned that he was the grandson of the celebrated Colonel Brandt, who commanded the Indian allies of the British during the war of the Revolution.

" In one of the battles which occurred in Pennsylvania the grandfather of Judge Wilson was, with others, captured, and the company of which he was a member turned over to the Indians as their share of the trophies of victory. With a view to having some sport with their captives, the Indians would cause the American soldiers to kneel down, when an Indian would mount his back, compel him to creep to the water and crawl in, when the Indian would duck his head sometimes strangling them to death. When it came Soldier Wilson's turn, being a very stout man, he rose and threw the Indian over his head into the water, which, while it amused the Indians upon the bank, very much incensed the one victimized, whereupon he demanded that he and the remaining soldiers who had survived the ordeal should be tomahawked. Accordingly they were ranged into line, when Wilson said to his companion that he was going to appeal to the Indians and make the Masonic sign of distress. His companion laughed at the idea but joined in and gave the sign, when instantly the Indian chief rushed to their rescue and they were saved. The Indian chief proved to be the celebrated warrior Brandt, the grandfather of the one present who witnessed the introduction into Masonry of the grandson of the soldier whose life his grandfather had saved, many years later, and in a territory wholly unknown to the civilized world at the time of the incident to which I have referred."

Similar tales are related of Tecumseh, the famous Shawanee warrior and orator, in connection with the war of 1812, during which he was an ally of the British, with the rank of Brigadier General.

There is a circumstance connected with the life of Major-General Israel Putnam (U.S.A.) which is not generally known. In the French and Indian Wars he commanded a corps of partizans on the frontiers. In a severe skirmish it was his fate to become a captive to the Indians. So gallant a warrior was worthy of no ordinary death. After being insulted and tortured in their villages he was led to the stake. The faggots were piled around him; the flames leaped and played over his wasted form. He had taken his last look of earth, and was consigning his soul to God when he beheld a French officer approaching. As a last resort he hailed him in a way that speaks with more than trumpet tones to the heart of a genuine Brother. Quick as lightning the cords were severed, the burning faggots were dispersed, and the officer rescued Putnam at the imminent peril of his own life.

So powerful is the word that binds our Brethren in the hour of peril! Putnam always said that he owed his life to Masonry, as he felt confident the Frenchman never would have incurred the risk of displeasing the Indians so much, to save any but a *Brother*. Through life his zeal and services to the "good cause" were equal to the debt he owed, and after a long life spent in the service of his country, "on the square," he met the grim tyrant with the firmness of a Mason, and the hopeful resignation of a Christian.

At the eventful battle of Buena Vista (in the Mexican war), a scene occurred which is worthy of being recorded. During the fiercest moments of the fight, a young soldier of the 2nd Kentucky Infantry, the ranks of which were more than decimated during the engagement, fell wounded, but apparently not mortally, on the ground. A score of lances pointed to his heart, but at that trying moment the young man thew himself upon that faith which so rarely fails. He made the sign, and the next instant a Mexican dashed past the gleaming instruments of death, and raised his prostrate *foe*, now his *brother*, and bore him off. The youth, however, ultimately perished with his protector, but the act itself still lives as a memento of the force and purity of the Masonic tie.

Among the prisoners taken by the Union troops at the time Picket made his great charge at Gettysburg, was a Virginian sergeant. He was a Mason. Captain John A. Kellogg, of the Sixth Wisconsin, gave him a drink of something reviving from his canteen, and put some rations in his empty haversack. Their parting was that of brothers.

In December, 1864, when Kellogg was a colonel commanding his regiment (says the relator of the anecdote), I accompanied him on a ride along the picket line, a few miles to the left of Petersburg. By some means and without knowing it, we got beyond the picket lines. We were brought to a halt suddenly by the unmilitary salute : " Is that you, Captain Kellogg ? "

Looking up and about two rods to the right we saw a lieutenant and a dozen men in grey, who had apparently just taken their arms in preparation for serious business.

" That's my name, sir," answered the colonel.

" Beg pardon—Colonel Kellogg. You were a captain at Gettysburg. Allow me to extend congratulations upon your promotion."

It was becoming interesting, and both of us were making plans for a shooting match between a dozen confederate pickets with guns in their hands, and two officers with only revolvers, and they not in hand.

" Guess you don't remember me, colonel ? '

"I guess that is so," said Kellogg; and he was more nervous than I ever saw him in battle.

"I'm the sergeant you gave a nip from your canteen and whose haversack you filled at Gettysburg. They have made me a lieutenant since then. I'd like to have a visit with you, but the officer of the day is due here. Guess you had better get back to your lines."

"Thank you, lieutenant," said the colonel, saluting, and as we turned to leave, the confederate gave the command: "Shoulder arms! Right dress! Present arms!" Then both of us lifted our hats. There was fraternity for you.

My friend, General John Corson Smith, writes:—When in Murfeesboro.' (Tennessee), among the Confederate prisoners under my charge I found the adjutant of an Alabama regiment wearing a Masonic charm, I asked him if he was a Freemason, and receiving an affirmative answer, without letting him know that I was member of the Craft, I accepted his personal parole within the lines, and sent him to the house of Judge Ready, the father-in-law of the Confederate General, John H. Morgan. When about to be sent to the rear for exchange, the adjutant asked me why I had so much confidence in him as to parole him. I answered "Because I knew you to be a Freemason."

From the same informant I learn that during the memorable raid made by Grant's army, on Petersburg (Virginia), in April, 1865, when Lee's lines were broken, a young Confederate officer lay in the road severely wounded, and when, without a moment's warning, a company of Federal Cavalry rode down towards him at full gallop; he saw death staring him in the face. His first thought was that possibly there might be a Mason among them, and he gave a sign of distress, known only to Masons. Then the Federal captain rode quickly to his side, dismounted and parted the company in the centre, without molesting the man in the least. He was quickly picked up, though a prisoner, taken to the rear and tenderly cared for, and in the course of time entirely restored to health.

General Smith also states that at the battle of Pea
Ridge, Lieutenant-Colonel (afterwards General) Frank J.
Herron, of Iowa, was lying wounded, and an Indian, of
General Albert Pike's command, was about to tomahawk
him, when he gave a Masonic sign. He was made a
prisoner and subsequently exchanged.

From the same source of authority I derive the following :
—" General Smith D. Atkins, of Illinois, relates that during
the Atlanta campaign, when pressing the enemy, he saw a
little white apron nailed to a cabin door, and riding up to
the cabin he asked a woman he found there its significance,
and was told that her husband was in Forest's Cavalry,
which was then fighting ; that her husband was a Freemason, and on leaving his home had said : ' There are
many Freemasons in the Federal army, and if she would
nail a white apron upon her door and let the Federals know
she was the wife of a Freemason she would be protected.' "
It is unnecessary to say that she was unmolested.

The late Charles A. Dana tells the following story of
General A. Rawlins, who was General Grant's chief of the
staff from the time the latter became a brigadier-general,
until he resigned his commission as Commander of the
Armies of the United States, to become president of the
great nation, the unity of which he had done so much to
preserve : " At the battle of Champion's Hill, on leaving
Logan, Rawlins and I were joined by several officers, and we
continued our ride over the field. On the hill, where the
thickest of the fight had taken place, we stopped and were
looking around at the dead and dying men lying all
about us, when suddenly a man, perhaps 45 or 50 years old
who had a Confederate uniform on, lifted himself up on his
elbow and said :

" ' For God's sake, gentlemen, is there a Mason among
you ? '

" ' Yes,' said Rawlins, ' I am a Mason.' He got off his
horse and kneeled by the dying man, who gave him some
letters out of his pocket. When he came back Rawlins had
tears on his cheek. The man, he told us, wanted him to

convey some souvenir, a miniature or a ring—I do not remember what—to his wife, who was in Alabama. Rawlins took the package and some time afterwards he succeeded in sending it to the woman." General Rawlins—as I am told by his comrade in arms, General J. C. Smith—was made a Mason in Galena, Illinois (1858), and while Secretary of War, U S.A., died at his post of duty in Washington City 1869

CHAPTER IV.

*Tell us then no more, that our Lodges are the receptacles of
sacrilegious and revolutionary miscreants,—I see them
frequented by men of unaffected piety, and undaunted
patriotism. Tell us no more that our brethren of the
Order are traitors, or indifferent to the welfare of their
country,—I see them in the form of heroes, at the head of
our fleets and our armies ; and the day will arrive when
a Freemason shall sway the sceptre of these Kingdoms,
and fill, with honour and with dignity, the British
throne.*

—SIR DAVID BREWSTER.

ALTHOUGH the Lodges held on board ships of war were few
in number, the Craft has always been largely supported by
members of the sea service. Anything like an exhaustive
list, however, even of the British Admirals alone (without
noticing the other ranks), who are or were Freemasons, would
take up too much space, and a selection must be made. The
names I am about to present are mainly derived from the
actual records of the Grand Lodge of England, but there are
three important exceptions, to which I shall assign priority
in my list.

Sir George Brydges (afterwards Lord) Rodney, at an
interval of his career (a political contest having ruined his
estate) found it necessary to retire to the continent, where
he became a member of the Secret Society and Masonic
Club in the Rue Saint Nicaise, at the French Capital. He
was elected under an assumed name, but on disclosing his
real one, at the instance of the Duc de Biron, Marshal of
France, his debts were paid, a banquet was given in his
honour, the street was illuminated, and couplets were
chanted to celebrate his departure for his native shores.
Generals Dumouriez, and Paoli (the Corsican Patriot), were
also members of the Club.

On his return to England, Rodney was again placed in

command of a squadron, and achieved a series of victories which culminated in his defeat of the French fleet under the Count de Grasse, in April, 1782, which saved Jamaica and ended the war at a blow.

The evidence relating to Nelson's connection with the Craft is as follows :—Among the furniture in possession of the Lodge of Friendship. No. 100, at Yarmouth, is an oblong block of white marble. On each of the long sides is an incised inscription. That on one side commemorates the foundation of the Lodge of United Friends, No. 564 ; while on the opposite side of the stone there appears :—

```
• In Memory of Broʳ Vᵗ NELSON
  of the Nile, & of Burnham Thorpe, in
  Norfolk, who lost his life in the arms
  of Victory. in an engagement with
  yᵉ Combin'd Fleets of France & Spain,
  of Cape Trafalgar, Oct. 21, 1805.
  Proposed by Broʳ. John Cutlove.
```

Unfortunately, the minute books covering this period have all disappeared, but it can be proved *aliunde* that John Cutlove was initiated in the Lodge of United Friends, on April 12th, 1799. Yet as Mr. Hamon Le Strange, from whose interesting work (*Freemasonry in Norfolk*) the foregoing is derived, well observes : " It is extremely unlikely that, in a place where Nelson was so well known as he was at Yarmouth, the members of the Lodge would have dared to place on the stone, commemorative of their own constitution, an inscription claiming him as a brother, which, if untrue, would have exposed them to ridicule and contradiction from many who knew the facts." From the same writer, we learn (and all the details of the story are well authenticated) that there is still in existence a masonic snuff-box, which was given by Lord Nelson to a friend, when they dined together at Yarmouth.

It is also on record that in March, 1801, the Admiral came into Yarmouth Roads with seven sail of the line, and that before leaving the station an event occurred to which he refers in a letter, addressed from Yarmouth Roads to Mr. Pillans, "Grand Master of the Ancient Order of Gregorians," which then flourished greatly at Norwich, thanking him for his election into that Society. Mr. Le Strange, whose words I reproduce, goes on to say,—"After the battle of Copenhagen, Nelson returned to Yarmouth, and landing there from the *Kite*, remained in the town for a time. He was also there when he returned to England after the battle of the Nile, so that there were ample opportunities for him to have been initiated at Yarmouth.

The terms "Gregorian" and "Gormogon," which occur in the fourth book of the *Dunciad*, are explained by Pope and Warburton, as meaning "A sort of Lay brothers, *slips* from the Root of Freemasons." The "Gregorians" are also mentioned by Crabbe in the *Borough*, as "a convivial sect," and "a kind of Masons, but without their sign."

It is at any rate abundantly clear that Nelson was admitted a member of one of the many festive societies which then existed, and are now forgotten rivals of the Freemasons. Hence, as it seems to me, the probability is enhanced—if we carefully bear in mind the lapidary evidence supplied by the Lodge of United Friends—that he also joined our own Fraternity, of which, his old friends, Sir Peter Parker, Admiral of the Fleet, was Deputy Grand Master; and the Duke of Clarence, Admiral of the White, (honorary) Past Grand Master, at the time he was received into the Order of the Gregorians.

As these sheets are passing through the press, I have been favoured with the following extract from the minutes of the Union Lodge, York (still existing, as the "York Lodge," No. 236) :—

December 16th, 1805.—"Brother W. Master proposed that a public procession should take place on the interment of our departed Brother and Hero, Lord Nelson, Secd. by Br. P.M., & Thirded by the S. Warden. The W.M. then expressed his wish that a uniformity of dress should be observed on the occasion. And that the Rev. J. Parker be requested to preach a sermon on the occasion at the Parish Church of St. Helen's."

There is also an interesting banner in the possession of the Lodge, a sketch of which, supplied by the courtesy of Mr. Alfred Proctor, has been reproduced in the present work.

Allusions to the great seaman being a Freemason, were of frequent occurrence in the earliest Masonic journals which appeared after his decease, and it is to the same source of authority that I must now turn, for the sole evidence upon which the third Admiral on the list I am proceeding with, can be included in the ranks of the Fraternity.

The *Freemasons' Magazine* of November 17th, 1860, in recording the death of Sir Charles Napier, mentions that he was a constant visitor at the Lodge of Friendship. There are a large number of Lodges, however, distinguished by this title, and an exhaustive inquiry into the matter has been impossible. The story therefore, is one of those relations, which, to adopt the words of Bede (in the preface to his *Ecclesiastical History*),

" I will not warrant, but deliver purely on common report."

Admiral Sir Charles Napier (passing over the long series of brilliant services preceding his promotion to flag-rank), in command of Dom Pedro's fleet, defeated that of Dom Miguel off Cape St. Vincent, in 1833. As second in command he assisted at the capture of Acre, in 1840. In 1847 he received the command of the Channel Fleet, and, on the outbreak of the Russian War in 1854, that of the Baltic.

The next names are chiefly taken from those which have been registered in the books of the Grand Lodge, and to a lesser extent from the lists of members which are given in the histories of certain private Lodges, and other authentic ources.

Many officers of the United Service figure, as may be expected, on the roll of the Phœnix Lodge, Portsmouth, the annals of which have been recorded with a loving hand by Mr. Howell. Among the Admirals who were initiated in or joined this Lodge, may be named Sir Charles Morice Pole (1787), first captain of the grand fleet under Lord Bridport, and who commanded in the Baltic, 1801. Sir Roger Curtis (1787), signalised by his bravery when commanding the

Brilliant, frigate, at the siege of Gibraltar. Amidst the blaze of a burning flotilla, the explosion of magazines, and the presence of death in every frightful form, he boarded a Spanish ship and brought off a portion of its crew in his boat, which had not moved many lengths from the vessel before the latter went into the air. To this heroic act the poet laureate of the day referred, when (speaking of Britain) :

> "She snatch'd in victory's moment, prompt to save,
> Iberia's sinking sons from Calpe's glowing wave."

Sir Roger was flag-captain in Lord Howe's great battle of June the 1st, 1794. On telling the Admiral that the line was complete, Howe replied, "then up with the helm in the name of God," and the *Queen Charlotte,* dashing through the French line, fired from both sides with her guns double-shotted, when 700 Frenchmen fell in the *Montagne* alone. Curtis, afterwards Commander-in-Chief of the Channel Fleet (1799), and still later at the Cape, was at one time sent on an embassy to Morocco, and in spite of his position found it impossible to proceed with his task. But on making himself known as a Mason all difficulties were removed, and he was allowed to pass freely through the country.

Sir Hugh C. Christian (1788) commanded, with Sir Ralph Abercrombie, at the reduction of St. Lucia, and died when in chief command at the Cape.

Robert Winthrop (1791), commanded a small squadron on the coast of Holland in 1799, and the *Stag* frigate in the expedition against Ferrol the next year.

Sir Thomas Byam Martin (1792), in command of a frigate, captured *La Tamise,* 1796, and *L'Immortalité,* 1798. Present in the action with the Russian fleet, 1808 ; Commander-in-Chief, Mediterranean and Portsmouth ; Admiral of the Fleet, 1849.

Sir Lucius (son of Sir Roger) Curtis (1827), served at the reduction of the Isle of Bourbon, 1810. Admiral Superintendent at Malta, 1843 ; Admiral of the Fleet, 1864. This gallant officer, who was twice Master of the Phœnix Lodge (1833–34) and Provincial Grand Master of Hampshire from 1840 to 1869, often spoke with much eloquence as an expositor of Masonic principles, of which some examples will be laid before the reader. At a meeting of the Craft in an adjoining Province, August 23rd, 1850, he said :—

"Let them go to any part of the world they pleased, they would be sure to find Freemasons. and by making themselves known, as everywhere the same signs and signals were used. they received as much assistance as would be accorded to them even in their own country. On this matter he spoke from experience, and had himself been placed in situations to prove the value of being a Mason, and the exercise of true Masonic principles. He would give one instance of this being shown where it was little expected. A General in the Army. well-known to him some years since. left Gibraltar with his family as passengers in a small vessel for Sicily. and on their passage the vessel was taken prisoner by an Algerine pirate. Entreaty and intercession failed to induce the pirates to grant them their lives. and the order was given for all the hands to walk the plank. or in other words to be thrown overboard. when as a last resource General Gardiner. who was a Freemason. thought he would try what effect the sign of unity might have upon the pirate captain. He made the sign. it was acknowledged. and the result was that their lives were spared and the Algerine landed them all safely in Sicily. As regards himself he was taken prisoner during the war, and. while a captive. being without shoes or stockings, and but half clothed, he had made himself known. and was acknowledged by a Mason, and from that time he was clothed and fed by Brethren so long as he remained a prisoner."

Six years later, at a meeting of his own Provincial Grand Lodge, Sir Lucius Curtis expressed himself as follows :—

"On one occasion (during the late war) an officer of a French ship, in the heat of battle. showed the sign and his life was saved. Also. in the Peninsular campaigns. a sergeant's knapsack. which had been captured, on being opened and his Masonic certificate being seen. it was again repacked and returned perfect. When he (Sir Lucius) was in command at Malta, the Pope's Bull against Freemasonry was promulgated; it excommunicated all who joined the Order. Many of his subordinates were members of the Romish Church, and they applied to him, as their superior. to absolve them from their allegiance to a faith. the head of which condemned an institution so well deserving the support of all good men. He knew an English naval officer whose vessel was captured by the Algerines. and he. as well as his crew. was ordered to walk the plank. Some females on board were to be otherwise disposed of. In his extremity he showed his sign. and the vessel and all were given up to him."

Hyde Parker (1832) commanded the *Prometheus* sloop in the expedition to Copenhagen, 1807, and served gallantly during the last American war.

Sir James Whitley Deans Dundas (who was initiated at the same time as his brother, General C. W. D. Dundas, in 1837) accompanied Sir R. Abercrombie to Egypt in 1800, and up to 1815 not a year passed without his distinguishing himself in some encounter. In 1854 he commanded the Fleet which operated against Russia in the Black Sea. He was Junior Grand Warden of England, in 1839.

Sir John Ackworth Ommaney (1843, Senior Warden 1844) was in command of the *Albion* at the Battle of Navarino, and of the Mediterranean station, 1837–41.

The Hon. Augustus Hobart (1847), who became famous as Hobart Pasha, Admiral in the Turkish Navy. Sir J. C. Dalrymple Hay (Provincial Grand Master of Wigtonshire, joined the Lodge in 1851); Controller of the Navy.

Albert Hastings Markham (1886; Master, 1889; District Grand Master of Malta, 1893), was presented by the Royal Geographical Society with a gold watch, May 1877, for having planted the Union Jack in the highest latitude ever reached by man. Commodore of the Training Squadron, 1886–89, and second-in command, Mediterranean, 1892. (China and Arctic medals). Author of the "Life of Sir John Franklin," and other works.

Of other flag officers who are known to have been Freemasons, the highest in naval rank was the Duke of Clarence, Admiral of the Fleet, 1811, and Lord High Admiral, 1827. He was initiated at Plymouth in 1786, and subsequently occupied the chair of the Prince of Wales's Lodge from 1827, until he was called to the throne as William IV., in 1830.

The following Admirals were also members of the fraternity:—Sir W. G. Fairfax (joined the Royal Navy Lodge, Deal, 1762), Captain of the *Venerable* (Admiral Duncan's flag-ship) in the glorious fight off Camperdown, in 1797.

Joseph Bullen (a founder of the Lodge of Honour, Bath, 1820), during his distinguished career, had more than 60 encounters with the enemy. Sir George Cockburn (Lodge of Antiquity, 1812), commanded a squadron during the last American war, which co-operated with the military

E

force under Major-General Ross, who fell by his side at Baltimore, 1814. In the following year he hoisted his flag on board the *Northumberland*, and took Napoleon to St. Helena, where he remained Governor and Commander-in-Chief until 1816 ; Admiral of the Fleet, 1851. Sir Thomas Fellowes (Cumberland Lodge, Bath), commanded the *Dartmouth* at the battle of Navarino. Sir E. A. Inglefield (Junior Grand Warden, 1887, a member of St. John's, Halifax, Nova Scotia, and many other Lodges), was Commander-in-Chief on the North American station, 1878, and retired from the navy with six medals, in 1885. Sir David Milne (Provincial Grand Master of Berwickshire, 1836 ; Senior Grand Warden of Scotland, 1838), was present in Lord Rodney's actions, 1779 and 1782, and as 2nd lieutenant of the *Blanche*, in 1795, when she effected the capture of the French frigate *La Pique*. The boats of both ships at the end of the conflict were either destroyed or unable to float, so Lieutenant Milne, followed by ten seamen, swam to the conquered vessel and took possession of her. Second-in-Command at the battle of Algiers, 1816, Commander-in-Chief North America, 1817, and at Devonport, 1842. Died (being at the time Grand Master of the Knights Templar of Scotland) 1845.

Sir Pulteney (brother of General Sir John) Malcolm, after distinguishing himself in numerous engagements, became Commander in-Chief on the St. Helena station, 1816-17 ; in the Mediterranean, 1828-31, and again in 1833-4. Sir Edward Nagle (Doyle's Lodge of Fellowship, Guernsey, 1807), a brave and esteemed officer. Sir John Ross, the famous Arctic navigator. Sir Michael Seymour (Grand Master's Lodge, 1796), lost an arm in Lord Howe's great battle, 1794. He captured in the *Amethyst*, frigate, the French frigates *Thetis* (1808), and *Le Niemen* (1809), and for his valour and heroic conduct was created a baronet. From 1833 until his death in 1834, he was in command on the Pacific station. Sir William Sidney Smith, of whom it has been truly said, that a more chivalric character is not to be found among the heroes of modern times, was Chancellor of the *Chapitre des Trinosophes*, at Paris, in 1818, and became a joining member of the Grand Master's Lodge in

1829. The exploits of this remarkable man, whose name, like that of Nelson, was long a terror to our enemies, would fill a volume, and it will be sufficient to refer to his gallant defence of St. Jean d'Acre, 1799, when he frustrated the repeated attempts of the French to carry the place by storm. It was of this feat of arms, and of the victorious Commodore (as Sir Sidney then was) that Reginald Heber wrote :

> " Britannia's champion !   bath'd in hostile blood,
>   High on the breach the dauntless SEAMAN stood."

Shortly after he was made a vice-admiral he received the distinction of D.C.L. from the University of Oxford, and on this occasion it was remarked, "Now that Sir Sidney Smith is made a doctor of Civil law, we hope that he will not abandon the practice of the cannon law, in which he has hitherto been so eminent." Sir Sidney, who vainly endeavoured to effect a re-union of the knights of all the European Orders, particularly those of St. John of Jerusalem and Malta, succeeded to the Regency of the Knights Templar of France in 1838, and held the office at his death, which took place at Paris, in 1840.

Sir Houston Stewart, who, in early life served in the *Impérieuse*, under Lord Cochrane, commanded the *Benbow* at the reduction of St. Jean d'Acre, in 1840, and the British squadron at the capture of Kinbourn, in 1855. In 1856-60, he was Commander-in-Chief on the North American station, and while holding that appointment became a member of a Lodge—St John's, Halifax, Nova Scotia— which is renowned for the number of illustrious names connected with the Army and Navy, which have been inscribed on its roll ; Admiral of the Fleet, 1872.

Sir William Hewitt, from 1847 until the premature close of his career in 1888, participated in almost every war in which England was engaged, and received the Victoria Cross for conspicuous bravery with the Naval Brigade before Sebastopol. He was Commander-in-Chief, successively, in the East Indies, and of the Channel Fleet. During the interval between these appointments, he was present with Sir Henry Keppel at the annual festival of the Moira Lodge, London, held (on the birthday of the 2nd

E 2

Earl of Moira) December the 7th, 1885. Each of the two Admirals wished the other to return thanks for the visitors, but in the end there were speeches from both. The Admiral of the Fleet was able, curiously enough, to refer to a third guest at the table—Mr. W. H. Read—as having made him a Mason "just forty years ago," at Singapore; and the Vice-Admiral (Hewitt), in the course of a spirited address, expressed the great benefit he had personally derived from having been admitted a member of the fraternity.

James Walker served in the battles of Camperdown and Copenhagen, and in the *Vanguard* fought and captured, near St. Domingo, in 1803, the *Duquesne*, a French ship of the line, which he afterwards commanded. This officer, when a lieutenant (during the peace of 1783) was a passenger with several others in a *diligence*. The carriage was attacked by robbers, near Aschaffenbourg, and the lieutenant rushed into the midst of them, but being unsupported by his fellow-travellers, he was overpowered and left for dead. He was afterwards found and conveyed to a place of safety at Frankfort, where he was supplied with assistance and money by the Freemasons. Sir Adolphus Slade (St. John and St. Paul, Malta, 1827) commanded the Turkish Navy, and was the author of "Turkey and the Crimean War." Lord Alcester served in the Burmese and New Zealand wars, and in the expedition to the Baltic, 1854; Commander-in-Chief, Mediterranean, 1880, and at the bombardment of the forts of Alexandria; Senior Grand Warden of England, 1890.

Of living British Admirals, and excluding royal personages, the veteran Sir Henry Keppel, G.C.B., who entered the Navy in 1822, is entitled to the first place, as Senior Admiral of the Fleet. He was made a Mason in Lodge Zetland in the East, Singapore, in 1846, and that he has retained a lively interest in the Craft throughout his long life, may be inferred from the circumstance that I am indebted to him (in conjunction with Admiral Markham) for some of the professional details which are given in this portion of the book. He also fully authorizes my placing on record in these pages, "that in his opinion Freemasonry did a great deal of good in the Navy, that it was a useful and valuable link between the officer and the man, and that he had never known an instance where one of the latter class presumed on his fraternity with one of the former." In these sentiments Admiral Markham heartily concurs. The autobiography of Sir Henry Keppel has recently appeared, under the title of "A Sailor's Life under four Sovereigns," and the pages are full of adventure, from his experience as a midshipman in the West Indies, to the time when he commanded at the great boat-action, and destruction of the Chinese fleet, at Fatshan, in 1857.

The naval brethren on the active list include Admiral of the Fleet, Sir F. W. Richards, G.C.B., 1st Sea Lord of the Admiralty ; Admirals R. Duckworth King, superintendent of Malta dockyard ; A. H. Markham (of whom previously) ; Sir Harry H. Rawson, K.C B., in command of the Channel squadron, and who in 1897 commanded the expedition to Benin ; W. H. C. St. Clair (a present Senior Grand Deacon) ; F. S. Vander-Meulen ; G. H. U. Noel, 2nd-in-command on the Mediterranean station ; and Lord Charles Beresford, a Grand Warden of 1887.

The Admirals on the retired list who are Freemasons, comprise Henry Boys, 2nd-in-command Channel squadron, 1878 ; Sir William Graham, a former Lord of the Admiralty and Controller of the Navy ; and P. H. Colomb, a great student and exponent of naval history, author of many learned works, and the inventor of the present system of night signalling in the navy.

Passing from the naval to the military heroes who have thrown a lustre on our Society, I shall begin with the Hon. Henry Seymour Conway, who fought at Dettingen, Fontenoy, and Culloden ; and serving in the Seven Years' War, was left in command of the English Army on the return to England of the Marquis of Granby, in 1761. Appointed Commander-in-Chief, with a seat in the Cabinet, in 1782. No man was more generally liked. He died in 1795, being then the oldest general officer in the Army, and the premier Field-Marshal.

Lieutenant-General Sir Eyre Coote—whose name appears on the roll of the "Antient Boyne Lodge" at Bandon, in the sister kingdom—the preserver of our Indian Empire, in 1759 gained the decisive victory of Wandewash over the French under Lally and Bussy. It led to the capture of Pondicherry, and was the decisive battle which established the supremacy of the British in the Carnatic.

The Duke of York—initiated in the Britannic Lodge by his uncle, the Duke of Cumberland, Grand Master, Admiral of the White, in 1787—was placed at the head of the British Army in Flanders in 1793, and again in 1799. During his earlier command he was powerfully reinforced by an expedition under the Earl cf Moira (1794), and to the name of the Bayard of the English Craft may be added those of many other victorious British Generals who were Freemasons.

Sir Ralph Abercrombie, mortally wounded at the battle of Aboukir Bay, 1801, was admitted a member of Lodge Canongate Kilwinning, in 1793. Of his former aide-de-camp, General Hutchinson (afterwards Earl of Donoughmore), who succeeded to the command in Egypt, a notice has been given on a previous page.

Lord Lake—Prince of Wales's Lodge, 1787—overthrew the Mahratta Army and the French General, Perron, in 1803, and captured Delhi; after which, in a series of brilliant actions, he triumphed over Scindiah and Holkar.

About the same period the future Duke of Wellington first exercised an independent command, and his military genius was fully established by the battle of Assaye, after which achievement he became the hero of India. The Duke was made a Mason in early life, in Lodge No. 494 on the Irish roll, held at Trim, in the county of Meath. His signature, " A. Wesley," is still preserved among the most valued records of the Lodge, the chair of which his grandfather, father, and brother each filled in turn.

Lord Cathcart, to whose position as Master of the Alloa Lodge I have already referred, commanded the expeditions to the North of Germany in 1805-6, and the Baltic in 1807, also in the latter year at the siege and capture of Copenhagen.

Sir John Stuart, the hero of Maida (1806), unquestionably the most glorious battle of the eventful period at which it occurred, was Master of St. Luke's Lodge, Edinburgh, in the following year.

Sir John Moore, who fell at Corunna, received the light of Masonry in St. John's Lodge, Halifax, Nova Scotia, in 1780, when a captain in the 82nd Foot. On Moore's death the command devolved on Sir David Baird, who served in the East Indies, Egypt, the Cape of Good Hope (where he held the chief command), at Copenhagen (where he was wounded), and, finally, at Corunna, where he lost an arm.

Like Sir Ralph Abercrombie, Baird was an initiate of Canongate Kilwinning, and his interest in the Craft continued, after arriving in the East Indies with the regiment to which he then belonged. A large portion of the Coast army was at that time concentrated at Arcot, and many of the officers were Masons. They determined to open a Lodge to be called "Carnatic Military," which was accordingly done, in November, 1784, and among the founders and first members were "Matw. Horne, brigadier-general, late Grand Master of the Coast of Coromandel ; " and " D. Baird, captain 73rd Regiment, M.M.S."—the concluding letters signifying, no doubt, "Master Mason, Scotland." After Sir David's death, a monument to his memory was erected by Lady Baird, the foundation stone of which was laid with Masonic honours in 1832. The 4th of May was selected for the purpose, because on *that* day General Baird took Seringapatam by storm.

Lord Lynedoch, who raised three regiments and founded the United Service Club, served throughout most of the campaigns in the Peninsula, and commanded at the battle of Barrosa.

" Barrosa's heights for splendid deeds,
May boast Trafalgar's fame :
Where British troops. like Neptune's sons.
A glorious conquest claim. '

Viscount Combermere commanded the allied cavalry under Wellington in the Peninsular War, and in 1825 was appointed to the military command in India, where he won fresh honour by the capture of Bhurtpore, in 1826. His admission into Masonry took place at an early age, and in later life he was for a long period Provincial Grand Master of Cheshire. In the latter capacity he delivered many interesting addresses, declaring in 1839 that "in all his services as a military man he had never met with a bad soldier who was a Brother Mason ; " and in 1852 he said, " Another year has rolled over, and many changes have taken place. Among the foremost to be regretted was the death to the nation of his commander, the Great Wellington. He had been associated with him since 1793. Perhaps it was not generally known that the Duke was a Mason. He was made in Ireland, and often when in Spain, where Masonry was prohibited, in conversation with himself, he regretted how sorry he was that his military duties had prevented him from taking the active part which his feelings dictated ; for it was his (the Duke's) opinion that Masonry was a great and royal art, beneficial to the individual and the community."

Sir Robert Sale (whose father and brother, Colonels in the Madras service, were also Freemasons) was nicknamed " Fighting Bob," for wherever there was fighting he was always in the thick of it. He was present at the battle of Mallavelly, the storm of Seringapatam, the capture of the Mauritius, and of Rangoon. He also served in the Affghan campaigns of 1838 and 1841, and commanded the storming party at Ghuznee, but is best remembered by his country-men as the " hero of Jellalabad." Killed at the battle of Moodkee in December, 1845.

After Sir Charles Napier, the conqueror of Scinde (who will again be referred to), come the Brethren who held independent commands during the Indian Mutiny.

General the Hon. George Anson (a Waterloo officer), the Commander-in-Chief when the outbreak occurred, and who died shortly afterwards, was Provincial Grand Master of Staffordshire. Sir Archdale Wilson, of Delhi, when a lieutenant in the Bengal Artillery, saw the light of Masonry in St. John's Lodge, Sangor, Central India.

Sir John Inglis, the defender of Lucknow, received (as lieutenant) the 1st and 2nd degrees in St. Andrew's Lodge, Toronto ; (as captain) the 3rd in the Phœnix, Portsmouth ; and (as lieutenant-colonel in the same corps, 32nd Foot) joined the Kyber Lodge, Peshawur, in 1852.

Among the other members of this Indian Lodge at the same date was Lieutenant-Colonel William Rose Mansfield,

53rd Foot, afterwards Lord Sandhurst ; and a little later, Lieutenant Frederick S. Roberts, Bengal Artillery (a subsequent Master), an officer of great distinction (though not holding a separate command) during the Mutiny, and whose name has since been inscribed on the roll of fame, as Field-Marshal Lord Roberts of Kandahar.

Sir James Hope Grant, who filled many responsible positions in India, but is still better known as having commanded with conspicuous success the expedition to the North of China in 1860, was admitted into Masonry (when Lieutenant-Colonel, 9th Lancers) in Doyle's Lodge of Fellowship, Guernsey, in 1851.

John George Neil, after a succession of gallant services at Benares, Allahabad, and Cawnpore, fell at the relief of Lucknow, when moistening from his own flask the lips of a private soldier who had sunk wounded or exhausted by his side.

Long prior to the Mutiny, however, the names of distinguished military brethren serving in India, who were earnest and devoted members of the Fraternity, might be numerously quoted. For example, that of the Hon. Sir Charles Colville, commander of the Army of Bombay, who laid the foundation-stone of a Masonic temple at Poona in 1825, appears on the roll of the Benevolent Lodge, city of Bombay, in the same year. This gallant officer, who was one of Wellington's favourite brigadiers, commanded a brigade and afterwards a division in the Peninsular War. He was also present, in command of the 4th division, at Waterloo, and the task was subsequently confided to him of storming Cambray, the only French fortress which did not immediately surrender. Sir John Malcolm, equally distinguished as a military officer, author, and diplomatist, joined the same Lodge on taking up the government of the Presidency in 1827 ; and a little later it received as an initiate the brightest ornament of the Bombay Army, Lieutenant (afterwards Sir) Alexander Burnes.

The following Commanders-in-Chief in Western India, were also Freemasons :—Sir Thomas McMahon (1839), who, after serving under Abercrombie and Wellington, accompanied Lord Moira to India, where for twelve years he held the office of Adjutant-General, and was actively engaged in the Mahratta War of 1817–18 ; Sir Willoughby Cotton (1847), who, after serving on the staff at Copenhagen and in the Peninsula, commanded a division in the first Burmese War, and also under Lord Keane in Affghanistan ; Lord Frederick FitzClarence (a former Grand Master of Scotland), (1852) ; Sir W. R. Mansfield (1860) ; and the Duke of Connaught (1886).

Sir Thomas Hislop, commanding the Madras Army, was a member of the Lodge of Perfect Unanimity in that Presidency in 1816 ; and the Marquis of Tweeddale was appointed Provincial Grand Master of Eastern India, while filling the same military Office, in 1842-48. The former commanded the Army of the Deccan in the Mahratta War, and signally defeated the combined forces of the enemy at the battle of Maheidpore, in 1817 ; the latter, who served in the Peninsula, was wounded at Vittoria and Busaco, and again in the American War.

The name of Sir John Doveton, a very distinguished officer of the Coast Army, who served in all the campaigns against Tippoo Sultan, and commanded the Hyderabad Contingent, under the Marquis of Hastings, in the Pindari War, appears on the roll of " Perfect Unanimity " for 1807 ; and that of Major William (elder brother of Sir Henry) Havelock, under the year 1838. The latter served throughout the Peninsular War, and was present at most of the actions in which the Light Division was engaged. At the combat of Vera in October, 1813, a Spanish force was held in check by a formidable abattis, defended by two French regiments. Havelock, who had been sent to ascertain their progress, called on the Spanish to follow him, and putting spurs to his horse, cleared the abattis at a bound, and went headlong among the enemy. Then the Spaniards, cheering for " *el chico blanco* " (" the fair boy," for he was very young and had very light hair), with one shock broke through the French, and this just as their centre was flying under the fire of Kempt's skirmishers. The gallant youth also fought at Waterloo, and as Lieutenant-Colonel, 14th Light Dragoons, fell mortally wounded at the head of his regiment in the desperate charge on the Sikhs at Ramnugger, in November, 1848.

With a solitary exception all the military brethren at any time in command of the entire Indian army have been incidentally referred to. Sir Eyre Coote, Lords Lake, Moira, Combermere, and Dalhousie, head the list. Then follow Sir Charles Napier, General Anson, Sir William Mansfield, and Lord Roberts. A glorious head-roll of soldier Freemasons, to which I shall now add the name of Sir William Lockhart, the present Commander-in-Chief in India, whose services are too fresh in the public recollection to require any recapitulation in these pages.

Examples of successful British Generals in other portions of the globe are afforded by Sir Benjamin Durban, who in 1794, while a subaltern in the 2nd Dragoon Guards (Queen's Bays) was initiated in the Union Lodge, Norwich. He served under Sir R. Abercrombie, Lord Cathcart, Sir David Baird, and Sir Robert Wilson (all of whom were Freemasons), and was present at most of the battles of the Peninsular War. He was appointed Governor and Commander-in-Chief at the Cape in 1842, and the principal event in his tenure of office was the occupation of Natal.

General George D'Aguilar, who was admitted into the Craft in the Rodney Lodge, Jamaica, in 1811, when a captain in the 81st Foot—after serving in numerous campaigns, and for 26 years on the General Staff, commanded the expedition which, in 1847, assaulted and took the forts of the Bocca Tigris in the Canton river, together with those of the Staked Barrier, and of the City of Canton.

Lord Chelmsford, who commanded at the battle of Ulundi, which terminated the late Kaffir War, was received into Masonry in St. John's Lodge, Halifax, while serving at that station in 1845, as 2nd Lieutenant in the Rifle Brigade.

Sir Charles Warren was selected in 1884 as first Master of the Quatuor Coronati Lodge—now regarded by students of all nationalities as the centre of Masonic light—and in the same year as commander of the Bechuanaland Expedition, returning with an increased military reputation, and at once entering upon his lodge duties, in 1885.

Lord Kitchener of Khartoum, upon whose exploits as a soldier it will be wholly unnecessary to dilate, is a Past Grand Warden of England, and (either himself or a namesake) to be numbered with Sir John Doyle, Sir C. J. Napier, and Sir James Hope Grant, in the list of eminent military commanders, to whom Doyle's Lodge of Fellowship has afforded a Masonic home.

The roll of British Freemasons who have commanded armies in the field, will be brought to a close with the name of Field Marshal Viscount Wolseley, the present commander of the forces, who was initiated in the "Military Lodge," No. 728, Dublin, in 1854, and served as its Master (while holding the chief command in Ireland) in 1893 and 1894. He is also a Past Grand Warden of England, a distinction which he shares with his illustrious compeers, Lord Roberts of Kandahar, and Lord Kitchener of Khartoum.

Among the military brethren, however, who have greatly distinguished themselves, though in the lesser roles of Divisional Commanders, or Brigadiers, may be named William Kingsley, colonel of the 20th Foot, who was promoted Major-General, 1758, and greatly distinguished himself at the battle of Minden, where his regiment, from its gallant conduct, acquired the highly honourable appellation of KINGSLEY's STAND. It was directed by the Grand Lodge of England that the sum of fifty pounds should be sent to Germany to be distributed among the soldiers in the army of the Duke of Brunswick, who were Masons, and other recommendations of the Deputy Grand Master. The money was sent to Major-General Kingsley (being a brother) for that purpose.

Sir Simon Fraser, who died a lieutenant-general in 1782, was the son of Lord Lovat, beheaded at Tower Hill for his participation in the Scottish rising of 1745. He had himself also been an adherent of the Pretender, but was pardoned, and when the 78th Regiment, or Fraser's Highlanders, was raised in 1757, he joined it as lieutenant-colonel, bringing with him 700 of his clan. It served at Louisburg and Quebec, after which latter victory, in the winter of 1759, the Masters and Wardens of the Regimental Lodges in the garrison (to the number of eight or nine), agreed to choose an acting Grand Master. Their choice fell on Lieutenant Guinnett, 47th Foot (undoubtedly the first subaltern who ever occupied a Masonic throne); and in the second instance on " Brother Simon Fraser, colonel of the Highland Regiment," who was duly installed in his high office by " Brother Dunckerley, of his Majesty's ship the *Vanguard.*"

Thomas Desaguliers (Lieutenant-General, 1777), served in the Royal Artillery for a period of fifty-seven years, and was present as a captain at Fontenoy, and as a Brigadier at Louisburg and Belle Isle. " The brave, the learned Desaguliers," was a Fellow of the Royal Society, as well as a practical soldier, and the only son of the "Grand Master" of that name, whom we know to have been a Freemason. It is possible that the extraordinary prevalence of Masonic Lodges in the Royal Artillery, during the last half of the eighteenth century, may have been due, in some degree, to the influence and example of Desaguliers, whose memory is still fondly cherished in the regiment as that of one of its brightest ornaments.

Sir John Byng, afterwards Earl of Strafford and a Field Marshal, was initiated at Frome in 1797, when a captain in the 33rd Foot, the colonel at the time being the Hon. Arthur Wellesley (also a Freemason), under whom he subsequently commanded a brigade in the Peninsula and at Waterloo.

Sir James Kempt, Provincial Grand Master of Nova Scotia, 1819, commanded a brigade in seven battles, and a division at Waterloo.

Sir Joseph Thackwell (initiated in the Lodge of Harmony, Richmond, 1811), after serving in the Peninsula and at Waterloo, commanded the Cavalry in the Aftghan campaign of 1839, and also at Maharajpore, Sobraon, and throughout the Punjaub War of 1849.

Sir William Kier Grant joined the Russian and Austrian armies in Italy in 1799, and was present in a long series of battles and campaigns. He afterwards served fifteen years in the East Indies, the first six as Adjutant-General under the Earl of Moira, and was the first Master of the Moira Lodge, Freedom and Fidelity, constituted by and named after that nobleman, on his arrival in Calcutta as Governor-General and Commander-in-Chief in 1813.

Sir Alexander Leith, who received the Gold Cross with one clasp for his services in the Peninsular War, and on the reduction of the army in 1815, was presented by the officers of the 31st Foot with a silver cup, may have been a member of the Scottish Lodge which then existed in the corps. But of his being at least a Scottish Mason there is no doubt, as in August, 1827, when Master of the Glen Kindie Lodge, Aberdeenshire, a special meeting took place at his own house, and the late John Hill Burton, Historiographer Royal of Scotland, together with the late Colonel W. J. B. MacLeod Moore (who, at the time of his death, in 1890, was Grand Master of the Knights Templar of Canada), received in one night all three degrees appertaining to the Fraternity.

Sir John Lysaght Pennefather was initiated in the Sussex Lodge, Jamaica, in 1828, when a captain in the 22nd Foot. This regiment he accompanied to India in 1841, and commanded the Infantry Brigade (of which it formed a part) at the battle of Meeanee, where he was shot through the body. He also served throughout the Eastern Campaign of 1854, in command of a brigade at Alma, and of a division at Inkerman.

Sir Charles Staveley—a member successively of Lodges at Montreal and Hong Kong—commanded the 44th Foot in the latter part of the Crimean Campaign, and a brigade in the North China Expedition of 1860. He also served (as second-in-command) throughout the Abyssinian War. Considerations of space forbid my proceeding with all the names I had marked for quotation, but there is one more for which room must be found—Major-General A. G. Yeatman-Biggs, of the Royal Artillery, who after distinguishing himself greatly in China, Egypt, and the Cape, was appointed to the command of the 2nd division of the Tirah Field Force, which bore the brunt of the arduous campaign in the North West Frontier of India, so recently brought to a successful termination, under the personal direction of Sir William Lockhart.

At the time of his death, which resulted from disease contracted while on active service, General Yeatman-Biggs was District Grand Master of Bengal, and Grand Superintendent of the Royal Arch.

That many members of the Royal Family were received into the Society during the last half of the eighteenth century, has been mentioned in a previous chapter, and to the names already given may now be added those of Albert Edward, Prince of Wales—Admiral of the Fleet and Field Marshal—Most Worshipful Grand Master of England; the Duke of Connaught—General in the Army—Provincial Grand Master of Sussex: and two Past Grand Wardens who, alas, have passed over to the silent shore, the Dukes of Albany and Clarence, Colonels in the regular forces.

Three sons of William IV. were also members of the fraternity. Major-General the Earl of Munster; Lieutenant-General Lord Frederick Fitz-Clarence; and Captain Lord Adolphus Fitz-Clarence, R.N. Lord Frederick, who was elected Grand Master of Scotland in 1841, and again in 1842, made a Grand Visitation to the Lodge of Edinburgh in the latter year, and witnessed the initiation of his brother, Lord Adolphus, "commanding H.M. Yacht *Royal George*, who was afterwards passed and raised at the same sederunt."

A formidable difficulty has next to be encountered. The names of naval and military worthies to whom the opportunity of exercising high command against an enemy has been denied, but which, nevertheless, deserve honourable mention as being those of noteworthy Freemasons, is very numerous—a few of these, however, can alone be found room for in this volume. To begin with the sea service, whether Captain James Cook was a brother I cannot say, though Sir Joseph Banks (afterwards president of the Royal Society) had undoubtedly become one before he accompanied the former (as naturalist) on his first voyage, 1768–1771. But the reason why the name of the great navigator has been brought into the narrative will appear from the following :—

In some interesting *Memoirs* "by a Midshipman of the *Bellerophon*," the writer speaks of his father as an old naval officer who was serving under Cook when he was killed at Owhyhee. The old sailor was full of narrative, and the story he told of Cook's death will next be related. Before going on shore the day he was killed, he ordered the second lieutenant of his own ship (Williamson) to take the command of the boats of both vessels—*Resolution* and *Discovery*—

and pull in shore, there to await events, and if he observed any commotion after the captain's landing, to at once join him with his whole force. Under this arrangement Cook, with a small party of Marines, went on shore, where a quarrel took place with the natives, the English were over-whelmed by the savages, and the captain and two Marines were slain. "But while all this was going on" (to use the words of the actual narrator), 'Where, you will ask, was Williamson and the armed boats'? Why, pulling as hard as they could off to the ships, instead of landing to support their captain. It was the intention of the whole of us to bring him to a court-martial upon our arrival in England : but after Captain Cook's death, he came to be first lieutenant of the *Resolution,* and on our arrival at Kamschatka, he very knowingly established a Mason's Lodge, got all the men to become free-masons by bribing them with brandy, and got them to promise, as *brothers,* that they would say nothing of his cowardice when he came to England. So by this trick (concluded the aged reminiscent) 'he saved his bacon.'"

Paul Jones, might well have been referred to on an earlier page as a successful commander, but, though a British subject, his naval operations were not of a character to endear him to his fellow-countrymen, or to justify his name being placed in juxtaposition with those of the national heroes whose fidelity to the Craft has proceeded hand in hand with their loyalty to the throne. Jones attained the rank of Commodore in the American, and that of Rear-Admiral in the Russian service. He was greatly admired in the polished circles of Paris, especially by the ladies, " who were all wild for love of him, as he for them," but the special object of his adoration was the Countess Lavendal, to whom (enclosing a lock of his hair) he wrote from Russia in 1780 :—"*Before* I had the honour of seeing you, I wished to comply with the invitation of my Lodge, and I need not add that I have *since* found *stronger* reasons that have compelled me to seek the means of returning to France again as soon as possible." The Lodge mentioned, without a doubt, was that of the Nine Muses (*Neuf Sœurs*), founded by the philosopher, Helvetius, and the celebrated astronomer, de Lalande, which absorbed much of the literary, artistic and scientific talent of Paris. Voltaire was initiated in this Lodge, April 7th, 1778. Among the other famous members were Claude Joseph Verney, Jean Baptiste Greuze, and Benjamin Franklin.

Captain Nicholas Lockyer (at one time flag-lieutenant to Sir John Duckworth in the West Indies) had many good stories of his own adventures, and among them how his life was saved on becoming a prisoner to the South American Spaniards on the main, where he and his comrades were considered to be spies, and expected to be hanged the next day The officer of the guard over him was a Mason, so was he, and the former winked at his escape in the night.

Douglas Jerrold, author of " Black-eyed Susan," " The Chronicles of Clovernook," and " Mrs. Caudle's Curtain Lectures" (one of which was delivered on the evening of Mr. Caudle's admission into the Craft, and another on his return from a Masonic dinner), was a member of the Bank of England Lodge, No. 263. This great humourist served for two years as a midshipman on board the *Namur*, when he had for a mess-mate Clarkson Stanfield (also in later years a Freemason).

They both left the Navy in 1818, and, as all the world knows, while Stanfield took high rank as a painter, especially in pictures connected with the sea, the success of Jerrold was equally great as a man-of-letters, and particularly as an author of nautical dramas which have never been excelled.

Masonry found a very ready acceptance among the members of the East India Company's maritime service, and one of the lieutenants (in 1849) said " that it was always a matter of vexation and regret to him on his voyages that he was not a Brother, he being the only individual who was so circumstanced of all the officers of his ship." The Indian Navy is now defunct, but perhaps there has been no finer representative of it in recent years than Captain Sir Henry Morland, Grand Master (until his death) of All Scottish Freemasonry in India.

Passing from the sea to the land service, Captain George Smith, Inspector of the Royal Military Academy at Woolwich, and Provincial Grand Master for Kent, was the author of " The Use and Abuse of Freemasonry," which appeared

in 1783. In the same year he was charged (with another)
for "making Masons in a clandestine manner in the King's
Bench Prison." It was pleaded in defence that "there
being several Masons in the prison, they had assembled as
such for the benefit of instruction, and had also advanced
some of them to the 3rd degree. But a doubt arising
whether it could be done with propriety, the Royal Military
Lodge, No. 371, at Woolwich, adjourned with their
Constitution for that purpose to the King's Bench Prison
(Captain Smith being Master thereof), being one of those
itinerant Lodges which move with the Regiment, the Master
of which, wherever he is, having the Constitution of the
Lodge, was, by Captain Smith, judged to have a right to
hold a Lodge, make Masons," &c. Whereupon it was
resolved : "That in the opinion of the Grand Lodge, it is
inconsistent with the principles of Masonry that any Free
Masons' Lodge can be regularly held for the purposes of
making, passing, or raising Masons in any prison or place of
confinement." The Royal Military Lodge was erased from
the list, and in 1785 Captain Smith, who had committed a
still graver misdemeanour, was expelled the Society.

General William Augustus Bowles, an American adventurer, joined the British Army in Philadelphia (1776) and
received a commission, but was dismissed for a breach of
discipline. He soon after became connected with the Creek
Indians, whom he commanded when they assisted the
British at Pensacola in 1780. Subsequently he led a roving
life ; at one time an actor, at another a portrait painter,
visiting England in 1790. The following year he joined
the Prince of Wales's Lodge, and on his return to America
again became Commander-in-Chief of the Creeks. After
disturbing the peace of the neighbouring States for some
time, he was taken prisoner by the Spaniards and sent to
Madrid, and subsequently to Manilla, whence he escaped
and returned to his old life. He was finally captured in
1804, and imprisoned in Havana until his death. This
remarkable character was appointed Provincial Grand
Master of the Creek, Cherokee, Chicasaw and Choctaw
Indians, under the Grand Lodge of England, and his name
appears as such in the official calendars of the period.

John Shipp, a man who well deserves to be numbered among the "bravest of the brave," enlisted in the 22nd Foot, which he accompanied to India, and served against the Mahrattas under Lord Lake. He was one of the stormers at the capture of Deig, 1804, and thrice led the forlorn hope of the storming column in the unsuccessful assaults on Bhurtpore, 1805. His daring was rewarded by Lord Lake with an ensigncy in the 65th Foot, from which he was promoted to a lieutenancy in the 76th Regiment during the same year. He then went home, but found it necessary to sell out in order to pay his debts, so he once more enlisted, and returned to India as a private in the 24th Light Dragoons. In 1812 he was regimental sergeant-major, and three years later the Earl of Moira appointed him to an ensigncy in the 87th Foot. John Shipp had thus performed the unique feat of twice winning a commission from the ranks before he was 30.

He afterwards distinguished himself in the Ghoorka war, and on the staff of the "Grand Army" under the Marquis of Hastings, in the operations against the Mahrattas and the Pindarees (1817-18). In 1820, he was a member of the Lodge of Sincerity, Cawnpore, and in the following year he attained his former rank of lieutenant. In 1823 he was dismissed the service for insubordination, but allowed to sell out, and the East India Company granted him a pension of £50.

He next became an author, and his earliest work, "Memoirs of the Extraordinary Military Career of John Shipp," which appeared in 1829, has since passed through many editions. He also wrote "The Military Bijou, or the Contents of a Soldier's Knapsack," "The Eastern Story-teller," and "The Soldier's Friend."

Memoirs of the brothers (James and Alexander) Burnes will be found in a later chapter, and with the names of three more officers of the regular Army, and an equal number from the auxiliary forces, the present one will be brought to a close.

I shall first of all refer to Sir James Brooke, Rajah of Sarawak, who in consequence of a wound received in the Burmese war, quitted the Madras Army, and entered upon the adventurous career which resulted in his becoming the hero of the Indian Archipelago ; Captain Sir Richard Burton, of the Bombay establishment, the great writer and traveller ; and Major-General Sir Francis Worgan Festing, who commanded the regular troops during the earlier stages of the Ashanti war, and afterwards the Marines, during the subsequent operations under Sir Garnet Wolseley.

Sir James Brooke was a member of the " Zetland " Lodge at Singapore ; Sir Richard Burton, of " Hope," in Kurrachee, Scinde ; and Sir Francis Festing, of the " Phœnix," Portsmouth, the membership of which he retained from his initiation in 1859 until his death in 1886.

John Wilkes, distinguished for the violence of his political conduct, was a colonel in the Buckinghamshire Militia. On his return to England, after having been outlawed, in 1768, he was committed to the King's Bench Prison, where he was made a Mason by the members of the Lodge at the Jerusalem Tavern, St. John's Gate, in March, 1769. The following year he was elected a "General" of the Hon. Artillery Company of London. Edward Gibbon, the celebrated historian, was appointed a captain in the South Battalion of the Hampshire Militia, in 1759. He relates in his Autobiography, " I always exercised the battalion in the field. The discipline and evolutions of a modern battalion gave me a clearer notion of the Phalanx and the Legions, and the captain of the Hampshire Grenadiers (the reader may smile) has not been useless to the historian of the Roman Empire." Gibbon, who was afterwards successively promoted to the rank of major and lieutenant-colonel commandant, does not, however, always speak in equally high terms of the value of his Militia training, as he permits himself to say with respect to the habits of his brother officers :—

" Of seeming arms they make a short essay :
Then hasten to get drunk—the business of the day."

The famous author of the " Decline and Fall " was initiated in the Lodge of Friendship, present No. 6, in December, 1774, and became a Master Mason in March, 1775.

Sir Walter Scott, the Wizard of the North, obtained a commission in the Royal Mid-Lothian Cavalry, in 1797. If the French had been actually off the coast, adjutant Scott could not have shown more alertness than he did, in drilling both horses and men. He was a most pleasing companion in the mess room, where his unaffected cheerfulness and boundless store of anecdotes often set the table in a roar. Sir Walter was made a Mason in the Lodge of St. David, Edinburgh, on the 2nd of March, 1801, and the Lodge of St. John, Selkirk, elected him an honorary member on the occasion of his laying the foundation stone of the Free-masons' Hall, Selkirk, on the 4th of June, 1816. After his death a monument was erected to his memory at Edin-burgh, the first stone of which was laid with Masonic honours by the Grand Master of Scotland, in 1840.

"It is to the honour of Freemasonry that a man of Sir Walter Scott's talents and genius had such an affection for the Craft, that he spent, as he himself often testified, many of his most delightful hours within the walls of the Lodge—and it is equally to the honour of the Masonic body, that its members were among the foremost to confer posthumous honours on the memory of a Great Light which gladdens mankind by its appearance, only at long and distant intervals."

CHAPTER V.

On Fame's eternal camping ground
Their silent tents are spread,
And Glory guards with solemn round
The bivouac of the dead.

—ANON.

" Travelling " or " Moveable " Lodges were at one time common to the armies of most civilized nations, but attained their greatest lustre in connection with the forces of the British Crown. In their general tendency they were supposed to strengthen the bonds of friendship, and to diffuse among the officers—commissioned and non-commissioned— and the rank and file, a spirit of charity, fraternal kindness, and subordination.

No restrictions with respect to the class of persons who might be initiated in a Regimental Lodge were ever imposed by the Grand Lodge of Scotland. But by a law of 1768 the Irish Army Lodges were prohibited from making any townsman a Mason in a place where there was a registered Lodge ; and the town Lodges, in a similar way, from initiating "any man in the Army where there was a warranted Lodge in the regiment, troop, or company, or in the quarters " to which he belonged. The zone of exclusive jurisdiction, or radius within which no military could encroach upon the domain of a town Lodge, was afterwards enlarged, and from the year 1850 no Army Lodge has been allowed to initiate a civilian in any part of the British dominions, when there is a registered Lodge held within ten miles of the place where he resides, or where such Army Lodge then meets.

The powers of the English Regimental Lodges were not interfered with until after the union of the two Grand Lodges in 1813. Two years later a new code of laws was enacted, from which I extract the following :—

No military Lodge shall, on any pretence, initiate into Masonry any inhabitant or sojourner in any town or place at which its members may be stationed, or through which they may be marching, nor any person who does not at the time belong to the military profession, nor any military person below the rank of a corporal, except as serving brethren, or by dispensation from the Grand Master or some Provincial Grand Master.

There were Lodges in every branch or division of the land service. Roundly speaking, the Infantry of the Line head the list with a total of 220. Next follow the British and Irish Militia with 68, the Cavalry with 46, and the Royal Artillery with 28. Smaller numbers now became the rule. There was a solitary Lodge in the Foot Guards, and three only existed in the Royal Engineers. In the Royal Marines there were seven, and a similar number were attached to the Garrison and Veteran Battalions. The Fencible Regiments follow closely with six, and after these came the Auxiliary Corps (foreign) and the Foreign and Colonial Regiments with four and twelve Lodges respectively.

The number of distinct Lodges attached at different times to particular regiments is very noteworthy. For example, there were no less than seven in the 52nd and six in the 28th Foot, while among the other regiments of cavalry and infantry there were four with five, six with four, twenty-one with three, and forty-six with two Lodges each.

When there were several Lodges existing in a regiment at the same time, this fact will ordinarily coincide with a plurality of battalions, but not invariably. For instance, the 6th Dragoons held at the same time warrants of constitution from *both* Grand Lodges of England (*Moderns* and *Ancients*), together with a third from the Grand Lodge of the sister kingdom. The possibility, moreover, of two Lodges working simultaneously in an infantry battalion of the usual strength is evidenced by the proceedings at the centenary of the Grand Lodge of Scotland in 1836, when the members of Lodges "Hibernia" and "St. Andrew" in the 42nd Foot (or Black Watch) attracted admiration alike for their martial appearance and Masonic behaviour.

The examples of a divided, or in some cases a shifting allegiance, might be greatly multipled, but it will be sufficient to state that English, Irish, and Scottish Lodges were all at various periods attached to the 1st, 17th, 23rd, and 51st Foot. On the other hand, the Royal Artillery, with its long roll of twenty-eight Lodges, a total which is four times as large as that attained by any other regiment or corps, was unswerving in its fidelity to the "Ancients."

Two Irish warrants were held at the same time by the 9th Dragoons, and two Scottish by the 31st Foot. The territorial designations of the Militia battalions will in general afford a clue to the particular kingdom from which a warrant was supplied. Thus, in the English regiments all the Lodges were, to use the stock phrase—which means just the reverse of what the words themselves would seem to convey—either "Modern" or "Ancient," except two, one of which (*Irish*) was in the "South Lincoln" and the other (*Scottish*) in the Durham battalion.

None of the Lodges in the Irish Militia owed allegiance to any outside (Masonic) power; and the same (with a solitary exception) may be said of those in the Scottish regiments, the only deviator from the general rule being the Berwickshire battalion, which obtained a warrant from the "Ancients," in 1811.

The practice of distinguishing Lodges by their numbers did not become a general one in Scotland, until the beginning of the present century. Hence the military Lodges in that jurisdiction were commonly known by their *names*. Numbers as well as names were used in England, and the older Grand Lodge (*Moderns*) periodically closed up the gaps in her roll, and re-numbered the daughter lodges. But the junior body (*Ancients*) was in the habit of selling vacant numbers at the top of the list to Lodges that were lower down; the other gaps (of lesser importance) being refilled in a routine way, by allotting them to the petitioners for new Lodges. Examples of the former method are afforded by the cases of Nos. 86 and 213, both in the Royal Artillery, which, on payment of five guineas "to the Charity," became (in 1788) Nos. 7 and 9, respectively, and are now stationary Lodges, one being the "Union Waterloo" No. 13, at Plumstead, Kent; and the other the "Albion" No. 2 on the registry of Quebec. Of the way in which the lower numbers on the roll of the "Ancients" were refilled, the earlier history of St. Luke's Lodge, No. 225, Ipswich, will supply an illustration. This was originally held in the Westminster Militia, the warrant dating from 1804; but Lodges at the same number (309) had previously existed in the 52nd Foot (1797), and in the 2nd Royal Lancashire Militia (1803).

The Irish Lodges were always chiefly, and in many cases exclusively, known by their numbers, which were occasionally varied (as occurred under the junior Grand Lodge of England) by assigning vacant places on the roll to Lodges that were lower down on the list. For example, in 1817, the 21st Foot was given 33 (the number of its original and lapsed warrant) in lieu of 936; and the 64th, 130 in the place of 686. Also in 1823, the 17th Regiment went up from the number 921, to that of 258.

But the custom which particularly distinguished the Army Lodges of this jurisdiction was that of exchanging, whenever practicable, the numbers of their warrants for those of the regiments whereunto such Lodges were attached. Thus, in the 4th and 12th Dragoons, the 7th Dragoon Guards, the 25th, 26th, 30th, 36th, 42nd and 83rd Foot, the regimental numbers and those of the Lodges were identical. The only instances which are known to me of what may have been a somewhat similar usage in other Masonic jurisdictions, occurred under the "Ancients," in Lower Canada, and Jamaica, respectively. The regiments concerned were the 7th and 18th Foot, and in each case a Lodge attached to the corps, appears at a similar local number on the provincial list.

In their choice of names, the Lodges frequently adopted those of patron saints, such as St. George, St. Andrew, and St. Patrick, and in solitary instances, those of St. David and St Cuthbert. The territorial designations of the regiments were also very often selected, or the battles and sieges in which they had been engaged. There were the "North Hants," "Oxfordshire Light Infantry," "West Norfolk," and "Argyle" Lodges, in the 37th, 52nd, and 54th Infantry; "Salamanca," — 4th Dragoon Guards — also "Orthes," "Albuhera," and "Waterloo,"—6th, 57th, and 79th Foot—

together with "Mount Calpe," and "Gibraltar"—12th, and 39th—and "Minden"—20th and 51st.

Very appropriate designations were the "Queen's" in the 7th (or Queen's Own) Light Dragoons, "Royal Rose," in the Royal Fusiliers, "Fuzilier" in the 21st Regiment, "Cameronians" (which still happily survives) in the 26th, and "Amphibious," in the Royal Marines. "White's," "Barry," and "Rainsford," in the 30th, 34th, and 44th, were the names of the Colonels of the battalions to which these Lodges were attached

The existing Ambulatory Lodges will be shown in two groups, the first denoting those under the Irish, and the second the lesser number under the English obedience.

In Military Corps, Not Stationary.

26. 26th Foot, 1758			295. 4th Dragoon Guards. 1758		
174. 46th	..	1896	322, 29th Foot	...	... 1759
263, 20th	,,	1860	570, 5th Dragoon Guards 1780

316, 1st Foot, 1798		497, 89th Foot 1844
	743, 31st Foot, 1858.		

Although the *numbers* formerly attached to the Infantry regiments of the British Army have disappeared, the use of the territorial designations by which they are now known, would be impracticable in the present volume. The old numerical titles, have, therefore, been retained, and under the existing regimental system the identity of any "linked-battalion" (at a previous period) will, on reference to an army list, be revealed at a glance.

The majority of the existing Irish Regimental Lodges trace their descent from rather a remote date, but in no cases that I have been able to fully investigate, is there an instance under any jurisdiction of an Army Lodge having been at work continuously for a period of a century. Thus, the warrant of No. 295—4th Dragoon Guards—was returned to the Grand Lodge in 1830, and not again revived until 1877, at which date the only former member of the Lodge (when it ceased to work), was the full Colonel of the Regiment, Lieut.-General Sir Edward Hodge, who, I may observe, commanded it with great gallantry in the Crimea.

The warrant of No. 322—29th Foot—was similarly returned in 1820, and there was an intermission of labour until the revival of the Lodge at Thayetmyo (Burmah) in 1855.

The "Lodge of Charity," No. 570, in the 5th Dragoon Guards, became dormant about 1823, and in 1858 sent back its charter, which was re-issued in 1863.

The original warrant of the Lodge in the "Cameronians" —No. 309—was granted in 1758, but the Deputy Grand Secretary of Ireland informs me that there is no record of its having been at work between 1765 and 1805. Since the year 1810, however, there has been no break of continuity in its career, and under its old regimental number (26), for which that of 309 was exchanged in 1823, let us hope the Lodge may celebrate in due course the century of active life which it will so shortly have completed.

The oldest regimental Lodge, until its recent disappearance from the roll in 1886, was No. 128, established in the 39th Foot by the Grand Lodge of Ireland so far back as 1742. This, the "Gibraltar Lodge," is said to have been erected in the battalion when forming a part of the garrison during one of the eventful sieges of the "Rock." The 39th regiment—"*Primus in Indis*"—claimed to have made the first Mason in India under a European warrant, in 1757. It subsequently founded numerous Lodges in various parts of Hindostan. There is a stone let into the wall in Fort William, Calcutta, commemorative of the early history of this Lodge. All its working tools and jewels fell into the hands of the enemy during the Peninsular War, but were subsequently returned to the regiment. The original warrant—128—seems to have lapsed before 1758, as a new one, No. 290, was granted in that year. The Lodge then continued in active existence until 1785, and was dropped from the list in 1813, but six years later was granted a renewal of its original charter, No. 128.

The "Minden" (an Irish) Lodge, No. 63, in the 20th Foot, was founded in 1748, and revived in 1812, at which date "there had been no trace of it for 40 years in the Grand Lodge books." From 1819 it was again dormant until a second revival took place at Cannanore in 1824. A

third slumber, lasting for eight years, was terminated at
Bermuda in 1844 ; but a fourth and final one occurred in
1850, and ultimately the warrant, records, and jewels were
all lost in the Indian Mutiny.

Of the English Lodges which still exist, No. 316,
"Unity, Peace, and Concord," in the 1st Foot (now "Royal
Scots"), has probably attained the longest span of un-
interrupted life that has ever been accorded to an Army
Lodge, and will complete its centenary (having been allotted
a vacant warrant of earlier date) in 1808 To the position
of No. 743, "Meridian," in the 31st regiment, I have
previously referred : but, for reasons that will be sufficiently
intelligible, I am loath to omit from the list of living
Military Lodges one with which I have been so closely and
pleasantly associated, until its doom has been officially
pronounced by erasure from the roll.

Extinct (or dormant) warrants were sometimes revived by
the "Ancients," but not, so far as I am aware (in the case
of any Military Lodge), by the "Moderns," nor has the
usage survived under the United Grand Lodge of England,
into which these two bodies were happily blended in 1813.
The Scottish practice was substantially the same as that
observed with regard to the Irish and the "Ancient"
Lodges. For example, the warrant, No. 63, granted to the
23rd Royal Welsh Fusiliers in 1751, was "confirmed" in
1767 : and that of No. 108, "St. George," issued to the
31st Foot in 1761, was similarly "confirmed" in 1805.

It is, perhaps, not to be greatly wondered at that, with
very few exceptions, all the vast array of actual records
which would have thrown a much needed light on the
proceedings of the Army Lodges have disappeared. There
are no minute books of such bodies in the archives of the
Grand Lodge of Scotland, and what is stranger still—having
regard to the number of military warrants issued—their
absence is equally to be deplored in those of the Irish
jurisdiction. A few, indeed, are to be found in the
muniment room of the Grand Lodge of England, all of
which I have diligently perused, together with some others
that have fallen in my way. But the great bulk of the
evidence relating to the now almost defunct organizations

of whose diffusion of Masonic light in countries beyond the seas, it might have been truly said, in the century immediately preceding our own,

"Like mighty Missioners they come,
Ad partes Infidelium,"

is either entombed in that mausoleum of ungrateful toil, the lost or missing "records" of our fraternity, or lies scattered over the entire surface of the fugitive and ephemeral literature of the Craft.

Travelling, or Regimental Lodges, are referred to as taking part in Masonic processions, in the laying of foundation stones, and in other ways, not only in the British Islands, but in all our Colonial dependencies, as well as in India and the Far East. We find them working harmoniously with the Stationary Lodges which are encountered in their tours of service, and the instances are numerous where the presence of an Army Lodge has been of lasting benefit to a civil community. Of this a noteworthy example occurred in 1759, when the members of Lodge No. 74, in the 2nd Battalion of the 1st Foot, on leaving Albany, granted an exact copy of their Irish warrant to some influential citizens. It was changed, in 1765, for a Provincial Charter, and the Lodge—Mount Vernon—now holds the third place on the roll of New York.

A still earlier patent, and indeed the first Military Warrant ever issued, had been previously granted to the 1st Battalion of the same regiment. The Lodge thus established, in accordance with the more general Irish practice, never took a name, and was only distinguished by its number. In 1814 the 1st and 4th Battalions of the "Royals" were stationed at Quebec, and lodges were attached to both, "No. 11" (*Irish*), without any other distinctive appellation, and "No. 289" (*Scottish*) "Royal Thistle," respectively.

At the same date there was a third Lodge—"Unity, Peace, and Concord"—existing in the "Royals," which had been established in the 2nd Battalion, then serving on the coast of Coromandel, in 1808, and at the time of applying for it, an officer in the regiment wrote to the Provincial authorities as follows :—

"Lieut.-Col. Stewart. whom I find to be a Master Mason of
the Ancient and Most Hon'ble Order, assures me that there is a
warrant in the battalion. but it was unfortunately left in Europe,
owing to the sudden order the Regiment got to quit that quarter
of the globe. but it may shortly be expected to arrive when our
destination is known at home."

The warrant referred to, there can hardly be a doubt, was
No. 74, originally granted by the Grand Lodge of Ireland
in 1737, and which, though cancelled in 1801, would almost
certainly have been renewed, and in such case probably now
figure as older by upwards of half a century, than the
charter of any living Military Lodge, had the Masons of the
battalion preserved the same attachment to the old allegiance
which they have since evinced for the new.

The foundation stone of the North Bridge at Edinburgh
was laid with Masonic honours in 1762, and "The Military
Lodge of the Duke of Norfolk," in the 12th Foot, was
among those that walked in the procession.

The 25th, now the "King's Own Borderers," obtained an
Irish warrant in 1749, and the minutes of an existing
"Border" Lodge alone record the fact, that the lodge chest
of this regiment having been lost at Munster, in Germany,
a new one was "consecrated" at Berwick, in December,
1763.

At the first recorded meeting of the Royal Arch Lodge—
St. Andrew's—in Boston, New England, in August, 1769,
foreign soldiers were chosen as first officers of the Lodge.
William Davis, of No. 58 (*Ancients*), in the 14th Foot,
received "four steps," described as those of "Excellent,
Super-excellent, Royal Arch, and Knight Templar."

About the same time Royal Arch Lodge, No. 3, Philadelphia, was in close communication with (*Irish*) No. 351,
in the 18th Regiment, and the two bodies were in the habit
of lending their Royal Arch furniture to one another.

The 22nd Foot, after first of all receiving an Irish warrant, which it "lost in the Mississippi" about the year 1759,
next applied for a Scottish one, which, with the title of
"Moriah," No. 132, was granted in 1769. This, with other
Army Lodges, took part in the formation of what is now
the Grand Lodge of New York (1782), but during its earlier
career a more remarkable incident occurred, if we are

to credit the following, which appeared in the "New-castle Courant" of January 4th, 1770 :—

" This is to acquaint the Public. that on Monday the first instant. being the Lodge (or Monthly meeting) Night of the Free and Accepted Masons of the 22nd Regiment, held at the Crown near Newgate (Newcastle). Mrs. Bell. the Landlady of the House, broke open a Door (with a Poker) that had not been opened for some years past. by which Means she got into an adjacent Room, made two Holes through the wall. and by that Stratagem discovered the Secrets of Masonry ; and she. knowing herself to be the first Woman in the World who ever found out that Secret. is willing to make it known to all her Sex. So any Lady who is desirous of learning the Secrets of Masonry, by applying to that well-learned Woman (Mrs. Bell. that lived fifteen years in and about Newgate). may be instructed in the Secrets of Masonry."

It would be interesting to know how many pupils Mrs. Bell obtained, and why she appealed to her own sex in particular.

In the Province of Lower Canada, in 1772,

" A committee of the Grand Lodge having examined into the pretensions which a number of Masons in His Majesty's 21st Regiment have. for holding a Lodge in that corps, by the title of ' No. 32 of the Registry of Ireland ' ; record their opinion. that until they produce a better authority than that offered. they cannot be received among us. notwithstanding their willingness to submit to our laws."

The Lodge referred to was evidently No. 33, originally chartered *circa* 1734, which, after having lapsed, was renewed in 1817, as previously related ; and the episode of the year 1772, in my opinion, points to the loss of the warrant (which the brethren were clearly unable to produce), having taken place at an earlier date. So far as I am aware, though the plight of the Masons in the 21st Foot, could not, in those stirring times, have been an uncommon one, no other incident of a precisely similar character has been recorded.

Many years afterwards, " Fuzileer Lodge," No. 33, was again at work in the Royal North British Fuziliers, and accompanying that regiment to Tasmania, was granted a civil warrant, with the old name and number, and became the first Stationary Lodge in that Colony, in 1823.

The minutes of the Junior Grand Lodge of England, or "Ancients," will supply the next illustration :—

"December 15th, 1773 : Heard a letter from No. 148 (Royal Artillery) at Gibraltar, setting forth that a set of people who had their authority from the 'Modern' Grand Lodge. thought proper to dispute the legality of said warrant No. 148. That in the said garrison there were also held Lodges 11. 244. 290, 359. 420. and 466 (1st, 2nd. 39th. 76th, 56th, and 58th Foot). on the Registry of Ireland, and No. 58 (12th Regiment) on the Registry of Scotland."

Captain Murray, R.N., for the services rendered by him on this occasion to No. 148, " in proving the authenticity of their warrant." was voted a gold medal by the " Ancient "· Grand Lodge in 1777.

A few years later, as we learn from the same official records, the "Ancients" at Gibraltar, were more than holding their own in the rivalry which existed with the " Moderns." In a letter to the Grand Master, dated March 20th, 1786, Grand Secretary M'Cormick informed him that the Provincial Grand Lodge of Andalusia, which had been under the government of the " Moderns " for upwards of 20 years, had applied for a warrant under the " Ancients," and that its members (none of whom were below the degree of an ensign) had refused to act any longer under the authority of the " Moderns," though the Duke of Cumberland was said to be then Grand Master.

As will presently appear, the contest for supremacy between the brethren of the two English systems was in the same year (1786) settled in quite a different manner on the coast of Coromandel.

Passing over many years, and coming much nearer to our own times, the members of No. 960, in the 2nd Dragoon Guards, "in token of respect for their uniform Masonic conduct during their stay in Norwich," were fraternally entertained by the "Lodge of Eleusinian Mysteries," at that city, in 1825.

A Masonic ball, to which visiting brethren were freely invited, was given by the "Cameronian Lodge," No. 26, at Calcutta, on St. John's Day (in winter), 1838. In the same year, a meeting of No. 7, in the 7th Dragoon Guards, then stationed at Edinburgh, was visited by deputations from nearly all the Lodges in that metropolis. A little later, July, 1844, No. 26, on its return from India, was quartered at the same capital, and assisted at the ceremonial of laying a foundation stone, the proceedings of which were thus officially recorded :—

"Amongst the numerous Lodges in attendance, was that of the 26th or Cameronian Regiment, on the Registry of Ireland, which being a visiting Stranger Lodge, under the rule of a Sister Grand Lodge, was placed near the Grand Lodge of Scotland."

But the materials, if not entirely wanting, are nevertheless wholly insufficient, to admit of my doing more than present the barest sketch of the proceedings, in time of war, of the Army Lodges. According to a ballad of the last century :—

> " Our God and soldier we alike adore
> Just at the brink of ruin, not before :
> The danger past, both are alike requited.
> God is forgotten, and the soldier slighted."

Whether, indeed, these ancient lines may admit of modern application, I shall not pretend to determine. Military matters unconnected with Masonry are out of my province, but that the services to our own fraternity of Naval and Military Brethren are imperfectly recorded and too little recollected, is a proposition which I shall lay down without any apprehension of its accuracy being regarded as open to dispute.

The earliest period at which any large number of Regimental Lodges can be identified as having been present with Armies in the field, was that of the Seven Years' War, which was carried on from 1756 to 1763, by Frederick the Great, in alliance with England, against France, Austria, Russia, Sweden, Saxony, and most of the smaller German States.

There were many "stricken fields," but the battles which chiefly concern us were those of Minden and Quebec.

The famous battle of Minden was fought on August 1st, 1759, the English Infantry being formed into two brigades, the 1st of which included the 12th, 23rd, and 37th regiments, and the 2nd comprising the 20th, 25th, and 51st. With the possible exception of the last named, the whole of the six battalions are known to have had Lodges attached to them at the time.

F

While these British regiments (and others) were serving on the Continent, before, after, and during the continuance of the Seven Years' War, the Rite or System called the STRICT OBSERVANCE, was in existence. This was based upon the fiction that at the time of the destruction of the Templars a certain number of Knights took refuge in Scotland, and there preserved the due succession of the Order. For various reasons also, these Knights were said to have joined the Guilds of Masons in that Kingdom, and thus to have given rise to the Society of Freemasons. The great doctrine laid down for the followers of the Rite was "that every true Mason is a Knight Templar."

Lodges in British regiments must have constantly worked side by side with the Lodges under the STRICT OBSERVANCE—which for twenty years, at least, pervaded all Continental Europe. During the military operations, moreover, in which the allied Army was engaged, many prisoners were made on both sides, and that the Masons among them fraternised in each case with their captors, must be taken as a certainty. It may be stated, also, that wherever there were *depots* of prisoners-at-war—in the British Isles, equally with all other countries—Lodges composed of such *detenus*, invariably sprang into existence.

The degree of Knight Templar became a very favourite one in the Lodges of the British Army, and by these military and Masonic bodies—who must have derived their knowledge of it from associating with the Lodges and brethren under the STRICT OBSERVANCE—the degree was doubtless introduced into England and America.

Ferdinand, Duke of Brunswick, who commanded the allied forces at Minden, served in several campaigns under Frederick the Great, and was considered one of the best soldiers of his time. His initiation took place—December, 1740—in the Lodge of the "Three Globes," at Berlin. In 1770 he was appointed English Provincial Grand Master for the Duchy of Brunswick, but in 1771 he forsook "pure and ancient Freemasonry," and was admitted into the STRICT OBSERVANCE.

Lord George (afterwards Viscount) Sackville (1716-85) entered the Army at an early age, and was present at the battles of Dettingen and Fontenoy. From 1746 to 1749 he was Colonel of the 20th Foot, and in 1758, as Lieutenant-General, succeeded the Duke of Marlborough as commander of the British forces in the Army of Prince Ferdinand. At the battle of Minden he was at the head of all the British and German Horse. The enemy being thrown into disorder by the allied infantry, the commander-in-chief sent orders for Lord George Sackville to advance.

But the critical moment passed away, the British cavalry lost their share in the glory of the action, and the French retreated in some order. Yet it is supposed that had Lord George obeyed the command of Prince Ferdinand, the enemy would have been left without an army in Germany.

For this Lord George was deprived of all his military employments, and upbraided by the public with cowardice ; but on the accession of George III. he was restored to favour, and became Secretary of State for the Colonies in 1776, a post which he retained up to the conclusion of the disastrous American War. Of his Masonic career after 1748 we only know that he was Grand Master of Ireland in 1751, and that the same position was offered to him by the Schismatic Grand Lodge of England (or "Ancients") in the following year.

The 20th Foot, to use the numerical title by which it afterwards became (in more senses than one) distinguished, received in December, 1748, a warrant of constitution—No. 63—from the Grand Lodge of Ireland. It was granted to Lord George Sackville (Colonel and first Master), Lieutenant-Colonel the Hon. Edward Cornwallis, and Captain Milburne.

The practice of appointing the colonel (or commanding officer) of a regiment, the first Master was by no means unusual. Colonel Edward Huntingford occupied a similar position in a Lodge established in the 28th Foot, at Louisburg, in 1758. The Hon. William (afterwards 6th Lord) Napier became the Master of "St. Andrew, Royal Arch"—Scots Greys—in 1770 ; the Hon. Sir Bydges Henniker (Lieutenant-General, 1808) of a Lodge in the 9th Dragoons, at Macclesfield, in 1794 ; and Colonel George Congreve, C.B., who commanded the 29th Foot at the battles of

Ferozeshah, Chillianwallah, and Goojerat, of one which was revived in that regiment, after a protracted slumber, in 1855.

At the battle of Minden the 20th Foot was on the right of the line in the 2nd brigade, commanded by the colonel of the regiment, Major-General William Kingsley (p. 26). The great mortality sustained by the battalion caused the following general order to be issued by Prince Ferdinand :—

"Minden, 2nd August, 1759.—Kingsley's regiment of the British line, from its severe loss, will cease to do duty."

But the zeal and *esprit de corps* which animated the survivors of the 20th is shown by the subsequent general order :—

"Minden, 4th August, 1759.—Kingsley's regiment, *at its own request*, will resume its portion of duty in the line."

After the great victory referred to, No. 63 adopted the title of the "Minden Lodge," under which it celebrated the centenary of its warrant in 1848.

On March 20th, 1750, Major James Wolfe (afterwards Major-General and commander of the expedition against Quebec) had been appointed Lieutenant-Colonel, 20th Foot, in succession to the Hon. Edward Cornwallis ; but as there are no records to guide us, we cannot tell whether Wolfe, like the other colonels who were his contemporaries in the regiment, was a Mason and a member of No. 63.

The scene will now be shifted to North America, for which country Edward Cornwallis had sailed in 1749, taking with him 1,140 settlers, who were safely landed in Nova Scotia, of which province he became the founder and first Governor.

This gallant officer, whose zeal for Masonry was again apparent in his new sphere of action, accepted the Mastership of a new Lodge shortly after his arrival at Halifax. A Provincial warrant was received in July, 1749, "and on the same evening Captain Lord Colville, and a number of the Navy gentlemen, were entered Apprentices in this Lodge."

In 1760, Cornwallis became a Lieutenant-General, and eight years later he was for the third time a founder of a new Lodge. This appeared at the (English) No. 426, in the list for 1768 as—"Twenty-fourth Regiment of Foot (General Cornwallis), Gibraltar, Spain"—the general at the time being both colonel of the regiment, and governor of the garrison of which it formed a part.

In the beginning of the present century, another Freemason, Sir David Baird, was colonel of the regiment, and also at the same time of the Westminster Militia, in which there was a Lodge. Upon the embarkation of troops for the Baltic, the " Westminster," being stationed at Harwich, offered to a man to volunteer with " their own general," as they called him, but as this could not be permitted, they testified their sincerity, when the Militia Transfer Bill was passed, for directly afterwards, out of 288 men, the number allowed to volunteer, 223 enrolled themselves in the 24th Foot, Sir David Baird's regiment.

Returning to the New World, Alexander, 4th Lord Colville, who was initiated by Colonel Cornwallis in 1749, became in the following year Master of the " 2nd Lodge at Boston," which he represented at every meeting of the Provincial Grand Lodge, until his appointment as Deputy Grand Master of North America in 1752. He was present at the capture of Louisburg in 1758, and served in the expedition against Quebec in 1759, and in command of the fleet at the re-capture of Newfoundland—one of the best conducted, most splendid, and most important successes of the war—in 1762, after which he was promoted rear-admiral of the White.

The siege of Louisburg has a two-fold interest for the military reader; in relation to the story of the gallant Wolfe, who acted as one of the brigadiers ; and in the fact that this was the last place held by the French against England, on the East Coast of America. For the Masonic or the general reader, the series of joint naval and military operations, beginning with the siege of Louisburg in 1758, and ending with the recapture of Newfoundland in 1762, may likewise possess an interest, in connection with the travelling Lodges of Freemasons which accompanied the British forces.

The regiments engaged at Louisburg were the 1st, 15th, 17th, 22nd, 28th, 35th, 40th, 45th, 47th, 48th, and 58th

Foot, two battalions of the 60th (Royal Americans), and Fraser's Highlanders (78th). Six of these are known to have had Lodges attached to them, the 1st, 15th, 17th, 35th, 47th and 48th. The 28th received an Irish warrant in 1734, but it had presumably lapsed in 1758, as a new Lodge under a Provincial Charter was formed in the regiment, by Richard Gridley, Colonel of infantry and Chief Engineer, in that year. The 40th received a " constitution " in 1759, the 78th in 1760, the 60th in 1764, the 45th in 1766, and both the 22nd and 58th, in 1769. Hence it will appear, that all of the thirteen regiments had Lodges attached to them some years in advance of the commencement of the Revolutionary war. But we must not too hastily conclude from the absence of entries relating to them in the official lists, that the six I have last named, were without Lodges in 1758. The historian of the 43rd Foot, writing in the same year, complains that " the time passes very wearily " at Nova Scotia, and adds, " When the calendar does not furnish us with a loyal excuse for assembling in the evening, we have recourse to a Freemasons' Lodge, where we work so hard that it is inconceivable to think what a quantity of business of great importance is transacted in a very short time." This Lodge I have not succeeded in tracing, and there are others in the same category of earlier and later date. A Lodge without any known " constitution " was at work in the 6th Foot in 1744, and another in the 12th, in 1747 ; while so late as December, 1786, a sermon (afterwards published), on " The Pleasures and Advantages of Brotherly Unity," was preached before the Master, Wardens, and Brethren of the similarly unregistered " 54th Regimental Lodge of Free and Accepted Masons, in the parish church, St. John, New Brunswick."

At least six registered Lodges accompanied the British land forces in the expedition against Quebec, and there were probably others, as besides those which may have existed without written " constitutions," the practice of " congregating all Free and Accepted Masons " on such occasions, and " forming them into one or more Lodges," was of frequent occurrence in the Masonic jurisdiction of North America. Military Lodges were formed in this way at

Louisburg, Lake George, and Crown Point, all of which may have been, and the first and last almost certainly were, present with the army before Quebec.

But there is documentary evidence to show that in the winter of 1759, after the capitulation of what has been termed the "Gibraltar of America," the "warranted" Lodges in the regiments there, to the number of eight or nine, assembled and elected an acting Grand Master. This temporary measure was succeeded in the following year by one of a more permanent character, in which Thomas Dunckerley, gunner of the *Vanguard*, took a leading part, and of this worthy, whose long and meritorious services to the Craft have never been excelled, a brief sketch will be interwoven with the general narrative.

Dunckerley, who was of humble parentage, having entered the Navy at an early age, attained the position of gunner in 1746, and we find him serving in the same capacity in the *Vanguard* (which seems to have been his favourite ship) for a period of six years. He was present as one of the crew of this vessel at the reduction of Louisburg and the capitulation of Quebec. The ship then returned to England, and in January, 1760, Dunckerley, having obtained leave of absence, went to London and attended his mother's funeral. The next day a declaration by his mother on her death-bed that his actual father was the then King, George II., was related to him. The records of the Grand Lodge show that in the same month a Lodge was established in the *Vanguard*. This vessel, with other ships of war, shortly after sailed for Quebec, arriving just in time to prevent that capital from being retaken by the enemy.

On the 24th of June, 1760 (St. John's day), Colonel Sir Simon Fraser, 78th Foot, was elected to preside over the Canadian Lodges, and (to use the words of a land "gunner" in a letter to the Grand Secretary) " Bro. Dunckerley, of His Majesty's ship the *Vanguard*, who was possessed with a power from the Grand Lodge of England to inspect into the state of the Craft wheresoever he might go, honoured them with his approbation of their conduct, and installed Brother Fraser in his high office."

It is reasonable to suppose that Dunckerley was desired by

the Deputy Grand Master of England to visit and report upon the Lodges at Quebec ; nor were roving commissions, empowering a seafaring brother to exercise the functions of a Provincial Grand Master, " where no other Provincial is to be found," wholly unknown either before or after Dunckerley fulfilled the mission with which his biographer, Mr. Henry Sadler, rightly (as it seems to me) suggests that he was entrusted.

During the same year Dunckerley returned to England, but the King's death had just occurred, and his efforts were ineffectual to establish the truth of the strange story which had been revealed to him.

The *Vanguard* sailed for the West Indies in October, 1761, but in the meantime Dunckerley had been appointed to the *Prince*, a larger ship, in which the second Sea Lodge was established, May 22nd, 1762. The new Lodge appears to have closely followed the fortunes of its founder, for in the second edition of the Engraved List for 1764, No. 279, which in the previous issue was described as " on board the *Prince*," is now represented as being held " on board the *Gaudeloupe.*"

Both "Sea Lodges" were ultimately revived by Dunckerley on *terra firma*, the one in the *Vanguard* being now the " London," No. 108, and the other in the *Prince* and *Gaudaloupe*, which adopted the title of the "Somerset House," and after amalgamating successively with the " Old Horn Lodge" (p. 28) and the " Royal Inverness," in a Volunteer corps of which the Duke of Sussex (Earl of Inverness) was the commander, has become the " Royal Somerset House and Inverness," present No. 4.

In 1767, to a great extent through the exertions of General James Adolphus Oughton, who had known him for many years, Dunckerley was granted a pension by the King, which enabled him to devote the whole of his time to the welfare of the Masonic Institution.

The rank of Past Senior Grand Warden was conferred upon him in 1786, and as a Provincial Grand Master his services were so appreciated that in 1795, when there were thirty-four provinces in all, he had for his share no less than eight of the number. In the Royal Arch degree he also took a profound interest, and was the Grand Superintendent over sixteen counties, together with Bristol and the Isle of Wight.

A third "Sea Lodge" was established in 1768 "On board His Majesty's ship *Canceaux* at Quebec," but notwithstanding the popular tradition which has found expression in an earlier page, there is no evidence to show that Dunckerley was either a party to its formation or interested in its success.

This Lodge, which was "to be held in the most convenient place *adjacent* to the said ship," never paid for its "constitution," or returned any list of its members, and was struck off the roll in 1792. A great desire to found Regimental Lodges appears to have existed in the Army at Quebec, and to a lesser extent a corresponding impulse to establish Naval Lodges, might be naturally looked for among the officers of the Fleet. It is important also to recollect that Lord Colville, a former Deputy Grand Master of North America, and most zealous Freemason, who, as a Commodore, had commanded at the re-capture of St. John's, Newfoundland, in 1762, shortly afterwards, as an Admiral, was appointed Commander-in-Chief on the Station, a position which he retained until the close of 1768.

No other sea Lodge was ever constituted, though a petition for one, "Naval Kilwinning," to be held "on board H.M. ship *Ardent*" was received from Lieutenant Crawford, and other naval officers, in 1810. But the Grand Lodge of Scotland, after consulting with the sister jurisdictions, "notwithstanding the respectable station of the applicants, felt herself constrained to refuse."

The first Military Lodge which sprang into existence at Quebec, was St. Andrew's, established October 20th, 1760—in the 78th Highlanders, by Sir Simon Fraser, Colonel of the Regiment, and Provincial Grand Master. Others soon followed, and the number of "itinerants" (as they were frequently styled) was still further augmented by the presence of many "sojourning" Military Lodges from the British Isles. The latter, it may be observed, were required to have their warrants registered in the books of the Provincial Grand Lodge, to pay five shillings at the making of every new brother, and to conform to the regulations of the local authority. A similar usage prevailed in other Provincial jurisdictions.

As before remarked, the strife between the two Grand Lodges of England, was carried across the Atlantic, and ultimately the "Ancients" were victorious all along the line, but the "Moderns" held their ground in that portion of North America which has now become the United States, until the War of the Revolution : and in Canada, down to the final decade of the last century.

For their success in the struggle for supremacy, the victors were mainly indebted to the Army Lodges, of whose fidelity to the cause of the "Ancients" at Boston and New York, in 1768 and 1781-2, examples have been given in a previous chapter.

Between these dates—in 1775—hostilities commenced between Great Britain and America. At the battle of Bunker's Hill, Lord Rawdon (afterwards 2nd Earl of Moira) fought stoutly on one side, and Major-General Joseph Warren (who was killed) on the other. Colonel Richard Gridley, who, for his distinguished services at the sieges of Louisburg and Quebec, had received a pension and grant of land from the British Government, planned the works that Warren laid down his life to defend, and was also wounded in the action. The war was carried into Canada, and Major-General Montgomery (also a leading Freemason) fell at the assault of Quebec.

The following year witnessed the British occupation of New York, and the introduction of so-called "Ancient Masonry" into that State.

Here it may be convenient to explain that while the members of Lodges under all the jurisdictions of the British Islands, with the exception of the original Grand Lodge of England, were commonly known as "Ancient Masons ;" the terms "Ancient York Masons," and "Ancient York Masonry" were at first only employed by the English Schismatics, and did not come into common use —in America—until the close of the century.

Pennsylvania was next occupied in force (1777). The American army took post at Valley Forge, twenty-six miles from Philadelphia, and tradition affirms that Lodges were held in this camp, which Washingon often attended. There can hardly be a doubt that such was the case, but unfortunately no records of the Continental Field Lodges for the period are in existence.

It was for a long time believed that the founder and first president of the American Republic was made a Mason in the "Lodge of Social and Military Virtues," in the 46th Foot, holding a warrant—No. 227—from the Grand Lodge of Ireland, granted in 1752.

In the officers' mess of this gallant corps, a Bible is preserved. It reposes in a walnut case, with glass lid, to which the following inscription is attached :—

"On this sacred volume Washington received a degree of Masonry. It was twice taken by the enemy. and both times returned to the regiment with all the honours of war."

The 46th Foot formed a part of General Grey's expedition against New Bedford (Mass.) in 1778, and it was by soldiers in its ranks that the family bible of the "Wests" residing in that town, was carried away. At the above date, the march of events seems to entirely preclude the possibility of Washington having been a *subsequent* visitor to the Lodge in the 46th Foot, while his presence at any earlier period, before the bible had passed out of the possession of the West family, is an hypothesis which, unless we throw over the inscription, it would be useless to discuss. Washington, who received the three degrees of Masonry at Fredericksburg, Virginia, some years before the arrival of the 46th Regiment in America, was indeed initiated in an English Colony, and in a Lodge working, in a secondary sense, under English authority. That the tenets of the Craft obtained a firm hold on his mind, his after conduct proved, for when war broke out, and he became divided from his brothers of the Mother Country,—in feeling, in communion of soul, he was their brother still. The Masonic chest of the 46th, by the chances of war, fell into the hands of the Americans. The circumstance was reported to General Washington, who directed that a guard of honour should take charge of the chest, with other articles of value belonging to the 46th, and return them to the regiment.

A similar incident occurred at Dominica in 1805, when the 46th was attacked by a French force, which it gallantly repelled, but in the action had again the misfortune to lose its Masonic chest, which the enemy succeeded in securing on board their fleet without knowing its contents. Three years afterwards, the French Government, at the earnest request of the officers who had commanded the expedition, returned the chest with several complimentary presents, offering by that act the acknowledgment and homage of an enlightened nation to the purity, value, and usefulness of Masonry.

The "Lodge of Social and Military Virtues," after undergoing many other vicissitudes, was at work in the same regiment at Sydney (N.S.W.) in 1816.

The next year we meet with it on the coast of Coromandel, where, retaining its old name, it sought for and obtained a local charter—No. VII.—which afterwards merged into an English Warrant (1836) with the number 634. At some time after the year 1822, when the regiment marched from Cannanore to Hyderabad, a number of the members died, others were invalided, and the Lodge chest was forgotten until accidently re-discovered by a member of the mess committee in 1829. The finder, Captain Lacy, who was a Mason, brought home the chest when the regiment returned to England in 1833.

The Irish warrant was renewed in 1834, there being at the time only one member originally connected with the Lodge, but the torch which had been re-lighted, after burning brightly for a few years, began to flicker, and finally went out, in the sense that the Regimental or Travelling warrant, which had again accompanied the 46th to the New World, was returned to the Grand Lodge of Ireland in 1847, and two days afterwards a new one of a military, though stationary character, at the same number, was issued for the purpose of forming a permanent Garrison Lodge at Montreal.

In 1855, No. 227 joined the Grand Lodge of Canada, receiving a civil warrant, and two years later it was resolved :—"That the 'Lodge of Social and Military Virtues' shall henceforth be called the 'Lodge of Antiquity,' shall wear gold instead of silver jewels, and take precedence of all numbered Lodges."

In 1869 a Grand Lodge was established for the Province of Quebec, and the first Lodge on its roll is " Antiquity," originally in the 46th Foot, while the two next—" Albion " and " St. John's "—were formerly in the Royal Artillery. It is gratifying to relate that the venerable " Lodge of Antiquity," now No. 1 Quebec, observes with great *eclat* its Annual " Military Night," at which large numbers of the officers of the Volunteer Force appear in uniform.

It is worthy of remark that the 46th was not the only British regiment which, during the revolutionary struggle in America, was afforded an opportunity of witnessing a practical illustration of the beautiful and humanizing principles of Freemasonry.

In a skirmish with the enemy, the " constitution " and regalia of a Lodge attached to the 17th Foot fell into the hands of an American general. Actuated, however, by the genuine principles of Masonry, he immediately returned them with the following letter :—

"WEST JERSEY HIGHLANDS,
23rd July, 1779.

" BRETHREN,—When the ambition of monarchs, or the jarring interests of contending States, call forth their subjects to war, as Masons we are disarmed of that resentment which stimulates to undistinguished desolation, and, however our political sentiments may impel us in the public dispute, we are still Brethren, and (our professional duty apart) ought to promote the happiness and advance the weal of each other.

Accept, therefore, at the hands of a Brother, the Constitution of the Lodge ' Unity, No. 18,' held in the 17th British regiment, which your late misfortunes have put it in my power to restore to you.

I am, your Brother and obedient Servant,
SAMUEL H. PARSONS.

To the Master and Wardens of Lodge ' Unity, No. 18,' upon the Registry of England."

The history of this Lodge illustrates very forcibly what may be called the " confusion of jurisdiction," which is apparent in the proceedings of so many of the travelling Lodges of that period.

Lodge " Unity " in the 17th Foot, was originally chartered by the Grand Lodge of Scotland, as No. 168, in

1771. The regiment landed at Boston in 1776, and was at Philadelphia in 1777 and 1778. During this latter period the Lodge (which remained on the Scottish roll until 1816) accepted a warrant from the Provincial Grand Lodge of Pennsylvania, under the "Ancients," with the local "No. 18."

A little earlier, Colonel (afterwards General) Samuel H. Parsons, was a founder and the first treasurer of "American Union" (a Military) Lodge, warranted by Colonel (afterwards General) Richard Gridley, Deputy Provincial Grand Master of Massachussetts, under the "Moderns," on February 15th, 1776. In the following April, the members of the Lodge were on duty with their regiment in the State of New York, and an application having been made for a confirmation of their warrant, it was denied. A new one, however, was granted, with the title of "Military Union," No. I. But the altered name gave umbrage to the members, who, while they apparently acquiesced in the change, never used the later appellation except under necessity. At the time referred to, it should be recollected that the mother country and her American provinces were at war, and that Sir John Johnson, Provincial Grand Master of New York (a military commander of some repute, only son of the more famous Sir William Johnson, also a Freemason), was in sympathy with the government of the country from which his Masonic power emanated. Pending the provincial conflict, Johnson had appointed Dr. Peter Middleton his deputy, and by the latter, the confirmation of a Lodge warrant, distinguished by the title of "American Union," must, from the nature of things, have been deemed unadvisable.

The further proceedings of this Lodge will again come before us, but a notice of it in this place, will convey (let me hope) some idea of the complications which occurred among the Army Lodges—on both sides—during the War of Independence. It could be supported by much additional evidence, that the asperities which characterised the rivalry of the two Masonic systems, found no place in the Army Lodges. To quote the words of a somewhat impassioned orator, "the 'Ancient and Modern' contest turned to ashes in the red-hot furnace of liberty"; and as we have already seen, the warrant and paraphernalia of an *Ancient* Lodge in the British Infantry was fraternally restored by a member (and at that time a past master) of a *Modern* Lodge in the American army.

After the war, the 17th Foot proceeded to Nova Scotia, and in 1786, a letter was received by the Provincial (which, later in the same year, became the) Grand Lodge of Pennsylvania, from Lodge No. 18, held at Shelburne (N.S.), claiming to have remained under its obedience, "and soliciting the Grand Lodge to address a letter on their behalf to General Parsons on the subject of a Lodge warrant, and civilities which they had experienced from him."

This Lodge was apparently left behind on the return from foreign service of the 17th Foot ; and it is probable that a majority of the members remained in Nova Scotia either as military settlers or as volunteers to other corps. The instances, however, of "Regimental" becoming "Stationary" Lodges, both in Canada and the United States, are very numerous.

The first Lodge on the existing roll of Quebec (as already related) was formerly held in the 46th Foot, and the two next in the Royal Artillery. But perhaps the most curious case of all has been that of a still surviving Lodge, which was originally constituted in the 60th Foot, then at Detroit, Michigan, in 1764, by the Provincial Grand Master of New York.

Michigan was French until 1763, British until 1796, under a territorial government until 1810, under Indiana for five years, and then "Michigan Territory" until 1837.

Zion Lodge, No. 1, attached to the 60th, or Royal American Regiment, was thus established by the "Moderns," in 1764, but thirty years later (1794) at the instance of another Army Lodge—then in the Artillery, now "Albion" No. 2, Quebec—it went over to the "Ancients," becoming Zion Lodge, No. 10, on the (Provincial) roll of Lower Canada. This warrant was granted two years before the surrender of the territory of Michigan to the United States, but the Lodge, which was evidently "left behind" by the 60th, at a much earlier date, experienced a similar fate when the British was succeeded by an American garrison at Detroit in

1796. In 1806, the Quebec warrant was surrendered, and a new one, at the No. 62, obtained from the Grand Lodge of New York. In 1819, it became No. 3, and in 1826 united in the formation of the Grand Lodge of Michigan, on the roll of which body, this old "Travelling Lodge," formerly attached to the Royal American Regiment, now holds the first place, under its original title of "Zion," No. 1.

In this connection, although slightly anticipating the sequence of the narrative, the later fortunes of "American Union" may be briefly adverted to. It met for the last time as an Army Lodge, April 23, 1783, and was ordered "to stand closed until the W.M. should call them together." This occurred in 1790, when a colony from New England having become established north-west of the Ohio, the Lodge was re-opened at Marietta by Jonathan Heart, the Master, with Benjamin Tupper and Rufus Putman officiating as wardens. Heart continued in the chair until the following year, when he joined the Army of St. Clair, and was killed at the battle of Fort Recovery. The Lodge united with others at the formation of the Grand Lodge of Ohio, of which General Rufus Putman was the first Grand Master, in 1808, and under its old title of "American Union" retains the place of No. 1 in the Masonic jurisdiction of that State.

Many and great were the vicissitudes of good and bad fortune experienced by the Lodges in British regiments in the course of the war with France, which, commencing in 1793, continued almost without intermission until 1815. A duplicate of its Irish warrant (No. 441) was granted to the 38th Foot in August, 1795, "the original having been taken by the French;" and a precisely similar order in the case of the 5th Dragoon Guards, whose Masonic chest, with warrant (No. 570) and jewels, had also fallen into the hands of the enemy, was made by the Grand Lodge of Ireland in September of the same year.

A Lodge was established in the 11th Foot, then stationed at Norwich, by the "Ancients" in February, 1798, and in the May following, while serving in Flanders under Sir Eyre Coote, the entire regiment became prisoners of war. From Ostend the officers and soldiers were marched to Douay and

Fort L'Escarpe, and they remained in France until 1799, when they were exchanged. Whether, indeed, the work of the Lodge was suspended during the period of their captivity cannot be absolutely determined, but the probability is quite the other way, as the Lodge was certainly in existence as late as the year 1807, and the custom of meeting as Masons has always prevailed to a very large extent wherever there have been prisoners of war.

Happily, indeed, the records of a few Regimental Lodges have escaped the general doom, and among them are those of No. 183, established in the 9th Foot by the Junior Grand Lodge of England, or "Ancients," in February, 1803.

In November, 1805, the 1st Battalion of the 9th Regiment embarked at the cove of Cork, in three transports, with the expectation of taking part in the war on the Continent. Two of the transports were, however, driven by contrary winds to the Downs, while the third, the *Ariadne*, having the head-quarters on board, was wrecked on the coast of France, near Calais, when the staff-officers and 262 soldiers were made prisoners of war.

Though the archives of the Lodge appear to have gone down with the *Ariadne*, a sufficient number of its members weathered the storm, and seem to have lost no time, after their involuntary descent upon French soil, in resuming their Masonic labours.

The regiment remained at Valenciennes until after the first abdication of Napoleon, and the proceedings of this "Captive Lodge" extend over a period of eight years, namely, from January 30th, 1806, until January 20th, 1814, under which latter date there appears :—

"The Lodge having heard the reports of the Different Brethren, closed, in perfect harmony and Brotherly Love, with 21 members present, and adjourned until the fate of War shall have decided the contents of Europe. *On the 25th January*, 1814, *the brethren were all dispersed. These affairs were decided on 31st March*, 1814, *by the triumphal Entry of the Allies in Paris and the overthrow of Bonaparte. The* ARK *was at Riom, in the province of Auvergne, with only Brs. Butler and Ware present, who separated, and Br. Butler brought the Lodge to England.*"

G

The above is a literal transcript of what purports to be the *last* entry in the minute-book of the Lodge during the captivity of the battalion to which it was attached, but the words italicized must evidently have been interpolated by the Master, Sergeant Edward Butler, at some later period.

Few minute-books of Regimental Lodges, as I have already more than once remarked, are available for examination. I think, however, if records of the kind were more numerous, we should find, in the generality of instances, the honour, reputation, and well-being of each Lodge to have been mainly dependent upon the enthusiasm and assiduity of one or two prominent non-commissioned officers. Edward Butler was the life and soul of the Lodge in the 9th Foot, and it fell to pieces directly this worthy sergeant obtained his discharge from the service.

The 96th Foot received a warrant (No. 170) from the "Ancients" in 1804, the fortunes of which are very curtly, though expressively, recorded in the following memorandum by the Grand Secretary :—

"6th Jan. 1809 : Warr^t. 170. Box and furniture lost at St. Croix. Members all lost or dead or disposed of, but Bro. Geo. Baxter. Quarter-Master."

The annals of the Peninsular war furnish many Masonic illustrations, and those of the Sixth Dragoon Guards, in which there was an Irish Lodge (No. 557), an especial one. The regiment, after a severe engagement, lost its baggage, among which was the chest containing the Lodge furniture, warrant and jewels. The commander -of the capturing party, when he saw the Masonic emblems on the chest, immediately sent for one of the prisoners, and demanded the meaning of the marks, which the soldier, as far as was prudent, explained. The French officer, on finding the chest belonged to a Freemasons' Lodge, directed it to be returned to the English regiment, with a flag of truce, and a guard of honour, forwarding at the same time a letter, stating that, although not a Freemason himself, he respected the Society, and that his brother officers would never forgive him if he did not treat the misfortunes of their Masonic Brethren with consideration.

A further anecdote, of the same eventful period, is connected with the 42nd Foot, but whether the writer who relates it was member of the Irish Lodge "Hibernia" (No. 42), or the Scottish Lodge "St. Andrew" (No. 310), both of which existed in the regiment at the time, is not revealed in the narrative from which I am about to quote. James Auton, "late Quarter-Master Sergeant, 42nd or Royal Highlanders," in his *Retrospect of a Military Life* (1841) tells us :—

" I was General Park's orderly this night. and had a good roof over my head, and the dry floor of a cart-shed. with plenty of dry straw for a bed : but my poor wife was absent, for the first time since we left home. She was detained, along with several other women, on the right bank of the Adour. until the bridge was repaired. While this was doing, one of the women belonging to the regiment begged her to take care of a little ass colt, with a couple of bundles, until she should get back to St. Severe to make some purchases : she complied, and before the other returned the bridge was repaired. Our regiment had passed, and she followed. driving the colt before her ; but before she got to the further end. the stubborn animal stood still and would not move a foot. Another regiment was advancing, the passage was impeded, and what to do she knew not. She was in the act of removing the woman's bundles from the beast's back, and struggling to get out of the way, determined to leave the animal, when a grenadier of the advancing regiment, casting his eye on a finely polished horn with the Masonic arms cut on it, and slung over her shoulder. stepped aside, saying ' Poor creature, I shall not see you left struggling here for the sake of what is slung by your side : ' at the same time handing his musket to one of his comrades, he lifted the colt in his arms and carried it to the end of the bridge. My poor wife thanked him with the tear in her eye. the only acknowledgment she could make for his kindness; but she has often thought of it since, and congratulated herself on having the good fortune to have that horn, empty as it was, with its talismanic hieroglyphic, slung by her side on that occasion : and thus to raise up a friend when she was so much in need of one."

In another popular work, *Adventures of a Soldier*, which appeared in the same year (1841), the author, Edward Costello, who also describes his experiences as one of the "rank and file" during the Peninsular war, observes :—

" At Castle Sarazin (between Toulouse and Bordeaux), we used to be on our usual excellent terms with the French quartered in the neighbourhood. I got acquainted here with a very smart fellow—a French sergeant belonging to the 83rd Regiment. A friendship was cemented between us, naturally enough, by our both being Freemasons."

To the testimonies of these private soldiers, as they both were when the incidents occurred which they afterwards described at a much later date in their books, I shall add the corroborative evidence of a commissioned officer who served in the same series of campaigns, and was the recipient of much fraternal attention when taken prisoner by the French.

Lieutenant-General Sir Charles James Napier, one of the most gallant soldiers of his time, entered the army at an early age, and in 1806, obtained a majority in the 50th Foot, which he commanded at Corunna, where he was made prisoner, after receiving five wounds. He also served in the Peninsula during later campaigns, in a floating expedition off the coast of America, and accompanied the English Army to Paris in 1815. In 1842, while commanding the forces in Bombay, he was sent to Scinde, where, in 1843, he fought and won the decisive battles of Meeanee and Hyderabad. In the spring of 1849, when the disasters of the Sikh campaign had awakened the anxieties of the people of England, all eyes were directed to the hero of Scinde, and he was appointed to the command of the Indian Army. But on his arrival in India the object of the war had been attained. He exerted himself, however, in reforming abuses which had grown up in the army, especially among the officers. A large number of courts-martial were held, on account of the laxity of discipline which had crept into the Indian Army, and one unfortunate officer, the sole support of his aged mother, was cashiered. That parent, having no other means of saving herself and son from ruin, applied to Sir Charles to allow her son to retire from the service by the sale of his commission. But the commander-in-chief was true to his duty as an officer and a Mason. With his right hand he confirmed the sentence of the court-martial, and with his left he sent to the distressed parent the value of her son's forfeited commission

In Doyle's Lodge of Fellowship, Guernsey, there is a portrait of the general, and the minute-book records under June 16th, 1807 :—" Emergency. Major Charles James Napier was entered, passed, and raised, he being about to leave the Island." In April, 1841, a letter was received from him, then in command at Chester, asking the date of his initiation, as he had lost all his papers when ship-wrecked; and a second, later in the same year, thanking the brethren of his mother Lodge for having elected him an honorary member.

In September, 1845, when Governor of Scinde, at the invitation of the Lodge of Hope, Kurrachee, he laid the foundation stone of a Masonic Hall, and afterwards delivered a most interesting address, premising that his position was a difficult one, owing to the suddenness of the call ; that his attention having been diverted to other objects for many years, he was probably one of the worst Masons present, but as there might be some less acquainted with the subject even than himself, he would endeavour to give a sketch of the history of Masonry from the earliest times.

On his return from India, Sir Charles was entertained at dinner by the Meridian Lodge, Dublin, and elected an honorary member of the Union Lodge, Limerick, in November, 1848.

The next year he was again in India, and a grand Masonic banquet was given in his honour at Simla on the 1st of October. The commander-in-chief, as he then was, appeared in full uniform, wearing the apron and insignia of the Royal Arch degree, and in response to the toast of his health expressed himself as follows :—

"Few Masons can say that they owe so much to Masonry as I do. I am an old and, I fear, a good-for-nothing Mason. I have been forty years a Royal Arch Mason, and yet I fear I could not work myself into a chapter of that high degree ; but with the aid of my friend, Colonel Curtis, I hope to rub off the rust, and be able to do so, for, as I said before, probably no man present can say that he is under the same obligation to Masonry that I am, and I am always glad of an opportunity of acknowledging the same to the Craft. I was once a prisoner, without hope of ever being exchanged, and expected to be sent to Verdun, to which place in France all prisoners were consigned, for, at this time, the two governments of France and England were so exasperated against each other that their anger fell on individuals, and there was no exchange of prisoners. A man who was taken lost all chance of promotion, or of ever seeing his friends again. In this state of despair and misery, knowing that my family must have believed me to have been killed, I was casting about in my own thoughts for some way in which I could communicate with my family ; it came into my head that I was a Mason. and I contrived to poke out a brother. He was a French officer of the name of Bontemps, I think. and a very good name it was, for, like a good and honourable brother, he managed to send a letter for me to England, by no means an easy matter in those days, for there were no railroads. or steam vessels, or steam engines then to carry letters like lightning everywhere. Besides, it was at this time an extremely dangerous and hazardous undertaking for a French officer. But my honest and good brother did it for me, and within three months my family knew I was alive."

Masonic banquets in honour of Sir Charles Napier were given on his final return from India by the brethren of the Rugby district, in 1851, and later in the same year (Trafalgar Day) by the Portsmouth Lodges, from whose address I extract the following :—" We hail you with a hearty welcome to the land of your birth ; as a Citizen you have our esteem, as a Soldier our admiration, as a Brother our honour and love."

Two years afterwards, with Military and Masonic honours, the departed warrior was laid in his tomb. "I meant to say," are the words of his younger brother, the historian of the Peninsular War, but to which he vainly attempted to give utterance at the time, "that a great and good soldier was in his grave ; that in his old age he commanded armies and led them always to victory. Neither in youth, nor in manhood, nor in his aged years, did he ever cease to love, and cherish, and confide in soldiers. And now they thronged round his grave, to do honour to the dead man whom, when living, they had by their courage, devotion, and discipline, raised to renown."

It was stated by Dr. Edward J. Scott, of Southsea, a past master of the Phœnix Lodge, one of the medical attendants of the deceased, that an hour or so before his death the hand of the great general was laid in his own, and that shortly before that event Sir Charles gave him the grip of a Master Mason, and thus died, evincing in his last moments an unfaltering sympathy with his brethren of the mystic tie.

The battle of Corunna, at which Major Napier was made a prisoner, was fought on the 16th of January, 1809 ; and later, in the same year, a similar fate was experienced by another British officer, the story of whose capture was related by Lieutenant-Colonel Lord Wantage, V.C. (who served throughout the war in the Crimea), on the occasion of his installation as Provincial Grand Master of Berkshire, in 1898 :—

" He stated that it was his lot in early life to be first interested in Masonry by an event that happened to his father, the late Lieutenant-General James Lindsay, when serving in the Walcheren campaign, in 1809. He was shot through the leg, and being quite disabled, fell into the hands of the enemy ; but no sooner was he carried from the field of battle, than he discovered that his captor was a brother Freemason, who, true to the traditions of the Craft, like the Good Samaritan, dressed his wounds, brought him into his own house, and took charge of him until the time of release, defraying all costs, without any security for payment."

At the close of the Peninsular War, peace was signed with France, but hostilities were soon resumed. Napoleon escaped from Elba, then followed the Hundred Days, and finally the battle of Waterloo, during which momentous conflict the influence of Masonry was brought into play on both sides, with very happy results, as the reader will have already gleaned from an earlier chapter.

With the downfall of Napoleon came the reduction of the British Army from a war to a peace footing. This led not only to the disembodiment of the entire force of Militia, which had taken the place of the regular troops in the United Kingdom, but also to the "mustering out " (or disbandment) of all the veteran and garrison battalions, of many of the regiments of cavalry and infantry, and the reduction of such as were retained on the fixed establishment to a much lower strength than had previously prevailed.

Many Military Lodges passed out of existence, but others, in lieu of an itinerant, assumed (and retained) a stationary character. Nor should it be forgotten that other causes were in operation, notably the frequent changes of regiments from one station to another, which conduced to the same end, namely, a reduction in number of the moveable and their conversion in other instances into irremovable Lodges.

To the examples already given of Lodges in foreign jurisdictions which were formerly held in regiments of the

British Army, I shall add one more. "Virgin Lodge," at Halifax, N.S., which, in 1786, became "Artillery Lodge," and, in 1800, "Virgin" again, is now No. 3 on the roll of Nova Scotia. Other existing Lodges formerly in the Royal, Bengal, and Bombay Artillery, are "Union Waterloo," Kent; "St. John's," Gibraltar; "Humility with Fortitude" and "Courage with Humanity," Calcutta; and "Orion in the West," Poona.

The "Amphibious Lodge," originally in the Royal Marines, is now peacefully moored in the inland town of Heckmond-wike, Yorkshire.

The "Royal York Lodge of Perseverance," London, established in 1776, only began its military career in 1793, when its fortunes were associated with those of the Coldstream Guards, in which regiment it continued at work until 1821, when it resumed its civil character.

"Mount Olive," in the 67th Foot, was transferred to the Royal Regiment of Cornish Miners in 1807, but the military was afterwards exchanged for a civil warrant, and it is now the "Lodge of Fortitude," Truro.

"Euphrates," London; "Unanimity," Preston; and "One and All," Bodmin; were held in the West London, 3rd Lancashire, and 1st Cornwall Militia, respectively.

"St. Cuthbert's," in the Durham Militia, was a Scottish Lodge, and in 1813, when the regiment was disembodied, continued to meet at Barnard Castle under the Scottish warrant until 1825, when an English one was applied for and received. This served the purpose of the members for eleven years, but in 1836 they made an effort to resume their old allegiance, in which, it is needless to say, they were unsuccessful.

These illustrations might be largely extended, but I shall content myself with adducing the case of the "Shakespeare Lodge," Warwick, which is the most singular of the series. Examples of Lodges having been "left behind them" by the military on a change of station are not uncommon, but those of Stationary being converted into Ambulatory Lodges by the simple process of regiments marching away with them, if not entirely unknown, are, nevertheless, of comparatively rare occurrence. Such an event happened in 1796, when the members of a Lodge at Norwich sold their furniture to some brethren in the Warwickshire Militia, making them, at the same time, a present of the "Constitution." On the removal of the regiment in the following year, the "Shakespeare Lodge," to use the title adopted in 1797, accompanied it, and was brought to Warwick in 1802. The next year the battalion was again ordered on service, but the Lodge remained at Warwick. The regiment returned in 1805, and three years later was quartered at Sunderland, when a resolution was carried in the Lodge at Warwick that it should be made stationary at that town. A protest was lodged by the members at Sunderland, and a counter-protest by those at Warwick. The latter had thirty-one signatures, the former only ten, so when the matter came before a committee of the Grand Lodge they decided in favour of the majority, and the removal of the "Shakespeare Lodge" from the Warwickshire Militia to the guardianship of non-military brethren at Warwick was recognised and approved.

It has already been suggested that the degree of Knight Templar penetrated into our British Military Lodges during (or before) the Seven Years' War. Whether derived from the Clermont or the Strict Observance systems is immaterial, though the traditions of both may be referred to as possessing attractions which, at least to Scotsmen, may have been irresistible. Thus, passing over the alleged reception of Von Hund by a former Grand Master of Scotland—Lord Kilmarnock—the sixth of the Clermont degrees and the whole fabric of the Strict Observance were based on the legend that Pierre d'Aumont was elected Grand Master of the Templars in Scotland, A.D. 1313, and that to avoid persecution the Knights became Freemasons.

It was, however, to their intercourse with brethren belonging to regiments which served in Ireland towards the end of the last century, that the Scottish Lodges owed their acquaintance with Knight Templarism.

This Order, then known as *Black Masonry*, was propagated, to a large extent, through charters issued by a Lodge of Freemasons at Dublin, which had been constituted by "Mother Kilwinning," for the practice of the Craft

degrees. The action of her daughter Lodge, encouraged,
not unnaturally, the belief in Kilwinning being a centre of
the so-called "High degrees," and in 1813 application was
made to the Mother Lodge to authorise the transfer of a
"Black Warrant" from Knights of the Temple, and of
Malta, in the Westmeath, to brethren of the same degree
serving in the Shropshire Militia. But the Lodge of Kilwinning, in reply to the "Sir Knights" of the latter regiment, strongly repudiated the existence of a maternal tie
between herself and any Society of Masonic Knighthood,
and expressed her inability to regard as Masonry anything
beyond the three regular steps. The Westmeath Militia
held at the time an Irish Warrant, No. 791—cancelled in
1826—and the Shropshire Regiment an English one, which
was made "Civil" and "Stationary" in 1820, and is now
the authority to assemble as Masons of the "Salopian
Lodge of Charity," at Shrewsbury. It is probable that all
the degrees, additional to the "three regular steps," obtained
a footing in the British Islands through the medium of the
Army Lodges.

In Scotland these additional degrees were, in the first
instance, wrought by the Lodges, and afterwards more often
in Encampments. A Lodge—"Aboyne"—was formed in the
Aberdeen Militia, in 1799, and an Encampment in 1812.
Both moved with the regiment, being at Dover, 1812;
Liverpool, 1813; London, 1814; and returning to Aberdeen in 1815. At the last named date, the degrees practised in the "St. George Aboyne Encampment," were
arranged in seven groups :—

I.—Master past the Chair. Excellent and Super-Excellent.
Royal Arch : II.—Ark. Black Mark. Link and Chain : III.—
Knight Templar. Knight of St. John of Jerusalem. Mediter-
ranean Pass. Knight of Malta : IV.—Jordan Pass. Babylon
Pass : V.—Knight of the Red Cross ; VI.—High Priest: VII.—
Prussian Blue.

Both Master Masons and Royal Arch Masons were
received indiscriminately as candidates ; if the former, they
received first the Group I. of Royal Arch degrees ; if the
latter, they began with Group II. When the Royal Arch
degrees were conferred, the meeting was called a Chapter ;
for all the others an Encampment.

In the English Lodges belonging to the regular establishment, the only degrees worked (with official sanction) were the first three, down to 1813 ; and the price they paid for the Union of that year, consisted in part of the acceptance of the Royal Arch and Installed Masters' degrees, as additions to the pure and ancient Masonry which had been bequeathed to them in 1717.

With the other section of the English Craft it was different. Under the "Ancient" (or Schismatic) Grand Lodge, both degrees were essential features of their system. There can hardly be a doubt, unless indeed it is a wholly gratuitous one, that the communication of the secrets of the Royal Arch, was the earliest form in which any mystical teaching was associated with the incident of a Master being placed in the chair of his Lodge. Out of this was ultimately evolved the degree of Installed Master, a ceremony unknown (except as a bye or side degree) in the "Modern" system until the first decade of the present century, and of which I can trace no sign among the "Ancients" until the growing practice of conferring the "Arch" upon brethren not properly entitled to receive it, brought about a *constructive* passing through the chair, which, by qualifying candidates not otherwise eligible, naturally entailed the introduction of a ceremony, *additional* to the simple forms inherited by the earliest of Grand Lodges.

The records of No. 441, in the 38th Foot, afford an illustration of the Irish practice. The working of the Royal Arch degree was resumed in the *Lodge*, in 1822, when a letter was read from the Deputy Grand Secretary, of which the following passage appears in the minutes :—

"There is not any warrant issued by the Grand Lodge of Ireland other than that you hold : it has therefore always been the practice of Irish Lodges to confer the Higher Degrees under that authority."

The Minden Lodge, No. 63, in the 20th Regiment, also continued the work of the Royal Arch under its original (Craft) warrant until 1838, when a separate charter was issued by the Grand Chapter of Ireland.

The Scottish custom must next be referred to, of the issuing by private Lodges of commissions—or, as they were afterwards termed, "dispensations"—an evil of great magnitude, which led to frequent complaints with regard to the practice of brethren traversing the country and picking up what members they could for their own Lodges, to the detriment of those "locally situated."

The erection of branch Lodges by "dispensation" became very popular in Ayrshire, and one of the kind remained in active operation for eight years in the County Militia, with results so beneficial to the Mother Lodge—Renfrew St. Paul —as to justify the holders of the "dispensation" being at that Lodge's expense "treated to two bowls of toddy" on the occasion of their surrendering it.

In December, 1808, a letter was read from the confidential agent of the Mother Lodge in the Ayrshire Militia, requesting that the members in that regiment might be granted a dispensation, which was agreed to, with the proviso :

" That no Mason can be initiated, or become a member of the dispensation. nor no man can be made a Mason under it, who has been found guilty of any of the following crimes by a General or Regimental Court-martial, *viz.:* cowardice, theft. mutiny. or desertion."

It seems to have been usual on the part of Lodges granting dispensations, to exact a tribute of one-half of the amount received as entrance fees, but the Mother Lodge, "from a wish to indulge her brethren in the Ayrshire Militia," asked "no more than 3s. for each entrant, 2s. 9d. of which was to be retained to defray any necessary expenses."

The records of the Irish daughter of the Lodge of Kilwinning show, that not only members of the Militia or Volunteers, but also (in certainly one instance) brethren of the regular forces were empowered to form branch Lodges and make Masons during their absence from the seat of their Mother Lodge.

" 1783. July 22nd. Took into consideration several communications from our Bror.Lieut.-Col. Heath relative to a Warrant or Dispensation from us to hold a Lodge in the 1st or Royal Regt. Resolved that a Dispensation be granted by us to Bror. Lieut-Col. Heath. Capts. Trail and O'Brien, to convene a Lodge and act as Masons while absent from Dublin."

That dispensations were granted as well as held by the Army Lodges, has been shown in the present chapter, and

the subject will again claim our attention, but the suggestion may be at once thrown out, that the origin of the
custom can be traced to a Scottish source. Returning for a
moment to the Militia: in 1854, the 4th Middlesex and the
1st Lancashire Regiments were stationed at Portsmouth,
and the records of the " Phœnix Lodge " inform us, that
the whole of the officers of the two battalions were either
initiated or admitted as joining members.

To account for the decay of "Military Masonry," or to
vary the expression, the falling off in the number of
Regimental Lodges, is by no means an easy task.

The reduction of the Army from a war to a peace footing,
though one of the factors in the case, could not have exercised nearly as much influence as people have commonly
supposed. Nor will the fusion of the two Grand Lodges of
England, in 1813, altogether suffice to clear up what is
otherwise left unexplained with regard to the disappearance
of the Army Lodges. Statistics, indeed, reveal that fifty
Regimental Lodges were carried over at the Union, all of
which, with only six exceptions, were working under
" Ancient " warrants. It might, therefore, at first sight
appear, that the prevalence of Lodges in the British Army
was very seriously affected by the junior Grand Lodge of
England ceasing to exist as an independent institution.
The proportion of Military to Civil Lodges (on the English
list), which, in 1814, was one in twelve, had fallen to one in
three hundred in 1878 ; and has sunk to one in eleven
hundred (or rather less) in 1899.

The laws, too, that were enacted in 1815, forbidding the
initiation of civilians, or of military persons below the rank
of corporal, were great innovations on the established usage.
But in the Irish and Scottish jurisdictions, in neither of
which was there any similar amalgamation of Grand Lodges,
nor any restrictive legislation with respect to the initiation
of private soldiers and the customs of both continued to
conform to what had been the practice of the "Ancients,"
there was also, in each case, a decided falling off (after
Waterloo) in the number of Military Lodges.

Of these associations no very early records have been
preserved ; but, so far as there is evidence to guide us, the

Regimental Lodges of the last century would appear in nearly every case to have originated in the zeal of the rank and file, and in the few instances where a Masonic spirit has pervaded an entire regiment, the love for the Craft seems not to have spread downwards, but upwards, namely, from the soldiers' barrack-room to the officers' mess.

Towards the close of the century, however, signs are not wanting that a custom was springing up of Lodges being held in regiments, the membership of which was confined to the commissioned ranks.

The first "Officers' Lodge" (of which there is any known record) was established, by the Grand Lodge of Ireland, in the 32nd Foot. The warrant, No. 617, was issued in 1783, and subsequently "erased for neglect" at some time after 1785 and before 1792 (p. 52). Before, after, and during the whole of this period there was a Scottish Lodge, No. 73—presumably the resort of the non-commissioned officers and privates—in the same battalion.

The annals of the Grand Lodge of Scotland supply the next illustration. A charter (No. 274) for the "Orange Lodge" was granted to the officers of the 51st Regiment in 1801 ; there being at the time two other Lodges in the corps of the same name, under Irish and "Ancient" warrants, each of which, it is somewhat singular to relate, bearing the number 94.

Whether, indeed, the symptoms point to a gradual loosening of the Masonic bond uniting the British soldier with his officer, is more than I am competent to determine. The soldier who has seen service is certainly, in one sense, highly educated, and always good company. As for the requirements of discipline, and the necessity which is supposed to exist for officers to keep at a distance from privates in order to preserve their dignity, they recall a familiar saying of the sagacious Goethe, that the true reason why so many people are afraid to go among those whom they regard as their social inferiors is the vague dread that, if they should thus abandon the advantages of privilege, they might not be able to hold their own by their personal merit. An officer has reason to fear the familiar society of a private, when the latter is truly his superior in character and intelligence, but not otherwise. It is, moreover, a curious fact that the private soldiers of England, though taken from the humblest classes of society, and few in number when compared to the hundreds of thousands forced into the ranks of Continental Armies, have yet surpassed all foreigners (of their own station in life) as much in letters as in arms. We have several highly interesting books of military adventure written by private soldiers, and conveying vivid pictures of their habits, feelings, and opinions, as well as the hardships to which they were exposed in the field. Three works of this kind were written by military brethren who have been referred to—Privates John Shipp, John Autun, and Edward Costello

But, as we have already seen, from the year 1815 the practice of admitting private soldiers, except as serving brethren, was absolutely forbidden by the Grand Lodge of England; and, while under the Irish obedience there is no actual law on the subject, there is every reason to suppose that from much about the same date the regulations of all the Military Lodges—regimental or garrison—have contained a clause to a similar effect.

It may, indeed, have been merely a singular coincidence, that subsequently to the Masonic Union of 1813, when private soldiers were disqualified for membership, the practice by commissioned officers of meeting as brethren without the companionship of the lower ranks attained a great vogue. There were "Officers' Lodges" in Bengal, Madras, and Bombay, and the proceedings of these bodies, together with some collateral evidence bearing on the same topic, derived from the minutes of a Cavalry Lodge, will claim our attention in the next chapter.

The English law of 1815, forbidding the admission of civilians, was probably obeyed by the regiments on home service; but by those abroad, more especially in the East, it was for many years totally disregarded.

The "Lodge of Hope," Poona, was formed by civilian members of "Orion in the West," Bombay Artillery, in 1825, and in the same year "Humanity with Courage," an offshoot of "Courage with Humanity," Bengal Artillery, was flourishing so greatly at Penang, in the Malay Peninsula, that every civilian of respectability was ranged beneath its banner. The "Union Lodge," in the 14th Foot, then stationed at Meerut, returned as a member, A. J. Colvin—judge and magistrate—in 1826.

The Irish practice of only curtailing the freedom of their Military, when calculated to be prejudicial to the interests of their Stationary Lodges, appears to have always prevented any friction between the two bodies, and has enabled the former, on several occasions, to be the means of establishing local (or civil) Lodges in continents or islands where the regiments to which they were attached happened to be sent on duty. The 1st Royals (as mentioned in the present chapter) constituted a new and stationary Lodge at Albany (New York) in 1759; and, possibly at a still earlier date, many were formed by the 39th Foot in Hindostan. Within more recent times (1857) the 4th, or "King's Own," was serving at the Mauritius, and twenty-eight gentlemen of Port Louis were initiated in, or affiliated to the regimental Lodge. The "King's Own" left the island in 1858, but before its departure the brethren of the Military installed the officers of a Civil Lodge, consisting of nineteen members of the parent body, who remained behind in the Mauritius.

In the same way, the "Lodge of Yokohama," the earliest in Japan, was an offshoot of the "Sphinx Lodge" in the 2nd battalion of the 20th Foot, which initiated a sufficient number of civilian members to enable the work of Masonry to be carried on at the departure of the regiment from that country in 1866.

Many of the vicissitudes experienced by the Army Lodges have already been laid before the reader. Some of these bodies ceased to work owing to the loss of their warrants, others through the regiments to which they were attached being ordered on foreign service, and perhaps the greatest number from sheer inability to continue their labours with an insufficiency of members. But there was a further reason why certain of the Lodges came to an untimely end.

The consent of the commanding officer to their original formation appears to have been always essential, and at any moment afterwards, as it would seem from the evidence at my command, at the *fiat* of the colonel for the time being, the permission could be revoked. Between the years 1806 and 1846 Lodges were closed in this summary way in the 3rd and 11th Dragoons, the 13th, 18th, and 85th Foot, and the 1st Lancashire Militia.

Of a "closure" by even higher authority there are a few examples. The warrant, No. 295, in the 4th Dragoons, now revived, was returned to the Grand Lodge, "owing to the disapproval of the military authorities," in 1830. The case of the 38th Foot was a very singular one. An Irish Lodge, No. 441, in this regiment, after many periods of dormancy, was revived at Limerick in 1840, but the Commander in-Chief in Ireland, Sir Edward Blakeney, set in motion by the Lord-Lieutenant, peremptorily ordered the meetings to cease, and "all documents connected with the institution to be forthwith returned to the parent society." The warrant was, therefore, sent to the Grand Lodge, from which body, however, a hint was received in 1842, the 38th being then at Corfu, that it was as much at the disposal of the members as when in their own possession ; and the same year the box containing it, which had not been opened, was returned to the regiment, in whose custody (though the Lodge has apparently drawn its last breath) it still remains.

A Lodge was established in the 37th Company of the Royal Engineers in 1863, but the warrant was withdrawn, and the fee returned, by order of the Grand Master of England in 1864.

Of the Lodges formed in Volunteer regiments, two of the most famous are the "Edinburgh Defensive Band," erected in 1782, and the "First Volunteer Lodge of Ireland," which came into existence in the following year. The "Edinburgh Defensive Band" was raised towards the close of the American War of Independence, and about fifty of the members, in anticipation of its being disbanded, formed a Lodge of the same name under the Mastership of the colonel of the regiment, Andrew Crosbie, who figures in the pages of Sir Walter Scott as Plydell, the advocate of Bertram in *Guy Mannering*.

The "First Volunteer Lodge of Ireland" was established in 1783, and Henry Grattan, the famed Orator and Statesman, was balloted for, and elected in 1784. The members wore

H

the regimental uniform for nearly sixty-one years, when it was resolved that "the dress be black trousers and coat, satin faced, and velvet collar, with white vest." The "satin facings" were of the same colour as the uniform.

The Lodges existing at the present time in the Volunteer forces, both at home and abroad, are very numerous, but to the examples already given, I shall only add a third, namely, the "Fitzroy," in the Hon. Artillery Company of London. The exact rank, indeed, of this ancient and distinguished corps, has never been definitely settled. According to its historian, "the members are usually classed with the Volunteers, which, properly speaking, they are not; and it is still an open question whether the officers would rank before or after those of the Militia, or with them according to the dates of their commissions."

A list of the Lodges in garrison towns or fortified places, which are (or were) of a Military, though Stationary character, would carry me too far. It will be sufficient to say that wherever members of the Sea or Land Services were permanently stationed, there Masonry flourished. The names of the "Friendship" and "Inhabitants" Lodges, Gibraltar : "St. John and St. Paul," Malta; and "Pythagoras," Corfu, will be associated with very pleasant memories by those brethren who have served in the Mediterranean. Nor will the recollections of Lodges in other portions of the empire be less fondly cherished by the commissioned, non-commissioned, and warrant officers, who, during their tours of duty, have enjoyed the benefit of Masonic fellowship in the East and West Indies, Australasia, North and South Africa, the Far East, and in the several provinces which are now collectively known as the Dominion of Canada.

A remarkable feature of the Masonry of our own times, has been the extraordinary increase in the number of what are commonly described as "Class Lodges." Graduates of Universities, Lawyers, Medical practitioners, and the members of nearly every other calling or profession, are accustomed, at stated periods,

"To meet upon the Level, and part upon the Square."

Nor will it be supposed that such a prevailing custom is one which has been more honoured by brethren of the two (regular) services "in the breach than the observance." Among the "Class Lodges" in the London district, are the "Navy" and "Household Brigade," of both of which the Prince of Wales (Admiral of the Fleet and Field Marshal) was the first Master : *Nil Sine Labore* (Army Service Corps); "Army and Navy" (chiefly non-commissioned officers and pensioners) ; "Comrades" (Warrant and non-commissioned officers in the Household Cavalry and Brigade of Guards) ; and *Ubique* (Royal Artillery). The "Aldershot Army and Navy" and "Camp" Lodges, are examples of similar associations in the province (and county) of Hampshire.

Some usages of earlier date, however, still remain to be described, and among them the habit of congregating in Lodges, which was practised by prisoners of war in all countries of Europe. The *detenus militaires* in Great Britain and Ireland often visited the regular Lodges. A great many French officers who were interned at Bandon in 1746 and 1747 were admitted members of the "Ancient Boyne Lodge" in that Irish town. Captives of the same nationality experienced fraternal kindness at the hands of their British brethren at Leeds in 1761, at Kelso in 1810, and at Selkirk—where 23 of their number were enrolled as honorary members of the Lodge of St. John—in 1812.

The prisoners of war at Basingstoke, in 1756, "finding themselves a competent number," formed a Lodge, making, at the same time, their due submission to the (older) Grand Lodge of England, and a warrant was placed at their disposal, which, for pecuniary reasons, they were obliged to decline. After this a portion of the captives were removed to Petersfield, where, in 1758, they formed a second Lodge, and again made "due submission" to the Grand Lodge. On this occasion, however, no notice was taken of their proceedings by the latter, but the French brethren, taking silence for approval, "continued working and making Masons until the middle of 1759," when there was a further change of quarters, and some of the prisoners who had been removed from Basingstoke and Petersfield united in forming a third Lodge at Leeds, which still existed in 1761.

In the following year (1762) "a constitution or warrant" was granted by the Grand Lodge of York to similar captives "on their parole" to hold a Lodge at the "Punch Bowl," in that city, "prohibiting them, nevertheless, from making anyone a Brother who shall be a subject of Great Britain or Ireland."

In Scotland also the French prisoners of war held Lodges of their own, one of which, "St. John of Benevolence," was constituted, it would appear, by leave and warrant of the Lodge of Melrose ; while the other must have met, if not by the direct, at least by the tacit, permission of "St. John's," Selkirk, the minutes of which body record that the prisoners there held a Lodge from time to time, the proceedings of which were conducted by themselves in their own language.

A similar Lodge, under the Grand Orient of Marseilles, was established at Malta after its occupation by the British. This subsequently shifted its allegiance and became *Les Amis en Captivité* on the English roll, but its life was a short one, and it disappeared without ever having made any return to the Grand Lodge.

In parting with the subject it may be observed that considerable sums were voted on various occasions by the Grand Lodges of England and Scotland for the relief of French prisoners of war confined in Great Britain who, on inquiry, were ascertained to be deserving Masons, and consequently considered worthy of assistance. It is very greatly to their credit that the recipients of this benevolence, in all cases, faithfully promised, if opportunities should occur, to perform equally kind offices towards their British brethren, prisoners in France.

In bringing the chapter to a close two comparatively recent examples of Masonry in warfare may be recorded. The first, that Colonel William Fordyce and Lieutenant Hirzel Carey, of the 74th Highlanders, killed in action during the Kaffir War, were buried with Masonic honours by the "Albany Lodge," Grahamstown, on the 9th of May, 1852 ; and the last, that the "Lodge of Integrity," which accompanied the 14th Foot to the Crimea, continued to work during the war and in the depth of winter. Many distinguished officers first saw the light of Masonry in this Lodge, amid the booming of guns, and among the number, Lord Eustace Brownlow Cecil, who was initiated in the camp before Sebastopol, on the 24th of May, 1855.

CHAPTER VI.

Parent of Ganges, hear and smile !
Soon from the West's Elysian Isle
A warrior comes, whose mighty voice
Shall bid thy hundred realms rejoice !
Far as Imperial Indus flows,
His hand shall stretch the sacred Rose.

—ANON (see p. 180).

The earliest Stationary Lodges in India, which must all have partaken more or less of a military character, were established at Calcutta in 1730, at Madras in 1752, and at Bombay in 1758. But the records now existing do not permit of our going back with any certainty beyond the year 1774, at which date there were Lodges at the principal seats of civil Government, and also at some of the military stations, or with the army brigades. Shortly afterwards came the war in the Carnatic, and Masonry in India was very nearly swept away by it. In the beginning of 1787, there was a Lodge consisting of non-commissioned officers and privates in the 3rd Brigade, and another of a similar character at Fort William, Calcutta, while what was apparently an "Officers' Lodge," had been recently established in the 4th Brigade. At the close of the same year there were two Lodges "amongst the lower military" at Calcutta, and in 1788 a letter was addressed by the Provincial authorities to the (Regular) Grand Lodge of England, from which I extract the following :—

"With respect to the brigades, they have been divided into six of Infantry and three of Artillery. This regulation has lessened the number of officers in each, and they will be more liable to removals than formerly. The first circumstance will be a great discouragement to the formation of Lodges in the brigades, and the second would sometimes expose such Lodges to the risk of being annihilated."

About the same time, or, to be more precise, in 1784, an equally important "revival" of Masonry had taken place in Madras. It is worthy of recollection that for a short period this Presidency was predominant over all the other English Settlements in India; and during the latter half of the eighteenth century the continuous wars with the French, and afterwards with Hyder Ali and his son, cause the Carnatic to figure largely in Indian history.

Major (afterwards Brigadier-General) Matthew Horne, of the Coast Army, was Provincial Grand Master of Madras (under the Moderns) in 1776, during which year the governor, Lord Pigot, was deposed by the Council. Party spirit seems to have run high, and Major Horne closed the Lodges. Meanwhile "Ancient" or "Atholl" Masonry, so largely practised in the Army, had been introduced into Madras, and a Lodge under that banner was established at Fort St. George. Towards the close of 1784, however, the dissensions among the "Regular" Masons had subsided, and a new Lodge, under the older sanction, "Carnatic Military," was established at Arcot, with the idea of its taking the position on the English roll of No. 355, at Trinchinopoly, the warrant of which, accompanying the Master, Dr. Terence Gahagan, a surgeon of the Coast Army on field service, in 1781, had been captured with his baggage in the action between Colonel Owen and Hyder Ali.

Among the founders of this Lodge, as previously related (p. 103), were Brigadier-General Horne and Captain (afterwards Sir David) Baird. The latter, who entered the army in 1772, had been selected by Lord Macleod (son of the second Grand Master of Scotland), in 1778, to be captain of the Grenadier Company in the Scottish regiment just raised by him, and at first called the 73rd, but afterwards famous as the 71st L.I. The battalion reached India in 1780, and shortly after a small detachment (of all arms), including the Grenadier Company of Lord Macleod's regiment under Captain Baird, was sent to assist Colonel Baillie, who was in danger of being surrounded by the enemy, but the whole force was cut to pieces by Hyder Ali and his son Tippoo Sahib. Baird had been severely wounded and left for dead, but managed to find his way into the French Camp, from which, however, he soon passed with his companions into the power of Hyder Ali, who treated the captives with oriental barbarity. The unfortunate officers lived for three years and eight months in most terrible agony, knowing that many of them were taken from prison only to be poisoned or tortured to death. That there were other Masons besides Baird among the captives might be naturally inferred, but the circumstance is placed beyond doubt by such words as " Prisoner with Tippoo "; which are appended to the names of members in the records of some of the Coast Lodges. The inhuman treatment they experienced at the hands of Tippoo Sahib, who succeeded his father as Sultan of Mysore, in 1782, would seem, indeed, to be quite irreconcilable with the alleged fact, that the son of Hyder Ali was himself a member of our fraternity. The statement has been very positively made, and is said to be supported by documentary evidence which leaves no room for dispute, but as the story itself has a fabulous ring, it will be safest to relegate the supposition of Tippoo being a "brother," into the limbo of fancy, until at least some proof is forthcoming, upon which our judgment can be employed.

The prisoner of Hyder Ali and Tippoo Sahib (who was released in March, 1784), the stormer of Seringapatam, the General of the march across the desert, and the Commander at the capture of the Cape of Good Hope, will always deservedly remain a popular hero. There was a chivalrous gallantry in his nature which made the *jeu d'esprit* " not 'Baird,' but 'Bayard,'" particularly applicable to him.

General Horne had also been a prisoner of war, though his captivity was unattended by any similar hardships, and, indeed, left very pleasing recollections behind it, as he experienced the most fraternal kindness from French Lodges at Bourbon and the Isle of France, which is gracefully referred to at the close of a letter addressed by him to the officers of the Grand Lodge of England, on January 16th, 1785 :—

" Before I conclude, I beg leave to observe. in Justice to a very respectable French Lodge at the Island of Bourbon. That many of our distress'd countrymen who had been made Prisoners and carry'd to that Island. and who proved themselves to be Brothers. receiv'd from them very handsome relief and assistance. and those of us who did not stand in need of any in the Pecuniary Way, Met with great attention ; and every endeavour by the Principal Members to render our Situation on the Island pleasant and agreeable. Some of the Gentlemen knowing I had presided in the Madras Lodge, it was on their first meeting, resolv'd that the Officers of the Lodge should pay me a visit. and give me an invitation, and on my visit they complemented me with a General One and the freedom of the Lodge, which I found conducted with the True principles of Masonry, although some of their rules are different from ours."

The revival of "Regular" Masonry by the formation of "Carnatic Military," in 1784, led to a union, which took place in 1786, between the "Atholl" or "Ancient" Masons under Lieutenant-Colonel Joseph Moorhouse, President of the Provincial Grand Committee ; and the Regular Masons or titular "Moderns," under General Horne, Provincial Grand Master—the immediate result being the opening of a new Lodge, "Perfect Unanimity," the history of which, from 1786 to the present date, is, in effect, a history of Freemasonry on the coast of Coromandel.

Of this Lodge, Major David Baird was a member, and Lieutenant-Colonel Moorhouse the Master, in 1789. In the following year the latter, an officer in the Coast Artillery, being ordered on service, resigned the chair, and was killed at the gallant assault of the Pettah Gate of Bangalore, in March, 1791.

It will be seen that the Freemasons of Madras, in a very happy manner, anticipated the "Union" in England by twenty-eight years. But a great many cases occurred after the healing of the schism, in which the Madras Lodges were erroneously supposed to be at work under an "Atholl" banner. This arose from the fact that the Madras brethren, though in full communion with the "Moderns," nevertheless conducted their ceremonies according to the practice of the "Ancients."

A "moveable" warrant, No. VII.—"Unity and Friendship"—was granted to the 33rd Foot in 1802. There had been an "Atholl" Lodge in this regiment, "No. 90," but the warrant was lost at Helvoitsluys, in 1795, and the brethren of the 33rd, in applying for a Provincial Charter, seem to have been quite under the impression that they were communicating with "Atholl" or "Ancient" Masons.

On their return to England they appear to have reverted to their old allegiance, and resumed work under the No. 90, which had been re-granted and sent to Fort William, Calcutta (though evidently lost *en route*), by the Junior Grand Lodge of England, in 1798.

In 1799, "St. Andrew's Union" was established in the 19th Foot, at Madras, and numbered X. on the Coast. The regiment shortly after was transferred to Ceylon, and the troubles of the Lodge began by the master and nine of the members being massacred by the King of Candia, in 1804.

After this, the regularity of the warrant was impugned, as not being "Ancient," by the "Atholl" Lodge, No 329 in the Royal Artillery, which had been working at Colombo since 1802. At first the two Lodges had fraternized, owing to the similarity of their working, but subsequently they ceased to have any dealings with one another, and deserters from the enemy were eagerly welcomed on either side.

The Lodges in two other regiments, in 1809, while freely admitting that the work was "strictly Antient," nevertheless "declared the warrant to be Modern," and for that reason "would not sojourn" with the brethren of the 19th Foot. These were (Irish) No. 863, in the 89th, and one of the two "Orange" Lodges ("Ancient" and "Irish"), bearing the No. 94, in the 51st regiment.

In the following year (1810), the brethren of No. 863 asked "Carnatic Military" to initiate two candidates for them, and as the ceremony was commencing, a member of No. 863 ordered the brethren instantly to desist, "that they were working with Modern Masons, and that he would upset the Lodge in ten minutes if they proceeded any further." After this, it savours of paradox to record that in June, 1811, a new member of "Carnatic Military, being a Modern Mason, was put over the old ground." Three years later, in the same Lodge, two Captains, described as "modern brothers," were "conducted over the antient ground as far as Master Mason"; and to crown the whole, Lodge No. 863, in 1822, relinquished its Irish warrant, becoming in the first instance "Hibernia and Union," No. XI., on the coast of Coromandel, and in due sequence, No. 633 on the register of the United Grand Lodge of England.

A Military Lodge, "Strength and Beauty," No. VIII., was constituted at Vellore, in 1802, but it came to an untimely end, in 1806, when the warrant was found in the Fort, after the mutiny.

The "travelling" bodies established on the Coast often shared a similar if not quite identical fate; for example, the "Lodge of Philanthropists," in the Scotch Brigade, a regiment which, after being in the Dutch service from 1586 to 1793, was incorporated with the English Army and became the 94th Foot in 1802. From this Lodge—warranted in December, 1801—the following information was received by the Provincial Authorities in March, 1806 :—

"The regiment being so long on field service. Lodge No. XI. has been subjected to various distresses, particularly that of losing two-thirds of its members, amongst whom were some of its best and brightest ornaments."

There is no mention of the Lodge after 1807, and at the union of 1813 it was erased from the roll.

In 1808, a petition for a warrant was sent in "by some Master Masons, privates in His Majesty's Regiment of Royals at Wallahjabad." The application was granted, and the "Lodge of Unity, Peace, and Concord," which still survives, was established in the 2nd Battalion of what was then the 1st or the Royal Regiment, and is now the Royal Scots The petitioners, however, were not all private soldiers, but included a large number of non-commissioned officers ; and in the following year the officers of the battalion sought permission to form a second Lodge in the same corps, to be styled "The Officers' Lodge." The result of this petition has not been recorded, but the examples are numerous, especially in India, of Lodges being formed in regiments, the membership of which was restricted to commissioned officers. The "Lodge of United Friendship," No. V., was formed at Madras in 1812 by officers of the 16th Native Infantry ; "Orion in the West," No. XV., at Poona, by those of the Bombay Artillery in 1823 ; and the "Corinthian Lodge," No. XIV., at Cannanore, by non-commissioned officers of the 7th N.I. in the same year. The "lower military" also figure as the exclusive petitioners for a Charter, as we find that in September, 1818, an application (forwarded by "St. Andrew's Union," No. X., in the 19th Foot) was received from three brethren, " Privates in H.M. 73rd Regiment, praying for a warrant of constitution for the establishment of a regular Lodge in that regiment under the distinctive denomination of St. John's Lodge."

The petition was not granted at once, but merely because the Provincial Grand Master thought Ceylon was beyond his jurisdiction. A reply, therefore, was sent to No. X. (in the 19th Foot) "that the matter was to be laid over for the present."

In Bengal, at the close of the last century, there was an almost general defection from the Provincial Grand Lodge, and consequently from the older or legitimate Grand Lodge of England. Lodges "True Friendship" and " Humility with Fortitude" (composed of non-commissioned officers and privates), were the first who transferred their allegiance to the "Ancients," and the "Marine Lodge" (consisting of persons employed in the marine service of the government) soon followed their example.

On St. John's Day (in Christmas), 1809, these Lodges, accompanied by No. 338 (*Ancients*) in the 14th Foot, and a " Dispensation Lodge" working under a warrant granted by No. 338, walked in procession to St. John's Church, Calcutta, when a Masonic sermon was delivered by the Rev. James Ward. This appears to have stirred up the zeal of the " Moderns." Two of the old Lodges were revived, and these, on St. John's Day (in winter) 1812, accompanied by " Humility with Fortitude" and the "Officers" (formerly the " Dispensation ") Lodge, No. 347 in the 14th Foot, also walked in procession to the same church, and benefited by a like sermon from Dr. Ward.

The spectacle of two Lodges under each of the rival (English) Societies, being thus united in Masonic fellowship, must have afforded, no doubt, a presage of what was about to happen in the following year, with respect to the yet smouldering animosities between the "Moderns" and the " Ancients."

But the time was now at hand when Masonry in Bengal would take root in the land and flourish as it never had done before. This era is inseparably connected with the memory of a great ruler of India, an outline of whose general will precede that of his Masonic career.

THE EARL OF MOIRA.

The subject of this sketch, known successively as Lord Rawdon, Earl Moira, and finally as Marquess of Hastings, was the eldest son of the first Earl of Moira. He was born on the 7th of December, 1754, and received a commission as Ensign in the 15th Foot in 1771. Two years later he became a Lieutenant in the 5th Regiment and embarked for America to take part in the War of Independence.

For his gallantry at Bunker's Hill he was especially complimented by General Burgoyne, who stated in his despatch " Lord Rawdon has this day stamped his fame for life." A month later he was promoted Captain in the 63rd Foot, and shortly afterwards appointed Aide-de-Camp to Sir Henry Clinton.

Having greatly distinguished himself in numerous engagements with the enemy, he was advanced to the rank of Lieutenant-Colonel, and appointed Adjutant-General to the British Forces in America in 1778. For his services in this capacity he was entrusted with a separate command in South Carolina, gaining fresh laurels at the battles of Camden—where he commanded a wing of the Army—and of Hobkirk Hill—where he directed the whole of the operations, and defeated General Greene, one of the ablest of the American Generals.

His health now compelled him to return to England, and the vessel he sailed in was captured by the *Glorieuse* and taken to Brest, but he was soon exchanged, and in 1782 received promotion to the rank of Colonel and became Aide-de-Camp to the King.

When a man has greatly distinguished himself in his youth, and again in his old age, it is not often that his middle life should be a blank. Yet this, in the opinion of his latest biographer, is what happened in the case of Lord Rawdon, who, he tells us, never rose above mediocrity between 1781 and 1812.

The point, indeed, is one upon which some differences of opinion will be found to exist, though not among English

Freemasons; but it will be convenient to give in the first instance the remainder of the personal history of Lord Rawdon as a Soldier, a Statesman, and a Viceroy in the East, after which I shall conclude with a recital of those services which entitle him to rank as one of the brightest characters in the annals of our Fraternity.

On the death of his maternal uncle, the Earl of Huntingdon, in 1789, he succeeded to the estates of that ancient and noble family, and in the same year he acted as second to the Duke of York in his duel with Colonel Lennox, afterwards Duke of Richmond and Provincial Grand Master of Sussex.

By the death of his father, in June, 1793, Lord Rawdon became the second Earl of Moira, and in the following October was promoted Major-General, and entrusted with the command of a force intended to co-operate with the French Royalists in *La Vendee.* The expedition, however, proved a failure, and the troops did not even land.

The next year the Army in Flanders, under the Duke of York, was in difficulties, and the battle of Fleurus made the position of the allies desperate. Lord Moira was at this time encamped near Southampton with 10,000 men. At their head he sailed for Flanders, and succeeded in effecting a junction with the Duke of York, then nearly surrounded by hostile forces much superior in number. This was one of the most extraordinary marches of which military history affords an example. After the Earl had cleared the French armies and was passing the Austrian Corps, under Field-Marshal Clarfayt, the latter greeted him with the words:— " My lord, you have done what was impossible."

The march from Ostend was the last active service in which the Earl was engaged until he went to India. He was promoted Lieutenant-General in 1798, and General in 1803. About the same time he became Commander of the Forces in Scotland. In 1804 he was appointed Colonel of the 27th Foot, and, in 1806, Constable of the Tower.

Of his character as a high military officer, General Sir John Doyle, who knew him well, observed:—

" No man possessed in a higher degree the happy but rare faculty of attaching to him all who came within the sphere of his command. When they saw their general take upon himself the blame of any failure in the execution of his plans (provided it did not arise from want of zeal or courage), and when it succeeded giving the whole credit to those he employed, every man found himself safe : an unlimited confidence infused itself into all ranks, and his army became irresistible. Never was there a man of whom it could be more truly said—

    'Self was the only being seemed forgot.' "

His sagacity as a statesman was not inferior to his intrepidity as a soldier. In the House of Lords he proved himself a clear and able orator, and a judicious man of business. His benevolent and persevering exertions in 1801, resulting in a law being passed to relieve the distresses of persons imprisoned for small debts, will remain a monument of philanthropy upon our Parliamentary records.

Lord Moira married, in 1804, Flora, Countess of Loudoun in her own right, by whom he had six children. He was created a Privy Councillor and appointed Master of the Ordnance in 1806. His mother died in 1808, and upon that event he succeeded to the ancient baronies of Hastings, Hungerford, &c., which were vested in the Hastings' family.

In 1812, on the failure of Lord Wellesley to form an administration, he was sent for and empowered to proceed with the delicate task of establishing a Coalition Government of which he would have been the head. At first it seemed as if success was likely to crown his efforts, but the arrangements ultimately fell through. Lord Liverpool was appointed Prime Minister, and the crisis ended.

Soon afterwards he was created a K.G., and on the resignation of the Earl of Minto, was appointed Governor-General and Commander-in-Chief in India. He sailed from Portsmouth on the 14th of April, and landed at Calcutta on the 4th of October, 1813.

"On his acceding to the Government of India," to use his own words, "there were made over to him no less than six hostile discussions with native powers, each capable of entailing a resort to arms, and the independent Princes of India were so numerous and strong as to conceive themselves equal to expel the British." But at the termination of Lord Moira's rule—during which period he brought two wars of the greatest magnitude to a successful issue—every native state in that vast region was in either acknowledged or essential subjugation to our Government. James Mill, the historian of British India, remarks :—

" The administration of the Marquess of Hastings may be regarded as the completion of the great scheme of which Clive laid the foundation, and Warren Hastings and the Marquess of Wellesley had reared the superstructure. The crowning pinnacle was the work of Lord Hastings, and by him was the supremacy of the British Empire in India finally established."

The subject of this memoir, who for his public services had been created Marquess of Hastings, Earl of Rawdon, and Viscount Loudoun, in 1817, returned to England in 1823, where, however, in spite of increasing age and infirmities, he found himself unable to enjoy that repose to which his long and brilliant career in the service of his country had justly entitled him.

It was said of him that his ample fortune absolutely sank under the benevolence of his nature, and his liberality was declared by a judge from the bench, "absolutely to exceed all bounds." While he commanded at Southampton (1793-4), his private expenditure exceeded £30,000, yet such was his delicacy, that he would not accept either pay, emolument, or patronage, while the troops in his camp were kept in that state of indecision which did not promise real service, and this rule was strictly carried out during the whole time that his commission was in force.

It has been suggested by Major Ross, of Bladensburg (in the *Rulers of India* series), that his extraordinary attachment to the Prince of Wales greatly contributed to the ruin of his affairs. " Moira and I," the Prince would sometimes say, " are like two brothers, when one wants money he puts his hand in the other's pocket "; and to help his illustrious friend, he sold his estates in Ireland and much valuable property in England. Also, according to the same biographer, on the exile of the Bourbon princes during the French Revolution, he placed Donnington Park at their disposal. There they remained for several years, and to fully supply their wants, he left in each bedroom a signed cheque book, which the occupant could fill up at pleasure, without having to undergo the humiliation of asking for pecuniary assistance. It is satisfactory to state that the Royal objects of his bounty availed themselves but sparingly of this generosity. His expenditure in India was conducted on a very lavish scale, and when he returned to England, he declared himself to be, after nine years' unceasing toil in the East, a poorer man than when he went out. He was obliged, therefore, to seek further employment, and in 1824 became Governor of Malta. Two years later, his health gave way, and he sustained a serious injury through a fall from his horse. A cruise in the Mediterranean was prescribed for him, but he never rallied, and died on board H.M.S. *Revenge*, in Baia Bay, near Naples, November 28th, 1826. His body was brought to Malta and buried on the ramparts.

> " What hallows ground where heroes sleep ?
> 'Tis not the sculptured piles you heap ! "

He left a letter, in which, among other requests, he desired that his right hand might be cut off, and buried (at her death) with his wife. The wish was complied with, and it now rests clasped with her's in the family vault at the old Kirk of Loudoun

When, or where, the eminent man whose Masonic career it will become my next task to unfold, was received into the Society, cannot be positively affirmed. It has always been supposed that he was initiated in an Army Lodge, and if so his admission probably took place either in No. 86, attached to the 5th Foot, in which he served as a subaltern from 1773 to 1775 ; or in No. 512, in the 63rd regiment, to which he was transferred as captain after the sanguinary engagement at Bunker's Hill. These were both Irish Lodges, but it is with the annals of English Masonry in which for many eventful years the EARL OF MOIRA (as he will always be best known by students of the Craft), forms the central figure, that we are chiefly concerned, and to these I now pass.

At the annual Feast of the Society in 1790, Lord Rawdon was appointed Acting Grand Master, and retained that position under the Prince of Wales, who, on the death of his uncle, the Duke of Cumberland, was elected Grand Master, and installed in 1792.

At this time the French Revolution had given rise to many unhappy dissensions in Great Britain, and to check them, addresses to the Throne were presented by most of the corporate bodies in the kingdom and all the true friends of the Constitution. It was deemed proper that the Society of Masons, by adding their mite to the number, should evince that attachment to the King and Constitution which the laws of the institution enjoined. Accordingly, on the 6th of February, 1793, the Grand Lodge unanimously resolved that an address which had been drawn up by Lord Moira should be presented to His Majesty.

The following passages from this powerful exposition of Masonic principles will be read with interest at the present time, when the eldest son of the Sovereign once more presides over the destinies of the Freemasons of England :—

"It may be thought, perhaps, that being what we are, a private society of men connected by invisible ties—professing secrecy—mysterious in our meetings—stamped by no act of prerogative—and acknowledged by no law, we assume a part and hold a language upon this occasion to which we can urge no legal or a lmitted right. We are the Free Citizens of a Free State, and number many thousands of our body. *The Heir Apparent of the Empire is our Chief. We fraternize for the purposes of social intercourse, of mutual assistance, of charity to the distressed, and good-will to all ; and fidelity to a trust, reverence to the magistrate, and obedience to the laws, are sculptured in capitals upon the pediment of our Institution.*"

A grand feast was held at Freemasons' Hall on the 13th of May, 1795, the Grand Master in the chair. The Prince of Wales was accompanied by the Duke of Clarence, and Prince William (afterwards Duke) of Gloucester, who had been initiated in the Britannic Lodge by the Acting Grand Master on the preceding evening. As a final toast the Grand Master gave "the Earl of Moira," whom he styled "the man of my heart and the friend I admire," and sincerely hoped that the Acting Grand Master might long live to superintend the government of the Craft, and to extend the principles of the Art.

The Prince of Wales again presided at the grand festival of the Society in 1796, and was supported by Prince Ernest Augustus, afterwards Duke of Cumberland, and still later King of Hanover, whose initiation, he informed the brethren, had taken place the same day, at a special Lodge held for that purpose, in the house of the Earl of Moira.

Two works were published in 1797, which, though now seldom read, produced an immense sensation at the time.

I

They were written by the Abbé Barruel and Professor Robison, in the same year and without mutual consultation. It was the object of both to prove that a secret association had been formed and carried on for rooting out all the religious establishments and overturning all the existing governments of Europe; and that this association had employed as its chief instruments the Lodges of Freemasons.

These works were not without influence in inspiring a portion of the legislation in 1799, when an Act of Parliament was passed " for the more effectual suppression of societies established for seditious and treasonable purposes, and for preventing treasonable and seditious practices."

By this Statute—39, George III., c. 79—it was enacted that all societies, the members whereof are required to take any oath not authorised by law, should be deemed unlawful combinations.

Ultimately, however, societies held under the denomination of Lodges of Freemasons, were, under certain conditions, exempted from the operation of the Act. This was mainly due to the tact and address of the Earl of Moira, by whose efforts English Freemasonry was saved from extinction, or at the very least from temporary obliteration.

On the 15th of May, 1800, the King was fired at from the pit of Drury Lane Theatre, and at a Special Grand Lodge held in June, the Acting Grand Master stated that it had been convened for the purpose of considering a suitable address to be presented to his majesty.

In the course of his speech, and evidently referring to the works of Barruel and Robison, he " took occasion to allude to certain modern publications holding forth the Society of Masons as a league against constituted authorities "; and while admitting " that in countries where impolitic prohibitions restrict the communication of sentiment, the activity of the human mind might, among other means of baffling the control, have resorted to the artifice of borrowing the denomination of Freemasons to cover meetings for seditious purposes," he boldly affirmed, " not only that such a subterfuge had no sort of connection with the tenets of Masonry, but was diametrically opposite to the junction regarded as the foundation of the Lodge, namely—FEAR GOD, AND HONOUR THE KING."

In 1805, the Earl of Moira, who then combined the functions of Acting Grand Master of English Freemasons with those of Commander of the Forces in Scotland, became the happy medium through which his own and the Grand Lodge of the Northern Kingdom were brought into fraternal union. In the same year, November 27, and through the same channel, a correspondence in terms of amity, and brotherly communication was arranged with the Grand Lodge of Prussia. At this meeting of the Grand Lodge, the brethren, to mark their sense of the services rendered to Masonry by the acting Grand Master, "agreed that the fraternity should dine together on December 7th, it being the birthday of Earl Moira." The practice continued to be observed by a large number of the Metropolitan Lodges until his lordship's departure for India, and a survival of it still exists in the Moira Lodge, No. 92, which holds its annual festival on December 7, when the toast of the evening is, " The memory of Earl Moira, the patron of the Lodge."

A friendly alliance with the Grand Lodge of Ireland, similar to that established with the Grand Lodge of Scotland, was effected through the same instrumentality, in 1808. The previous Masonic intercourse of both these Grand Lodges had been confined to the Schismatic Grand Lodge of " Ancient Masons," seceders from the Grand Lodge of England about the middle of the last century.

The Earl of Moira, who was acting (or virtual) Grand Master of Scotland in 1806 and 1807, twice discharged the ceremonial duties incidental to that office in 1809. On October 25th, he laid the foundation stone of George the Third's Bastion at Leith, and on November 21st, the " Freemason's Hall " of Scotland was consecrated by him, and in the most solemn manner dedicated to Masonry. On each of these occasions the Earl delivered one of those eloquent addresses for which he was so justly famed.

Towards the close of the year 1812, Lord Moira having been appointed Governor-General of India, it was considered by the Fraternity as only due to his exalted merit to entertain him at a farewell banquet, and to present him with a valuable Masonic jewel, as a memorial of their regard.

I 2

On the day appointed—January 27th, 1813—the Duke
of Sussex, as Deputy Grand Master (in which office he had
succeeded Sir Peter Parker, Admiral of the Fleet, who died
in December, 1811), took the chair, and was supported by
above five hundred brethren, the company including six
royal dukes.

In happy terms the Chairman characterised the services
of the Earl during the one and twenty years he had
presided over the interests of the fraternity, as having shed
splendour upon the Craft, and saved the society from total
destruction ; while in terms still happier, the guest of the
evening acknowledged the compliment :—

" The prominent station which I hold here," replied Lord
Moira, " concentrates all the rays of the Craft upon my person, as
it would upon the person of any other placed in the same
elevation : and the illustrious Deputy Grand Master makes an
effort to persuade himself that the lunar brilliancy is the genuine
irradiation of the sun. My real relation to you may be best
explained by an Asiatic apologue. In the baths of the East.
perfumed clay is used instead of soap. A poet is introduced,
who breaks out into an enthusiastic flow of admiration at the
odour of a lump of clay of this sort. ' Alas ! ' answers the clay,
' I am only a piece of ordinary earth, but I happened to come in
contact with the rose, and I have borrowed some of its fragrance.'
I have borrowed the character of the virtues inherent in this
Institution : and my best hope is, that however minute be the
portion with which I have been thus imbued, at least. I am not
likely to lose what has been so fortuitously acquired. Gratitude
holds a high rank among those virtues : and. if I can be confident
of anything, it must be of this. that earnest gratitude towards
you cannot depart from my breast, but with the last pulse of
life."

THE MASON'S WIDOW.

Lord Moira was on the eve of starting for the seat of
Government in India. Thousands of miles were soon to
interpose between him and the home of his ancestors. Was
he ever to return to its shades a free, unembarassed,
independent man ?

In his splendid library at Donnington Park he was
busily engaged in sorting papers, destroying letters, and
signing certain lengthy parchments, prior to a long absence
from England. While so employed a servant entered and
said that a woman wished to see him.

" Her business ? "

" Military business, my lord, so she says."

" I cannot see her, be her errand what it may."

" I told her so, my lord, but she will take no denial."

" The shortest way to end this matter," said Lord Moira kindly, " will be for me to see her at once. Let her enter."

" What may you want from me ? " said the Earl, coldly, on her admittance to the library.

She explained that her second son, who supported the entire family, had been drawn for a soldier, and she wanted Lord Moira to get him off.

" I cannot help you," was the Earl's rejoinder ; " if your son has been regularly balloted for and drawn in the Militia, he must serve."

" Serve ! " exclaimed the poor woman bitterly and vehemently, as if her grief was getting the better of both reason and prudence. " Yes, that's the word—'serve.' My three brothers did so, and fell on the field of battle. My father did so, and his bones lie in the sands of Egypt. My husband did so, and fell in action at Corunna."

" A soldier's widow," said his lordship, musingly. " What was your husband's name ? "

" Isaac Wardroper."

" Did he ever serve in the 63rd ? "

" He did, and volunteered out of it for foreign service."

" The 63rd ! I should know something about that regiment," returned the Earl quickly. " I had a company in it." Then in more measured tones—" I think I recollect your husband, what was his rank ? "

" Pay-Corporal," was the reply.

" Right," said his lordship. " I remember him, a steady, well-conducted man." Then turning to the lawyer by his side, he asked in a low tone, " What would a substitute cost ? "

The legal gentleman made no reply, but his look at the parchments lying before them seemed to say, " How can you, with such a heavy mortgage as the one you are about to execute, think, even for a passing instant, of incurring the cost of a substitute ? "

Lord Moira coloured and turned away. " I cannot interfere," he said at last, "the law is peremptory and must be obeyed."

The tone of the Earl's voice, or the energy of despair may have suggested the movement, but again advancing, the woman said faintly,—"About a week before he went into action for the fifth time, my poor fellow gave these into my hands, and told me, that should he fall, and 1 be ever able to reach England, they might, perhaps, be useful to me."

She handed to his lordship, as she spoke, a certificate, drawn up on vellum, together with certain insignia, and waited in bent and hopeless attitude the result.

He to whom Masonry was so dear, whose devotion to its interests never varied, who held so high a place in the Craft, and in the affections of the Brethren, extended his hand, and examined narrowly and deliberately the various insignia; the vellum, its tenor, its signatures. The scrutiny, it would seem, left no suspicions behind it, for the Earl, with a smile, said firmly and cheeringly,—

"Your husband, it appears, was a Mason. Of that I am satisfied. He belonged, unquestionably, to a Military Lodge. There are such in the army, not many, nor perhaps much countenanced by the authorities; but they do exist. For you it is well. Go, and with a light heart. So good a son had best remain where he is. He will not be torn from you. I require no thanks. I can listen to nothing further; go, and have no fears about the future."

A substitute for Stephen Wardroper was procured—who provided him? who sought him? who paid for him? and who, before the week's end, sent a £10 note by post to the Mason's widow? The poor woman accurately conjectured, and so without a doubt will the reader.

On Lord Moira's passage to India, the vessel in which he had embarked, calling at the Mauritius, at the head of the Masons of that island, he laid the foundation stone of the Roman Catholic Cathedral of Port Louis.

The Earl, who was not only Governor-General and Commander-in-Chief, but also Acting-Grand Master of India, arrived in Calcutta on October 4th, 1813. His first Masonic act was to constitute a new Lodge, which was named after him—The "Moira Lodge, Freedom and Fidelity," to which he granted a warrant of constitution on November 8th in the same year.

The first Master was Major-General Sir William Keir Grant ; the Wardens, Colonel C. J. Doyle and Commodore John Hayes ; and one of the Founders (or earliest members) Major-General Sir Rollo Gillespie.

The Acting Grand Master, who was presented—December 11th, 1813—with an address of congratulation on his safe arrival in India, made a most eloquent speech to the brethren of Calcutta in reply, declaring "the diffusion of a spirit of benevolence and charity to be the object of their labours, and that the true work of Masons was the adoration of the Most High."

An address to the Countess of Moira was presented on the same occasion. This lady—the grand-daughter of John, 4th Earl of Loudoun, Grand Master of England, 1736—was also Countess of Loudoun in her own right, and succeeded to the family honours in 1786. The brethren expressed to her ladyship that they were unable to deny themselves the gratification of blending with their congratulations to Lord Moira the same cordial welcome to herself, and claiming her hereditary influence over their Fraternity with sentiments of equal veneration.

Under the benignant sway of the Earl of Moira, as Grand Master in India, which lasted for the period of nine years, the Lodges multiplied, and in those glorious days persons of all classes were eager to become members of the Society. The wisdom of the appointment was exemplified in its immediate effects. The influence of his lordship's great name, exalted rank, high acquirements, extensive benevolence, and Masonic eminence was seen in the new zeal it infused into the Fraternity. The constant appearance of the Governor-General and Commander-in-Chief among the Brethren in India, gave additional vigour to the spirit so inspired, and, working under the eye of a Grand Master so distinguished for every Masonic virtue, the ardour of that spirit continued unabated until the close of his administration, to the honour of the Craft, the increase of its numbers, and the extension of its charities.

On its being notified that the Governor-General was about to lay down his high office and return to England, the Marquess of Hastings—to use the title which had been conferred upon him in 1817—was presented with a farewell address, offering their united sentiments of regard and esteem for his person and virtues, by the Freemasons.

The Provincial Grand Lodge of Bengal and eight private Lodges took part in the demonstration, assembling on December 20th, 1822, at the Town Hall, Calcutta, and having been joined by several brethren of distinction, walking in procession to the Government House to the number of about three hundred. In most of the Lodges the military element must have predominated, but in three of them the membership was restricted to brethren of the sea and land services. These were "Courage with Humanity" (now No. 392), in the Regiment of Artillery at Dum-Dum, so called because "*Courage* was ever the leading feature in the Bengal Artillery, and *Humanity* the grand characteristic of the British soldier"; "Marine" (now No. 232), at that time composed, as its name would imply, of persons employed in the Marine service of the Government; and No. 921, under the Irish Constitution, attached to the 17th Foot.

The presence of military Lodges, as well as military brethren, lent a particular interest to the presentation of the address, and probably nothing has ever surpassed in pathos or dignity the leave-taking of the Governor-General and Commander-in-Chief as Grand Master of English Freemasons in the East. He did so in the following words :—

" Brethren.—The compliment which you have offered to me is peculiarly affecting and grateful to my feelings. It ought to be so. As you have yourselves observed, each of you has already affixed his name to the general Address with which I was honoured some days ago. There is, of course, a motive for your wishing to come forward again, and as I cannot but understand it, the quality of that motive is most flattering to me : you have desired to bear a more precise and emphatic testimony to my conduct. That observation which Masons reciprocally exercise over each other, not as a privilege, but as a duty, binds the Craft to be strict in a public profession of opinion, so that where it can commend, the commendation stands vouched by the known caution. Your approbation of me may be mistaken—may be undeservedly partial—may be exaggerated in phrase, but it must be sincere, and as such I take it to my heart.

" You have thanked me for the encouragement I have given here to Masonry, and for the vigilance I have exerted for its preserving an accurate course. That fostering care was incumbent on me, for the superintendence which I have held. But I have not considered the fulfilment of such an obligation as a dry duty.

" I have felt a lively interest in the promotion of what I believe to be highly beneficial to society. The veil thrown over Masonry renders its operation silent and unobserved ; yet the influence of a body, spread through all classes of society, pervading every circle and diffusing (though by its separate members) opinions digested and matured, from remote periods, in the Brotherhood, must be powerful in its effect. I think the traces of its useful sway are discoverable if we cast our eyes on olden times. Reflect on that semi-barbarism which was the condition of all the States of Europe in ages not long past. What apparent cause was there for a sudden and rapidly progressive mitigation, of the rude oppressions which characterised the day ? If none such can confidently be pointed out, is it not reasonable to recur to an agency which, while it is unobtrusive, must in its very nature be active ?

" The secrecy observed in Masonic proceedings, and the rigid scrutiny exercised into the private character of candidates for admission, excited the curiosity of the higher ranks, and at the same time removed every fear of their discrediting themselves by becoming members of the Fraternity. Once initiated they received lessons which never could have reached them in any other situation. They were taught that, throughout the necessary gradations in a community, and amid the unavoidable distinctions arising from talents or property, man was still the brother of man. This primary position once adopted, all corollaries from it were readily embraced. The doctrine imbibed in the Lodge became the rule of action for the man of might in his public sphere, and his example disseminated the principles of humanity and justice to the utmost extent of the circle. Surely this is not a visionary supposition. Observe the difference of character between the nations of Europe where Masonry has flourished and those in which it has been proscribed, and let the contrast, so favourable for the former, support my hypothesis. The proof will be still stronger if you advert to the despotism, the ferocity, the degradation of manhood in the Asiatic regions, where no casual ray of Masonry has ever pierced the gloom. In Europe, what were once Masonic principles alone, are so generally prevalent, that it would now be difficult to make it believed that they were once acknowledged only in a confined society. Yet it is well that the sanctuary for them should still exist. Our forms are only constant inculcations to us of the moral Rules which ought to be observed in all times, cases, and situations. If I may have been fortunate enough to have recollected them in the exercise of authority, as you would kindly persuade me, I am most happy.

"Now, in the truest spirit of fraternal affection. I bid you
FAREWELL, with this parting injunction—CONTINUE TO FEAR
GOD, TO HONOUR THE KING, AND TO KEEP PURE THE CRAFT."

The Marquess of Hastings left India, where he restored
Freemasonry and became the shepherd of the faithful, amid
the regrets of his fold. The parting scene, which has been
well depicted by Dr. Burnes, in his oration "On the
duties of the Masonic Soldier," will be found in the present
volume, and there is nothing in the annals of Indian Masonry
that possesses an equal interest for such military readers as
happen also to be members of the Fraternity.

If wisdom in council, eloquence in debate, valour in arms,
undeviating patriotism, and universal benevolence, are
deserving of record in the pages of history, and in the annals
of Freemasonry—then, in the character of the Earl of Moira
(first Marquess of Hastings), who was equally renowned as a
soldier, a statesman, and a great ruler in the Craft, we find a
happy combination of Masonic and patriotic excellence,
which no lapse of time ought to efface from our memory, as
it can never be surpassed.

The warrant of the "Moira Lodge, Freedom and Fidelity,"
which was the only instrument of its class, granted by the
Acting Grand Master of India (as shortly after he re-
established the Provincial Grand Lodge of Bengal), was
surrendered in 1823. A short notice of the first Master, Sir
William Keir Grant, has been already given (p. 109). The
Senior Warden, Colonel (afterwards General Sir Charles
William) Doyle, served in the Netherlands and Egypt, under
Abercrombie, and commanded a force of Light Infantry,
known as "Doyle's Triadores," in the Peninsula, with such
conspicuous success, that he was made a Spanish Lieutenant-
General. The Junior Warden, Commodore (afterwards
Sir John) Hayes, entered the Indian Navy, of which he
was one of the brightest ornaments, in 1781. He commanded a squadron of nine vessels at the capture of Java,
and the armed flotilla on the coast of Arracan (as a flag
officer) during the Burmese War of 1825.

The remaining member of the "Moira Lodge" whose
name has come down to us, was Sir Robert Rollo Gillespie,
of whom a brief memoir will next be presented.

From time immemorial the Craft has recruited from the ranks of the British Army, brethren who have been distinguished for their devotion to Freemasonry and its principles, no less than for their gallantry in the field of arms. Of this a brilliant example is afforded by the career of General Gillespie, who was born at Comber, in the County of Down, and became a Cornet in the 6th Dragoon Guards, and also a Freemason, in 1783. A few years later he was transferred to the 20th (Jamaica) Light Dragoons, with which regiment he saw much service in the West Indies, particularly at the capture of Tiburon in 1794, and afterwards at Port-au-Prince, where his life was threatened, and he was on the point of being put to death by order of the French Governor, General Santhonax, under the following circumstances.

He was selected by the British Commander-in-Chief as the bearer of a despatch with a summons to surrender the island, and having been sent under a flag of truce, so great was his anxiety to reach the shore from the English squadron, that the boat became stranded and overturned, with the result that both flag and papers were lost in the sea. Whereupon Gillespie swam ashore with his sword in his mouth, and though repeatedly fired at succeeded in affecting a landing without receiving any hurt. On being brought a prisoner before the Governor he was charged with being a spy, and sentenced to be hanged. Gillespie, however, espied on the buttons of the Governor (or one of his officers) a certain device, and at once resorted to the language of Freemasonry. The signal was acknowledged, he was immediately released, sumptuously entertained, and sent back to the squadron and his companions in arms, under a guard of honour, by order of General Santhonax.

In 1796, as a Major, he accompanied General Wilford to St. Domingo, when he was appointed Adjutant-General and much feared by the republicans. A gang of eight desperadoes broke into his quarters, murdered his slave-boy, and attacked Gillespie, who, however, defended himself with his sword, and killed six of his assailants, when the two others, after firing at and wounding him, fled. On his return to England, he attended a *levee*, and George III. noticing his diminutive stature,—" Eh, eh, what, what," said the King, "is this the little man that killed the brigands?"

After the Peace of Amiens, he exchanged, as Lieutenant-Colonel, into the 19th Light Dragoons, and proceeding overland to India, was appointed Commandant of Arcot, where his regiment was stationed. But he had not been there many days when, riding before breakfast on July 10th, 1806, he was met by an officer who reported a mutiny at Vellore. This was fourteen miles distant, and the retreat of the captive princes of Tippoo's family.

Starting at once with a squadron of the 19th, and some native cavalry, and directing the rest of the Dragoons with their "galloper" guns to follow, Gillespie hurried to Vellore to find that the Sepoy troops had massacred the Europeans, with the exception of a few survivors belonging to the 69th Foot, who had spent their ammunition and were making their last stand. With the aid of a rope, Gillespie had himself hoisted into the fort, where he encouraged the 69th until the arrival of the guns from Arcot, when the gates were blown open, and the Dragoons entering cut down over 800 of the mutineers. The Military Lodge at Vellore, as previously narrated, perished in this revolt.

In 1811, Gillespie, as Brigadier-General, accompanied the expedition against Java, and on the reduction of the Island was left in command of the troops. The next year finding that a confederacy of the Javanese Chiefs had taken up a position in a powerfully stockaded fort, defended by 100 guns, and 30,000 men, he promptly attacked and carried it with 1,500 troops, thereby, in all probability, saving the lives of all the Europeans on the island.

Returning as a Major-General, to India in 1813, after participating for a brief period in Masonic fellowship with his brethren of the "Moira Lodge," he was appointed, in 1814, to the command of one of the four columns which took part in the invasion of Nepaul. The progress of the column was arrested by one hill fort, Kalanga, garrisoned by a mere handful of the enemy. Two assaults were beaten back, and the British General and 500 of his men were killed.

The gratitude of a nation has reared in St. Paul's Cathedral a monument to perpetuate the memory of Sir Rollo Gillespie, and in the town of Comber, where he was born, his Masonic brethren have erected a column in loving remembrance of the hero whose last words were—" One shot more for the honour of Down." Thirty-five Lodges were present at the unveiling of the " Gillespie Monument " on the 24th of June (St. John's Day), 1844, and the members of the Society who assembled on that interesting occasion, are said to have formed the largest meeting of Freemasons ever witnessed in Ireland.

For a short time after the departure of Lord Hastings Masonry continued to flourish in Bengal, and ten (or more) Lodges of a military, though stationary, character are known to have existed in that Presidency (or jurisdiction) in 1827. Three, " Sincerity " (Cawnpore), " Hastings " (Allahabad), and " Northern Star " (Barrackpore), were in each case composed of officers in the cantonment and neighbourhood. The members of the others, one of which, " Independence with Philanthropy," was formed out of the lower ranks by the " Hastings " Lodge, Allahabad, were non-commissioned officers and men.

But the close of the same year ushered in the annihilation of all order and constituted authority for a time. The Provincial Grand Lodge sank into a profound slumber, and the military brethren of "Independence with Philanthropy" hoisted the standard of revolt by returning their warrant, intimating that future meetings would be held under a dispensation obtained from Lodge " Union " in the 14th Foot until a charter could be obtained from England, for which application had been made direct. The latter—formerly No. 338, " Ancients "—was carried over at the fusion of the two societies as No. 432, but, together with its earlier offspring under a previous dispensation, the " Officers' Lodge " in the same regiment, had ceased to exist in 1832. The petition of the former was successful and a civil warrant was granted, under which it still exists as the Lodge of " Independence with Philanthropy " at Allahabad.

Yet in general the letters of the Lodges remained unanswered and their requests unheeded, a state of affairs which continued until the year 1840—the commencement of a new era in the Masonic History of Bengal.

There are many obstacles to the success of Masonry in India, and perhaps the chief one is the peculiar nature of the society there, and its liability to perpetual fluctuation. Most of the Lodges are composed chiefly and some exclusively of military members, all of whom are liable to be removed from particular stations at a moment's notice.

Whether, therefore, an Indian Lodge, except in the principal seats of Government, will continue to prosper or fall into at least a temporary decay, is even in our own times dependent on the chance of any given number of those who form the last relief being members of the Fraternity. But in more remote days, when there were no railroads, and the European population of India was merely a fraction of what it now is, any sudden removal of Masons from a station, which was not counter-balanced by an accession of new brethren, almost invariably resulted in the extinction of a Lodge.

To these observations the Lodges in regiments were, of course, an exception, since wherever the regiments moved the Lodges and their members accompanied them. Still, it must be recollected that in practice, regimental Lodges were confined to the Queen's troops, excepting only the (Bengal and Bombay) Artillery. In regiments of Native Infantry (though the experiment has been tried in Madras) the number of officers is too scanty to allow the possibility of Lodges being permanently established in them.

It is, indeed, to these regimental Lodges that I must, as far as possible, restrict my remarks, but cases were of frequent occurrence in which their assistance was invoked by military brethren under circumstances of the following character.

As already stated, the Stationary Lodges were always in great peril, owing to the possible removal of the whole (or a large portion) of their members on military duty ; and to this must now be added that it was by no means unusual for the members, whose involuntary defection so often brought about a catastrophe at the station from which they were removed, to find themselves at a new one, where there was no Lodge. In this difficulty it was the custom for such brethren to apply to a regular Lodge for a dispensation, and to work under the protection of that body, until a warrant was received from home.

Some Masons at Delhi applied in 1834 to their brethren at Meerut for a constitution of this kind, which might serve their purpose until the receipt of a warrant from the Grand Lodge of England. At the latter station there were two Lodges, one of which, however, was itself working under dispensation, and could not therefore dispense grace to another. The other belonged to the 26th Foot, No. 26, under the Grand Lodge of *Ireland*. This Lodge declined giving a dispensation, for the somewhat Irish reason that the "Cameronian Lodge" had already granted one to another Lodge *of the propriety of which act they had great doubt*; and that until an answer had been received from Ireland, they could not commit a second act of doubtful legality.

The custom was, indeed, a very old one, and to the examples already given of its prevalence in numerous jurisdictions, it will be sufficient to add that in 1782, Lodges in the Nova Scotia Volunteers, Royal Artillery, and 82nd Foot were at work in Halifax (N.S.), "under dispensation from the warranted Lodges Nos. 155 and 211"—now Nos. 1 and 2 on the roll of the Grand Lodge of Nova Scotia. Also, that a Lodge, "No. 213 Junior," was held in the Royal Artillery, under a dispensation from the parent body at the same ("Atholl") number—now the "Albion," Quebec—at St. John's, Newfoundland, in 1785

The practice, which attained a great vogue, necessarily fell into disuse with the more general existence of Provincial Grand Lodges, and no survival of the usage after 1840 has been recorded. In that year there was a second revival of Masonry in Bengal. After the departure of the Marquess of Hastings, it had gone out of fashion, and the circumstances under which military brethren of all ranks in the leading Presidency again rallied round the Masonic Standard will be presently related.

In 1813, the 17th Dragoons was stationed at Kaira, in Goojerat, and a Lodge (*English*), No. 361, was attached to the regiment, which for many years continued to be the only one in the Presidency of Bombay. Of the thirty-four

members, sixteen were Knights Templar, and seventeen
Royal Arch Masons. Twenty-nine were non-commissioned
officers, and the remainder private dragoons. The degrees
worked, in addition to the "three regular steps," were those
of Past Master (in the Lodge); Royal Arch, Super-excellent,
Mark and Link (in the Chapter); and Knight Templar, St.
John of Jerusalem, and Knight of Malta (in the Encampment).

Six commissioned officers (of other regiments) and one
civilian were admitted to the membership of the Lodge in
1821, and in the same year a petition from the seven for a
Grand Lodge warrant was forwarded and recommended by
No. 361. A remarkable entry in the minutes occurs under
the date of August 22nd, 1821 :—-

"Proposed and agreed to that the half-monthly meeting be
entirely for the Br. Officers (Military) of Lodge No. 361. but
that all fees and dues for Initiation. &c.. exclusively to the
General Lodge fund. and that such Br. Officers as may have
already been admitted into our most Honble. Society. may
attend the regular monthly meeting if they desire it. and on the
half-monthly night calling such assistance from the old members
as they may require."

From that time, until the regiment left India (1823), there
were virtually two Lodges attached to it, one consisting of
commissioned officers and members of the Civil Service, the
other of non-commissioned officers and private dragoons.

In December, 1821, "the Brethren, Commissioned Officers,
and Lodge Officers" met, and it was arranged that the
former should fill the various offices on the occasion of the
Festival of St. John.

The "Benevolent Lodge," No. 746, was duly established
(on the recommendation of No. 361) in 1822, and all the
military petitioners for it were founders of another Lodge,
"Orion in the West," "installed" in the Bombay Horse
Artillery, at Poona, in 1823. In the latter none but
Initiates of the Lodge, or officers of the regiment, could
become members, and non-commissioned officers were only
admitted as serving brethren. In 1832, a subaltern of the
corps, being "the only uninitiated officer of the mess," was
admitted, "though under age," by dispensation.

The "Benevolent Lodge," held in the first instance at

Poona, was, a few years afterwards, removed to Bombay, at which capital there were thirteen non-commissioned officers who were too poor to establish a Lodge of their own, and too modest to seek admittance into what was considered an aristocratic Lodge. They met, however, monthly in the guard-room over the Apollo Gate, for mutual instruction in Masonry. This coming to the knowledge of the " Benevolent Lodge," the thirteen were elected honorary members of No. 746, for which they returned heartfelt thanks. At their first attendance, when the Lodge work was over and the brethren adjourned to the banquet, the thirteen were informed that refreshments awaited them *downstairs*. Revolting at the distinction thus made among Masons, they one and all left the place. The next morning they were sent for by their commanding officer, who was also one of the officers of the Lodge, and asked to explain their conduct. One of the party, William Willis—by whom this anecdote was related to me at Poona in 1859—told him that as Masons they were bound to meet on the Level and part on the Square; but as this fundamental principle was not practised in No. 746, of which they had been elected honorary members, they could not partake of their hospitality. The astonished Colonel uttered not a word, but waved his hand for them to retire. Ever after this the " Benevolent Lodge"—including the thirteen—met on the Level, both in Lodge and at the banquet table.

During the brief existence of this Lodge some very illustrious names were inscribed on its roll (p. 105), and among them that of a famous Initiate, a short account of whose career, combined with a memoir of his elder brother, upon whom the mantle of the Marquess of Hastings would seem to have fallen as a Ruler of the Craft, will be next laid before the reader.

James and Alexander Burnes arrived in India and were taken on the strength of the Bombay army, the former as a medical officer and the latter as a cadet, in October, 1821. The elder brother, Dr. Burnes, author of a *History of Cutch* and a *Visit to the Court of Scinde*, after meritorious service with the cavalry and infantry, returned to Europe on sick certificate in 1833.

Alexander Burnes, at an age when youths at home were just leaving college, had already advanced a long way on the path of fame.

> "Where souls are born to soar in loftier spheres,
> True valour waits not the advance of years."

After proceeding on a mission to Runjeet Singh, "The Lion of the Punjaub," at Lahore, the unwearied traveller, in January, 1832, commenced his adventurous journey into Central Asia. Among the countries he passed through was Affghanistan, and from Cabool, Burnes wrote to his mother:—

"The people know me by the name of Sekunder, which is the Persian for Alexander, and a magnanimous name it is. I am living with a most amiable man, a Nawab, named Jubbur Khan, brother to the Chief of Cabool."

Of this worthy he relates an anecdote which will be best given in the traveller's own words :—

"I had the pleasure of many sociable evenings with our host the Nawab, whom I found, like many of his countrymen, in search of the philosopher's stone. We heard from him the position of many metallic veins in the country. The good man declared that he must have some of our knowledge in return for what he told so freely. I informed him that I belonged to a sect called Freemasons, and gave some account of the Craft. It was an institution, I said, where, though we did not change the baser metals into gold, we sought to transform the baser and blacker passions of man into philanthropy and charity. He particularly requested that he might be admitted into the fraternity without delay, but as the number of brethren must be equal to that of the Pleiades, I put it off to a convenient opportunity. He confidently believed that he had at last got scent of magic in its purest dye, and had it been in my power I would have willingly initiated him."

On leaving Cabool "Sekunder Burnes" made his way to the City of Bokhara, where he received all possible kindness and hospitality. The story of his travels he sums up in a few striking words :—

"I saw everything, both ancient and modern, to excite the interest and inflame the imagination—Bactria, Trans-Oxiana, Scythia, and Parthia, Kharasm, Khorasan, and Iran. We beheld the scenes of Alexander's wars, of the rude and savage inroads of Jengis and Timour, as well as of the campaigns and revelries of Baber. In the journey to the coast, we marched on the very line of route by which Alexander had pursued Darius, while the voyage to India took us on the track of the Admiral Nearchus."

Burnes arrived in England in November, 1833, and was most cordially received as a true son of Britain who had performed glorious service in the East. His manuscript quickly found a publisher, and it was at once admitted that such a book of travels had not appeared for many a long year. Honours of all kinds were showered upon him. Such attention no lieutenant in any age had ever received before. It was enough to turn the head of any ordinary subaltern, but Alexander Burnes was cast in no ordinary mould, and he survived it.

In February, 1834, the young officer, in the course of an address delivered before St. Peter's Lodge, Montrose, gave some interesting particulars of the state of Freemasonry in the East, and stated that even in the most remote and rude districts of Asia which he had visited, he had traced that Masonry had once existed there, from tradition and the remains of various Masonic symbols which he particularised.

In the following August, at a meeting of the same Lodge, three of his brothers, Dr. James Burnes, K.H., Charles Burnes, of Montrose (afterwards Lieutenant, 17th Bombay Native Infantry), and David Burnes, M.D., of London (who joined the Royal Navy as a Surgeon in 1826, and retired from it in 1835), were enrolled as members, having been entered, passed, and raised in the course of the evening.

An offer of the Secretaryship of Legation, to be followed by the superior appointment of British Minister at the Court of Tcheran, was declined by Alexander Burnes. He laughed at Persia and her politics, exclaiming—" I look far higher, and shall either die or be so." India was his chosen field of action, and thither he returned with a "flaming despatch" from the Court of Directors in his pocket, in June, 1835.

The remaining events in the life of Sir Alexander Burnes (as he shortly after became) are matters of history. The Cabool tragedy of 1841 opened with his brutal murder by the Affghan mob, and this brief sketch of his career will be brought to a close in the words of his best biographer :—

" Carried off in the prime of life.—'only thirty-six years old, so young, yet so much already done for immortality '—so much time remaining, as it appeared to us short-sighted mortals, to maintain and to extend his fame."

Returning to Dr. James Burnes, there is nothing more remarkable in the annals of Masonry, than the absolutely unique position which he attained in the Craft within less than three years from the date of his initiation at Montrose. In 1836 he was appointed Provincial Grand Master for Western India, where, on his return, Scottish Masonry flourished, and English Masonry became quite dormant until the year 1848.

In 1840, Dr. Burnes was for some time in Bengal, and the revival of Masonry in India, which had languished in the leading Presidency ever since the departure of the Earl of Moira—first Marquess of Hastings—in 1823, has always been associated with the visit to Calcutta of the Provincial Grand Master of Bombay.

The addresses of Dr. Burnes to the Calcutta Lodges were of a very eloquent character, and one of them, delivered before the brethren of "Humility with Fortitude" (formerly an Artillery Lodge) in Fort William, is so germane to the scope of the present volume that I shall not scruple to reproduce a portion of it in these pages.

On the Duties of the Masonic Soldier.

"I have ever fancied Masonry as a sort of rosy wreath that might be entwined round the iron pillar of military discipline, imparting a grace and beauty to its form without impairing its integrity or strength; since it is a system utterly abhorrent of oppression and insubordination, encouraging attachment to the officer, and even devotion. should he be a Brother, at the same time that it enhances the self-respect of the soldier by making him feel that in consequence of his moral worth, there is a point at which he and his military superior may be on the level, where the good qualities of both may become prominently known to each, and where neither would obtain a place unless under the tongue of good report, well vouched for and true. Everyone knows that even in the fury of the late war, the charters, diplomas, and insignia of Lodges used to be returned with courtesy after an engagement. It was only last night that Colonel Logan, a brave officer of the Peninsula, mentioned to me an authentic anecdote which will interest you. A whole battalion of the 4th Foot had been taken prisoners and the officers stripped of everything; several of them were bemoaning their lot in a dreary abode, when, to their surprise, they saw a subaltern of their corps passing along with a gay step, in full dress. The explanation was very simple: having been discovered to be a Mason, his uniform and baggage had been immediately restored to him, and he was then going, by special invitation, to dine with the French Field-Marshal. Some of you may have heard of a party of ladies and gentlemen having been taken prisoners in the Bay of Bengal by the French frigate *La Forte*, but who were all afforded the means of escape on the captain discovering that there was the Master of one of the Calcutta Lodges amongst them. From the qualification required in Military Lodges, as well as the character of our Institution, the Masonic badge has become an honourable distinction in the ranks of the Army. On last St. John's Day I had the honour of being supported by Brigadier Valiant, commanding the Garrison of Bombay, and Colonel Griffith, Commandant of the Artillery, two distinguished officers and Masons, who asserted, in the presence of the Military Lodge, 'Orthez' (6th Foot), that Masonic Brethren had invariably been the best conducted soldiers. It is also within my knowledge that the Quarter-Master-General of this Army stated publicly at Agra that during his command of the Bengal European Regiment, no Masonic Brother's name had ever appeared in the defaulter's list. So much, however, for the effect of Masonry on the soldier.

How it has chastened the officer, I need scarcely recount here, since the annals of this city contain a glorious record of its triumph ; and many still glow with enthusiasm at the recollection of the august scene when Francis, Marquess of Hastings, the most chivalrous character of later times, impressed with devotion for the Craft and love for *all* his brethren, descended from his high estate as Governor-General and Commander-in-Chief in India, and within the walls of his own palace offered the right hand of friendship, with his parting benediction, to every soldier, individually, that wore an apron, acknowledging also his pride that Masonic principles had been discovered in the exercise of his authority."

In 1846, Dr. Burnes was appointed Grand Master of Scottish Freemasons in India, and three years later his colleagues on the Medical Board intimated to the Bombay Government their deep regret that ill-health was about to deprive the Army Medical Service of an officer who had been "so long its pride and ornament."

Whether, indeed, the Military is entitled to rank before, or with, but after, the Medical profession, in respect of the influence it has exercised on Freemasonry, is a point on which there will be a difference of opinion, but a combination of the two may be instanced with confidence, as the most favourable condition—certainly in former times— under which the highest distinction in the Craft could be attained.

Burnes and Grant, under whom Masonry so greatly prospered in Bombay and Bengal, were Army Surgeons on the Indian establishment, and of the same military and medical status was Terence Gahagan, a third Provincial Grand Master of earlier date, through whose energy and zeal, after the war in the Carnatic, Masonry was prevented from sinking into a second lethargy on the Coast of Coromandel.

Masonry over the whole of India could not fail to be profoundly affected by the Mutiny of 1857. A few days before the Siege of Lucknow, twenty brethren of the " Morning Star Lodge " celebrated the festival of St. John. At the close of September nine of the party had been killed in action and three lay grievously wounded in the hospital. Captain Bernard M'Cabe, 32nd Foot, who, as one of the "rank and file," had served throughout the Cabool and Sutlej campaigns in the 31st, died sword in hand while leading his fourth sortie.

The meetings of the Lodges were suspended, and the brotherly feeling of the members was enlisted in a new cause. A staff officer records in his *Diary* :—

"May 20, 1857.—Attended a grand meeting of Freemasons, when it was resolved that the services of all the Masons in Calcutta should be placed at the disposal of Government : and everyone pressed forward to show his loyalty by enrolling his name as a Volunteer."

It is curious and noteworthy that amid the general devastation which occurred during the Mutiny, the "Masonic Temples" in the various cantonments were often left totally uninjured. Everything English in Bareilly—people, houses, furniture—was ruthlessly destroyed, all save the house which the military brethren had used as a Freemasons' Lodge. The poor superstitious Sepoys understood that there was something *mysterious* transacted there, and that it might not be safe or lucky to interfere with it in any way. So there it stood in its integrity (on the return of those who fortunately for themselves had left Bareilly before the massacre), alone and unharmed amid the ruins of the English station.

CHAPTER VII.

Like God's own voice, in after years,
Resounds the Warrior's fame,
Whose Soul his hopeless country cheers,
Who is its noblest Name.

—ALBERT PIKE.

According to tradition the first Lodge in France was founded at Paris by the Earl of Derwentwater in 1725; but all that can be reasonably inferred with any approach to certainty is, that prior to 1738 there existed in Paris one, and in the Departments two, regularly constituted Lodges, together with some others more or less irregular, and that the fashion had been set, in the first instance, by refugees at the Court of the Pretender.

The first French military officer of the highest rank who joined the Fraternity was Marshal D'Estrees, "admitted at the expense of ten Louis d'Ors," in 1737. The two next were the Comte de Saxe and the Duc de Richelieu, also Marshals of France.

The first historical Grand Master was Lieutenant-General the Duc d'Antin, elected in 1738; and the second, Louis de Bourbon, Comte de Clermont—an officer of the same military rank—who was chosen to preside over the Grand Lodge of France in 1743.

Four of these brethren commanded French armies in the field. The Comte de Saxe in a series of glorious campaigns, and the other three in the lesser operations of the Seven Years' War. The two Marshals—D'Estrees and Richelieu—won renown at Hastenbach and Closter Seven; but the Comte de Clermont was utterly defeated by another commander of high military and Masonic standing, Ferdinand, Duke of Brunswick, at Creveldt—all these events occurring in 1757.

About this time new rites were multiplying in France

and Germany, and in the so-called "Scots degrees," which sprang up about 1740, we have the first of the legion of additions to Freemasonry on the Continent. Then followed the Chapter of Clermont (1754), the Knights of the East (1756), and the Emperors of the East and West (1758).

Many of the degrees afterwards absorbed within these various rites, originated in the Lodges established by prisoners of war, of which the most industrious and inventive were those working at Berlin in 1757 and at Magdeburg in 1759-61.

There was a great rivalry between the "Knights" and the "Emperors," and to this must be attributed the sorrowful picture of discord presented by the Grand Lodge of France from 1760 until the close of its career.

The Lodge "Montmorenci—Luxembourg," in the Regiment of Hainault Infantry, was the stem or trunk from which the Grand Orient of France budded forth in December, 1773. The Duc de Luxembourg, colonel of the regiment, and "Brigadier des Armees du Roi," was the Master; the wardens, his son and the Prince de Rohan-Guemenee, and among the members—who were all, with one exception, noblemen—may be named the Princes of Conde, Ligne, Tarente, Montbazon, Nassau, and Pignatelli; and the Dukes of Lauzun, Coigny, and Fronsac. Of the first officers of the Grand Orient, the six highest in rank—including the Duc de Chartres, Grand Master—and nearly the whole of the honorary Grand Officers, were members of this Lodge.

The Duc de Chartres—afterwards Duc d'Orleans, and who was guillotined as "Citizen Egalite, in 1793—commanded a division of the French fleet in the action with Keppel off Ushant, in 1778; and though his conduct won the applause of the populace, it is doubtful whether he did not behave with pusillanimity. This prince showed no anxiety to enter upon the duties of his Masonic office, and for several years the Duc de Luxembourg, who assumed the title of "General Administrator," was in all but name the real Grand Master.

In the archives of the Grand Orient are the records (*dossiers*) of about two hundred Regimental Lodges, together with a number of documents formerly belonging to the Lodges established in England (and elsewhere) by French prisoners of war. Others, of course, existed, which are only to be traced in the official lists. Of the older French Army Lodges there were seventy-six, the last on the roll being " Parfait Amitie " in the Royal Italian Infantry, constituted in 1787, of which the first Master was Andre (afterwards Marshal) Massena, adjutant of the regiment. About a third of the number were founded by the Grand Lodge, and the remainder by the Grand Orient, of France. The first on the list, " Parfaite Egalite," in the " Regiment Irlandais de Walshe," has the date of 1688, but was only taken on the roll of the Grand Lodge in 1772. The second, in the " Vivarais Infantry," was established in 1759, and with hardly a doubt must be regarded as the older of the two, and, consequently, the senior Lodge of its class in the monarchy of France.

Some of the regiments to which Lodges were attached served in America during the War of Independence, and among the higher military officers who accompanied them were the Duc de Biron (afterwards Marshal) and the Marquis de Lafayette, both prominent members of the Craft, and each of whom probably saw the light of Masonry in an Army Lodge (French or American) of the Revolution.

No Field Lodges were constituted in 1788 or 1789, and only eight between 1790 and 1801. Forty-three regiments had Lodges attached to them in 1804, of which one only was of earlier date than the Revolution, while no less than thirty-five had been warranted in 1802-4. The year 1804 witnessed the foundation of a new Masonic power in France, in the form of a Supreme Council—of the Ancient and Accepted Scottish Rite, an expansion of the Emperors of the East and West—by the Comte de Grasse-Tilly (son of the Admiral defeated by Lord Rodney), " Captain of Horse." This Rite has now obtained a firm footing in nearly every other country, and for the most part either rivals the grand authority of the Craft, or is only in nominal subjection to it.

When Glogau. in Silesia, was occupied by the French, in 1808, there was a military Lodge at work there, attached to the head-quarters of the 6th Corps of the Grand Army. The Master was General (afterwards Count) Jean Gabriel Marchand, and among the members were Joseph Delom, a distinguished member of the General Staff, and Louis Marcognet, General of Brigade, who subsequently held a high command at Waterloo.

In 1811 the number of Lodges in the French Army had risen to sixty-nine. At this time they were both opened and closed with the cry of " *Vive l'Empereur !* " There is ground for belief that Napoleon himself was a Freemason, and, according to Besuchet, his initiation took place at Malta in 1798.

Further Lodges were established in the two following years, but in 1815 they had all virtually ceased to exist. The Grand Master, Joseph Buonaparte, sailed for America, and the superintendence of the Craft was vested in a military triumvirate, consisting of Marshal Macdonald, and Generals Beurnonville (afterwards Marshal), and the Marquis de Valence.

A few Lodges were established in regiments after the Restoration, but in 1844 "Cirnus," in the 10th Regiment of the Line, the last of the long roll of French Military Lodges, disappeared from the scene. In the following year, the Minister of War—Marshal Soult—in a circular to the colonels of regiments declared " that it was contrary to the rules of the service for any of the military to become members of the Institution." Soult was himself a Freemason, and his diploma (or certificate) found in his tent after the battle of Vittoria, which afterwards fell into the possession of a Scottish Lodge, was returned to him through the British Ambassador in 1851.

Many other Marshals of France of the same (or a slightly later) period were also members and (in most instances) Grand Officers of the Society—for example, Augereau, Bernadotte, Beurnonville, Brune, Kellerman, Lefebvre, Lauriston, Massena, Mortier, Murat, Macdonald, Oudinot, Perignon, Poniatowski, Serrurier, and Sebastiani.

The Viceroy of Italy, Prince Eugene, was likewise of the brotherhood, and so were Generals Dumouriez, the Comte de Segur, Junot, and the Comte de Fernig, together with

Colonel Godefroy Latour D'Auvergne, the "First Grenadier of France."

Marshal Magnan was *appointed* Grand Master of the Grand Orient by the Emperor Louis Napoleon in 1862, and retained the office until his death in 1865. General Mellinet was his successor, but declined re-election in 1870.

Throughout the German Empire, Field or Camp Lodges are regarded as merely auxiliary to the regular or stationary Lodges. The former are in every case erected to serve a temporary purpose, and before a candidate is accepted for initiation, he is required to name one of the latter as the Lodge he will repair to for admission, when the warrant of the movable and transitory body is surrendered or withdrawn. They only exist in time of war, or when an appeal to arms is believed to be impending.

In the last century there were Military (which sometimes became Field) Lodges, one of the earliest of which, "*Parfaite Union*," was founded by French prisoners of war at Magdeburg in 1761. But at a much earlier date, both in North and South Germany, military officers of high rank were enrolled as members of the Society. Francis, Duke of Lorraine, afterwards Emperor of the West, was initiated in 1731, and Frederick, Crown Prince (afterwards King) of Prussia, in 1738. At his father's death the latter founded the "Royal Lodge," of which he was the Master until 1744, and many distinguished princes and soldiers received the light at his hands. The outbreak of war then diverted the attention of the great Frederick to other matters, but during his reign three grand Lodges grew up in Berlin, to all of which he formally extended his protection, and in the earliest of them—Grand National Mother Lodge of the Three Globes—he filled the Grand Master's chair.

Masonry has never really flourished in Austria, although it enjoyed the patronage of the Emperor Francis, a former Duke of Lorraine (p. 36). He died in 1765, and the suppression of the Craft in the Austrian hereditary dominions, which had been decreed but not executed in 1764, was relentlessly carried out (in the absence of his sheltering arm) in 1795. After his death, Francis was commonly referred to by the brethren in Vienna as "Grand

Master of the Old Lodge." This was the "*Trois Canons*" (at first styled the Grand Lodge), of which he became a member (on its formation) in 1742. It afterwards merged, about 1760, into the *Loge Royal Militaire de Vienne*, a title derived from the prevailing element in its composition.

A movable Lodge (*loge volante*) appeared on the scene in 1765. On the death of the Emperor Charles VI. (father of Maria Theresa), the French, Bavarian, and Saxon armies occupied Bohemia, and in November, 1741, Prague was taken by the allies. At the instance of the Commander-in-Chief, Count Rutowski (a natural son of Augustus II. of Poland, and brother of Marshal Saxe), who was Grand Master of Saxony, a military Lodge was formed at Leitmeritz and named "*Sincerite*" which soon after became dormant, but early in the sixties awoke to new life, and we find it working as a *loge volante* at Pilsen, in 1765, and afterwards at Ellbogen and Klattau. In the subsequent war of 1778, a regiment which had been in garrison at Klattau was ordered to Silesia. Among the officers were members of "*Sincerite*," who applied for and received a warrant from Prague, by virtue of which a Lodge, "Joseph of the Three Trophies," was founded, but which ceased to exist after the treaty of peace, when the regiment was sent back to Bohemia. "*La Parfaite Union*," formed at Magdeburg by prisoners of war, has already been referred to. Among the members were officers of Austrian, Hungarian, and Croatian nationality, who, on returning to their native countries, established Lodges there. Of these the first appears to have been the "Lodge of Military Friendship," which was founded at Glina, a small village in Croatia, at some time between 1764 and 1769.

Returning to the dominions of Frederick the Great, a Lodge—"*Minerva*"—was established at Potsdam in 1768, which at first consisted of military officers only. The first "travelling Lodge" was the "Flaming Star," founded in 1770, it being thought desirable "to take the brethren of military rank out of all the Lodges, and to erect a separate Lodge for them, which, in the case of war, might follow the camp, and exemplify the benefits of Masonry in the field." From this time all military candidates were sent to the "Flaming Star" for initiation.

In 1778 there was a concentration of the troops both in Saxony and Silesia, and the military duties of the Master—Captain C. A. Marschall von Bieberstein—taking him in the former direction, he was accompanied by the "Flaming Star," while a branch or "Dispensation" Lodge, under Major von Kleist, proceeded to diffuse Masonic light in the other.

In 1779 the brethren were re-united in a single (stationary) Lodge, which is still in existence at Berlin.

Seven Field Lodges, the most important of which were the "Golden Goblet," "Finger Post," and "Army Lodge No. 1," were formed between 1778 and 1797, and five others during the continuance of the War of Independence, ending at Waterloo. One of the latter was established by Count von Lottom, in furtherance of his desire to found a Lodge "on hearing that General Blucher was to command the Army Corps on the Prussian Coast of the Baltic." This great soldier was a member of "Field Lodge No. 1" in 1812.

Two military Lodges at Frankfort have yet to be referred to. One of these (consisting chiefly of foreigners) was formed by Count Schmettau in 1743, and the other was at work in the Royal Deux Ponts (successively a Swedish, French, and Bavarian) Regiment, about 1760. This *Regiment*, and doubtless the *Lodge*, accompanied the expedition of General Rochambeau to North America in 1780, as the latter was still in existence, and transferred its allegiance to the Grand Orient of France at the termination of the war in 1783.

Five additional Lodges in the Prussian Army were formed in the period ending with 1820, and the two last of the series in 1850 and 1861, but at the present time all the Field or Garrison Lodges which existed at any date in Germany, are either extinct or have long ceased to possess any Military character.

From the time of Frederick the Great, every King of Prussia except Frederick William IV. and the present German Emperor, has been a Freemason. The late Emperor William was admitted into the Craft in 1840, and in 1853 he initiated his son (and successor) Frederick William, in a special Lodge composed of the representatives of the three

Prussian Grand Lodges. Over one of these bodies, the "Grand National Lodge of German Freemasons," the latter presided as Grand Master from 1860 until 1874.

The other Royal Families of what is now the German Empire—and among them were many famous soldiers—have also been firm supporters and protectors of the Craft. The most conspicuous member of the Fraternity in Germany during the latter half of the eighteenth century, was Ferdinand, Duke of Brunswick (p. 130), who saw the rise and fall of the STRICT OBSERVANCE, and except in the earliest years of its existence was the pivot and ruler of its destinies. To his enthusiasm it owed its success—to his calmer judgment and punctilious honour its decay. Of that wonderful perversion of Freemasonry alone, no less than twelve reigning Princes were members in 1774.

A previous Grand Master and the founder of the "Grand National Lodge of German Freemasons" was J. W. von Zinnendorff, one of the most remarkable Masons that ever existed. He was a military surgeon, and the examples are more numerous than in any other walk in life, where brethren of the medical departments of armies have attained the highest distinction as Freemasons. Officers of high military position figure largely as German Grand Masters, and among the "rank and file" of the Craft in the "Fatherland" there have been many victorious commanders. Of the former class, it will be sufficient to refer to Generals Frederick August, Prince of Brunswick, who distinguished himself in the Seven Years' War, and afterwards commanded in Holland; J. H. von Schmidt, who fought with the Turks against the Russians in 1791, and was Chief of the Prussian Artillery in Napoleon's Grand Army of 1812; H. W. von Zerchau, also a veteran of the Russian Campaign; Count Henckel von Donnersmark, who held many important commands, saw much active service, wrote a famous military work, and was the leading "Master" at the reception of Prince (afterwards the Emperor) William, in 1840; K. F. von Selinsky, Aide-de-camp to General York in 1813, and who subsequently performed very gallant services; the O'Etzels, father and son; and (coming to our own times) August von Reinhardt, the present Grand Master of the Grand Lodge of the Sun at Bayreuth.

Of the latter class, the examples that might be given would far transcend the limits of the present work, so I shall content myself with citing the names of G. L. von Blucher, Prince of Wahlstadt and Field Marshal, for many years Master of the Lodge at Wesel, and who, throughout all his numerous campaigns, never wavered in his allegiance to the Society ; and General F. W. Osten Sacken, subsequently a Prince and Field Marshal, who was a most zealous member of the Minerva Lodge, at Leipsic.

General von Scharnhorst, a minor hero, but equally intense patriot, who was also a Freemason, accompanied Blucher as chief of the staff in the war of 1813. It was this officer who, with General Gneisenau, skilfully evaded the provision of the Treaty of Paris (1808), limiting the Prussian Army to 42,000, by training fresh bodies of men in relays.

The archivist of the Grand Lodge of the Three Globes at Berlin, who served throughout the late Franco-German War, informs me that during the armistice of 1871, in Vesoul, he attended a Grand Field Lodge, at which there were present about 180 German officers and military *employes*, and about 300 French officers, military *employés*, and civilians.

Military and Travelling Lodges (*loges militaires et voyageuses*) formerly existed in Holland, Sweden, Russia, and Belgium. The first Dutch Field Lodge was established at Maastrecht in 1745, the twenty-second and last at Alkmaar in 1814. The "Lodge of the Swedish Army" (*Svenska Arméens*) was formed at Greifswald (Pomerania) in 1761. During the continuance of the Seven Years' War the Lodge threw off shoots at Greifswald, Stralsund, and Christianstadt. A pension fund was established for wounded soldiers, and the recipients of its bounty wore silver medals, struck at the expense of the Lodge. Prince Frederick Adolphe, Duke of East Gothland, the King's brother, was its Master at the time of his decease. In 1781 its labours came to an end, and the members joined other Lodges at Stockholm.

The most famous soldier, whose name has been recorded in the annals of Swedish Freemasonry, was Marshal Bernadotte, who, as Crown Prince, was Grand Master until his succession to the throne, when he assumed the superior office of " Vicarius Salamonis," which is always held by the King of Sweden for the time being.

James Keith, after trying his fortune in Spain, entered the Russian service, and was Master of a Lodge either at Moscow or St. Petersburg in 1732. He was present with his brother the Earl Marischal at the Grand Lodge of England in 1740, and, on being recalled to Russia, bore with him a commission as Provincial Grand Master, which was granted by his kinsman, Lord Kintore.

In 1744, having attained the rank of Lieutenant-General, he left Russia, joined the Prussian Army as a Field Marshal, and after displaying the greatest talents and bravery, was killed at the battle of Hochkirchen, in 1758.

In 1761 a Field Lodge was formed in the Russian Army, which at that time had its head-quarters at Marienburg, in West Prussia. A second—afterwards the stationary Lodge of " The Three Towers "—with Major-General von Tscheplin as Master, was established at the same place in 1765. Others were erected at St. Petersburg in 1773 ; and at Kief, one of the ancient Russian capitals, in 1784. A fifth, under the presidency of Colonel von Scheffler, was at work at Gumbernen (East Prussia) in 1814 ; and the latest of all, " George the Victorious," was constituted in France in 1817.

The labours of all the Russian Lodges were suspended in 1794, but ten years later the liberal-minded Alexander, who, with good reason, is supposed to have been a Freemason, let it be understood that he would not interfere with the meetings of the Fraternity. From that time until its final suppression, Masonry flourished greatly in Russia, and the leading officers of the army were enrolled under its banner. Of this there are ample proofs, but the matter is placed in a very clear light by the testimony of Sir Robert Wilson, a distinguished British General and military writer, whose reputation for courage and ability (acquired under the Duke of York, Moore, Abercrombie, Baird, Hutchinson, and Wellington) was still further increased by the Russian and German campaigns of 1812–14, and the Emperor Alexander acknowledged the value of his services by hanging the cross of St. George round his neck in the presence of the army.

During an earlier campaign in Poland, of which Sir Robert wrote a *Sketch*, an incident occurred which is recorded under the date of June 7th, 1807 :—

"While Marshal Ney had been defending Gütstadt, General Platoff passed the Aller, near Bergfried, and surprised an enemy's post ; the French commanding officer saved his life by a sign of Masonry just as the lance was about to pierce him—a *brother* was near, and by an exertion preserved him."

General Platoff, the celebrated Hetman of the Cossacks, is again referred to by the same writer a month later in his *Private Diary* :—

"He told the King that I was not only his adjutant, but his brother ; and that he had no other name for me but ' Boatt Wilson,' which in the Russian language signifies ' brother.' "

What this implied is made very clear in the *Diary* kept by Sir R. Wilson during the subsequent campaigns of 1812–14, where, under the date of " February 16th, 1813, Kladova," we read :—" I was much gratified at finding *Brother* Platoff here.'

On an earlier page the English General writes :— " November 25th, 1812. This morning the Grand Duke Constantine arrived suddenly. He received me with most remarkable proofs of friendship, and with *Masonic* proofs of amicable bonds."

At a very early date Masonry entered the old Kingdom of Poland, where it was mainly fostered and propagated by military officers of rank. The greatest name of all, however, among the Polish Freemasons, is that of the gallant Joseph Poniatowsky, created by Napoleon, on the field of Leipsic, a Marshal of France. This prince lost his life in the river Elster, while covering the retreat of the French army in 1813, and a solemn Funeral Lodge was held in his honour at Warsaw in the following year.

The closing of all the Russian Lodges was summarily decreed by an Imperial Ukase in 1822. The suppression of Polish Freemasonry had been enacted in the previous year, and in either instance there appears to have been ample justification for the action of the Czar.

In 1817, Paul Pestel, with some other officers, organised, under the title of " Union of Salvation," one of the first (really) secret societies, the statutes of which were extracted from those of some Masonic Lodges. This was followed by the "Society of Russian Chevaliers," and the "Union for the Public Welfare." The Russian conspirators then turned to Poland, where, after the suppression of Freemasonry, General Uminsky had founded, in the province of Posen, an association called the "Reapers." By other Freemasons at Warsaw, under the guidance of Major Lukasinsky, there had been formed the "Patriotic Society," to which was also given the name of "National Freemasonry." The true object of these associations was the Independence of Poland.

The death of the Master Architect was the emblem of the dismembering of the Kingdom. His three murderers represented the three monarchies which had co-operated in the spoliation. The brothers of this (counterfeit) Masonry represented those that were sent after the murderers.

The plans of the Russian and Polish conspirators would probably have met with success, but in November, 1825, the Government were informed of the plot, and twelve commanders of regiments in the Southern Army, including Paul Pestel, who was the soul of the whole conspiracy, were arrested.

The association in the North, however, under its chief leader, Conrad Ryleief, a retired sub-lieutenant, was still active, and it was determined to cause a revolt when a new oath was exacted from the army by Nicholas, on the ground that the renunciation by Constantine, his elder brother, was an imposture.

The insurrection of December 26th, 1825, was quelled with a firm hand by the Emperor Nicholas. Paul Pestel and Conrad Ryleief were hanged, and with them expired the secret associations of which they were the chiefs. The "Patriotic Society" of Poland, together with its various off-shoots, shared a similar fate, and the tragic end of Major Lukasinsky was spoken of throughout Europe. Arrested at a meeting of the "Society," he was cruelly tortured, and nothing is known with certainty of his ultimate fate, but some peasants of the country through which the Grand Duke Constantine passed on his retreat from Warsaw, asserted that they had seen, chained to a cannon, and running behind it, a man who was manacled on the hands and feet.

The edict prohibiting the meetings of Lodges is still in force, and the period is yet far distant, in all human probability, when a revival of genuine Freemasonry may be expected to take place in the dominions of the Czar.

Four Field and two Garrison Lodges—all of which have passed out of existence—were established in Belgium, the first in 1832, the last in 1836.

No warrants for Field or Army Lodges have been granted at any time under the jurisdictions of Switzerland, Greece, Denmark, Hamburg, and Darmstadt. In the Austrian dominions Masonry is forbidden, and though the ban does not extend to Hungary, the Craft is viewed with such suspicion by the highest military authorities that few, if any, of the officers of the army (who are Hungarians) care to ruin their chances of professional advancement by applying for initiation.

Many of the national heroes, however, who served in the Revolutionary War, became Freemasons during their subsequent exile—for example, Generals George Klapka and Stephen Türr, both of whom were founders (and the latter the first Master) of Lodge "Mathias Corvinus," established in more peaceful times at Buda-Pesth.

In 1727, two Jacobite refugees, Philip, Duke of Wharton, and James (afterwards Marshal) Keith, were fighting in the Spanish trenches before Gibraltar, and it was by the former brother that the first Lodge in the Peninsula was established at Madrid in 1728. The Duke, after turning many political somersaults, had finally cast in his lot with the Pretender. One evening the Jacobite Peer very nearly threw away his life by advancing close to the walls of Gibraltar, and either daring or threatening the soldiers of the garrison. They asked who he was, and he readily answered "the Duke of Wharton," but though appearing as a rebel in arms, and aggravating that offence by the use of most intemperate language, not a shot was fired at him, and he was permitted to return to the trenches. After the siege the King of Spain appointed him as "Colonel Aggregate" to one of the Irish Regiments, a position which the second of our "Noble Grand Masters" continued to hold (having disdained the offer of a conditional pardon, and subsequently placed himself beyond the pale of forgiveness by the publication of a scandalous libel on the English King) until his death, in 1731.

After this the Craft fell into decay, but a revival took place during the Peninsular War, which, however, was summarily arrested in 1814 by Ferdinand VII., who at one stroke abolished the constitution, and declared the Free-masons to be guilty of treason. Among the brethren imprisoned at the time was General Alava—a member of the sea as well as of the land service—aide-de-camp to the Duke of Wellington, and of whom it is said that he was the only person who was present both at Trafalgar and Waterloo. Other military brethren of later date were General Gomez D'Antrada, Grand Master of Portugal, who, with eleven of his Masonic companions, was put to death at Lisbon in 1817 ; Colonel (afterwards Marshal) Rafael Del Riego, the immortal Spanish patriot, Grand Master of the National Grand Orient, who, in 1823, after three years of glory and honours, was charged with high treason and executed, the populace applauding ; Lieutenant-Colonel Galvez, who was hanged at Barcelona in 1829, for the crime of being a Freemason ; Tomás Zumalacarregui, the modern Cid, the great Basque Captain of the forces of Don Carlos in 1834–36, conqueror successively of the leading Generals of the Christino Armies ; Ramon Cabrera, who, on two occasions, nearly succeeded in securing the triumph of Don Carlos ; and Marshal the Duke of Saldanha, at the head of the Constitutionalists and Freemasons of Portugal after the Peninsular War—whose wisdom in council was only equalled by his valour in the field.

Among the Freemasons of Italy are to be named the unfortunate Admiral Caraccioli, who, during the sanguinary reaction at Naples in 1799, was hanged from the masthead of his own vessel, and his body thrown into the sea ; Generals Schipani, Mantone and Federici, who were also hanged. The Duke de la Torre, who with five other military brethren, was burned alive ; Eugene Beauharnais, Viceroy of Italy, and Grand Master of the Grand Orient "de la Division Militaire" at Milan, in 1805; Joachim Murat, King of Naples, and Grand Master of the National Grand

Orient, in 1809 ; General Ventura, who served in the French army under Napoleon, fought at Waterloo, and made his way through Afghanistan to Lahore, where he became the chief General of Runjeet Singh ; Guiseppe Garibaldi, Liberator of Italy, who was a member of every Lodge in that country, and of many in England, France, and America ; and Timoleo Riboli, for several years Grand Commander of the Supreme Council of Italy, Ex-Surgeon in Chief of the Army of the Vosges, Compatriot and Surgeon of Garibaldi.

Mexico owes her independence to Freemasons. Hidalgo Costilla, a priest, headed the first revolt against the Spaniards, but was captured and shot in 1811 ; Morelos, of Indian blood, *cure* of Caracuaro, assisted in bearing against Spain the flag of the Revolution, and was also executed ; General Xavier Mina, a native of Spain, with a party of volunteers, landed in Mexico and fought for its independence. After the battle of Tamaulipas, where he was defeated and made a prisoner, he was put to death, and his remains, with those of Hidalgo and Morelos, now repose in the " Grande Chapelle Sepulcrale " of Mexico City ; Ignace Comenfort and Benito Juarez, soldiers and Presidents of Mexico ; Generals Mariano Escobedo, and Manuel Gonzales, dignitaries of the Supreme Council ; and General Porfirio Diaz, the most distinguished Mexican commander of his time, who at present combines with the office of President, that of Protector of the Craft in the Republic.

The following military brethren of other countries were also members of the fraternity :—

General Paoli, the celebrated Corsican Patriot, a member successively of the " Nine Muses " (London), the Secret Society and Masonic Club in the Rue Saint Nicaise, at Paris (p. 91), and the " Prince of Wales's Lodge " (London) :

Simon Bolivar, the liberator of South America ; General Paez, President of Venezuela, the most enterprising of all the officers who fought under the republican banners against Spain ; Jose Maria Monson, Roman Catholic Chaplain in the Peruvian Army of Independence, and afterwards a Canon of the Cathedral in Trujillo ; Abd-el-Kader, the heroic Emir of Algeria, initiated in the " Lodge of the Pyramids " at Alexandria, whose life was a practical exemplification of

Masonic obligations and religious duties; General Lopez, the unfortunate Cuban hero, who was garrotted by the Spaniards in 1851 ; and General Garcia, one of the native commanders in the recent struggle between Spain and America for the possession of the " Pearl of the Antilles."

CHAPTER VIII.

*In their ragged regimentals
Stood the old Continentals.*

—" Lyric of the Revolution."

*Under the sod and the dew,
Waiting the judgment day,
Under the rose the blue,
Under the lilies the gray.*

—" Funeral Hymn."

In 1775, Washington was elected commander-in-chief of the American Army, and on the very same day that he received his commission, the battle of Bunker's Hill was fought, in which Major-General Joseph Warren, Grand Master of Massachusetts, lost his life. According to a national biographer. "this was the first grand offering of American Masonry at the altar of liberty, and the ground-floor of her temple was blood-stained at its eastern gate."

General Washington was initiated in the Fredericksburg Lodge, Virginia, in November, 1752, and became a Master Mason in August, 1753. In 1779 he declined the office of Grand Master of Virginia, but accepted that of Master of Alexandria Lodge, No. 22, in his native State, in 1788. As President of the United States he was sworn in—April 30, 1789—on the Bible of St. John's Lodge, New York. In 1793 he laid the corner-stone of the Capitol, and is described in the official proceedings as " Grand Master *pro. tem.*, and Worshipful Master of No. 22, of Virginia." His death occurred in 1799, and he was buried with Masonic honours on December 18th of that year. On the following day the news of his death reached Philadelphia, where Congress was sitting, and a national tribute was paid to his memory on the 26th of December. The Masonic Fraternity were among the chief mourners, and Major-General Henry Lee, a member of Congress and also a "brother," was the orator of the day. The now familiar words, "First in War, First in Peace, and First in the Hearts of his Countrymen," which so justly describe the estimation in which Washington was regarded by the American nation, were used on this occasion by General Lee in his address.

Henry Lee—father of the great Confederate General, Robert E. Lee—who was popularly known as "Light Horse Harry," commanded an independent partisan corps in 1778, and three years later joined the army of General Greene, in whose retreat before Lord Cornwallis, "Lee's Legion" formed the rear-guard.

Ten Lodges in all were at work in the American Army during the Revolution, the earliest of which, "St. John's Regimental" was granted a warrant by the Provincial Grand Lodge of New York, in July, 1775.

"American Union" (p. 142) in the Connecticut Line, though of later date, was the first Lodge organised in the Continental Army, with which it is described as having moved as a pillar of light in parts of Connecticut, New York, and New Jersey. Washington Lodge, in the Massachusetts Line—at whose meetings the Commander-in-Chief was a frequent visitor—was constituted at West Point, in 1779. The first Master was General John Patterson, and the first Wardens Colonels (afterwards Generals) Benjamin Tupper and John Greaton.

Army Lodge, No. 27, in the Maryland Line, received a warrant from Pennsylvania, in 1780. The first Master was General Mordecai Gist, and the Wardens, Colonel (afterwards General) Otho Williams and Major Archibald Anderson.

No records of the American Field Lodges of the Revolution have been preserved, except a portion of the minutes of "American Union," and some returns of the "Washington Lodge." The latter merely inform us that in 1782, two hundred and fifty names had been borne on the roll of the Lodge. The former are of a more interesting character. The principal officers of the army, and the general in command, are frequently named as visitors, and at all the banquets, while the first toast was "Washington" or "Congress," the second was invariably—"Warren, Montgomery, and Wooster," followed by the Dead March.

Dr. Warren (p. 138) was the first man of distinction to lay down his life in the cause of American liberty. Richard Montgomery was of Irish birth, and after serving at Louisburg, Martinique and Havana, entered the American Army as Brigadier-General, and was killed at the attack on Quebec in December, 1775.

The services of David Wooster as a naval and military officer extended over forty years, through four wars, with Spain, with France, with France again, and finally with England. He was mortally wounded, as a Major-General in the American Army, while leading an attack on the British troops in 1777.

There is an abundance of testimony to show that while Commander-in-Chief of the American Army, Washington both countenanced the formation and encouraged the labours of the Army Lodges, that he found frequent opportunities to visit them, and that he thought it no degradation to his dignity to stand there on a level with his brethren.

In December, 1777, the army retired to Valley Forge, and it was there—according to evidence which seems to be of a trustworthy character—that General Lafayette was initiated. The French officer, though he had been received very warmly and kindly by General Washington, experienced much uneasiness from the circumstance that he had never been entrusted with a *separate command*. During the winter he learned that there was a Lodge working in the camp. Time hanging heavily on his hands, and the routine of duty being monotonous, he conceived the idea that he would like to be made a Mason. His wish, on being made known to the Lodge, was soon gratified, the Commander-in-Chief being present and in the chair at the time of his initiation.

"After I was made a Mason," said Lafayette, "General Washington seemed to have received a new light. I never had from that moment any cause to doubt his entire confidence. It was not long before I had a *separate command* of great importance."

On the 27th of December, 1779—the head-quarters of

the Army being then at Morristown, New Jersey— " American Union Lodge" met to celebrate the festival of St. John. At this meeting a committee was appointed from the Lodges in each Line, and the Staff of the Army, to consider the expediency of a General Grand Master being elected to preside over all the Lodges in the Republic. There were present on the occasion thirty-six members of " American Union" and sixty-eight visitors, one of whom was General Washington.

The Masons of the various Lines met three times in convention, and though the name of Washington as Grand Master designate does not appear in their address to the Army, yet it was formally signified to the Masonic governing bodies of America then existing, that he was their choice.

The idea of a General Grand Master or Superintending Grand Lodge has often been revived, but on no occasion, except when it was first mooted by the Army Lodges of the Revolution, with the faintest chance of being carried into effect.

The principal northern forces under Washington were stationed on the banks of the Hudson, near Newburg, during the winter of 1782. So well established, at this time, had the Camp Lodges become, and so beneficial in their influence, that an assembly-room or hall was built, to serve (among other purposes) as a Lodge-room for the Military Lodges. The scheme was entrusted to General Gates to carry into execution, and all the regiments were called upon for their quota of workmen and materials. The building was used for the first time in the early part of 1783, and " American Union" met there in the June of that year, preparatory to celebrating with " Washington Lodge," at West Point, the festival of St. John.

A venerable brother, Captain Hugh Maloy, aged 93, residing at Bethel, in the State of Ohio, was still living in 1844, who had been initiated in 1782 in General Washington's marquee. On that occasion also, the General occupied the Master's chair, and it was at his hands that the candidate received the light of Masonry.

The following Generals of the Continental Army were among the Masonic compeers of the founder and first President of the United States :—

Richard Caswell, who led the troops of North Carolina—of which State he was afterwards governor and Grand Master—under General Gates, and was engaged at the disastrous battle of Camden in 1780.

Mordecai Gist, who fought gallantly for his country from the commencement to the close of the Revolutionary War, was Master of Army Lodge, No. 27 ; president of the convention of Masons from the Military Lines at Morristown, New Jersey ; and, finally, Grand Master of South Carolina.

James Jackson, who served with distinction in the Continental Army, was afterwards Governor and Grand Master of Georgia.

Morgan Lewis, who accompanied General Gates as chief of the staff in the campaign of 1776, and commanded a division in the subsequent war with Great Britain in 1812-15, was Governor of New York in 1804, and Grand Master from 1830 until his death in 1844.

Israel Putman (p. 86) commanded a regiment in the expedition which captured Havana, and was a prominent figure in the war of the Revolution. His tombstone bears the inscription : — " He dared to lead where any dared to follow."

Rufus Putman (p. 144), "the Father of the North-West," was for some time chief engineer of the American Army, and commanded a brigade under General Wayne in 1792. He was made a Mason in " American Union Lodge " in 1779, and elected Grand Master of Ohio in 1808.

John Sullivan, one of the most famous of the Generals of the Revolution, was elected Governor of New Hampshire in 1786, and Grand Master in 1789.

Anthony Wayne, whose popular title was " Mad Anthony," won great renown by his capture of Stony Point (New York), only bayonets being used. He succeeded St. Clair in command of the Western Army, and gained a brilliant victory over the Miami Indians in 1794. A monument to his memory was erected by the Masonic fraternity at Stony Point in 1857.

The Baron de Kalb, mortally wounded at the battle of Camden, was buried with military and Masonic honours by his victorious enemies ; Count Casimir Pulaski, the famous cavalry leader, killed at Charleston in 1779 ; and Benedict Arnold, whose unsurpassed gallantry and devotion during the earlier stages of the war, were, alas, totally obscured by the infamy which characterised his proceedings towards its close.

Commodore James Nicholson (an active member of the fraternity) was placed in 1776 at the head of the list of captains in the Continental Navy, a position which he retained until the close of the war. His brothers, Samuel and John, were also Masons and Naval captains. The former, who served with Paul Jones (p. 112), in the engagement between the *Bon Homme Richard* and *Serapis*, afterwards received the command of the frigate *Deane*, in which he cruised very successfully ; Stephen Decatur was a member of the same Lodge as Commodore James Nicholson, and like the latter a captain in the United States Navy from its first establishment. He commanded the *Delaware* sloop of war, and afterwards the *Philadelphia* ; Commodore Edward Preble, a member of the "Ancient Landmark Lodge" in Portland (Maine), entered the Navy in 1779, and commanded the American Squadron at the bombardment of Tripoli, in 1804 ; and Commodore Whipple, a member of " American Union Lodge " during its early days at Marietta, who burned the *Gaspe* in 1772, one of the most brilliant officers of the land or sea service.

The first field Lodge after the Peace of Versailles (1783), was formed in the " Legion of the United States," commanded by General Anthony Wayne, in 1793, and it is said that nearly all the members were killed in the Indian War. In 1814, some officers of the Northern Army applied to New York for a "marching warrant," which was referred to the grand officers, and later in the same year a Military Lodge was established by the Grand Lodge of Pennsylvania, to be held wherever the Master for the time being should be stationed in the United States.

General Andrew Jackson at various times commanded armies in the field, but is best known in connection with his decisive victory over the British at New Orleans in 1815, which put an end to the war. He subsequently became President of the United States and Grand Master of Tennessee.

General William H. Winder, who commanded on the losing side at Bladensburg, the other eventful battle of the same war (1814), was elected Grand Master of Maryland in 1821.

Generals Stephen Austen, the liberator of Texas, and "Sam" Houston, the recognised hero of the Texan War of Independence, were Freemasons; also Colonel David Crockett, backwoodsman and Member of Congress, who fought on the same side, and after a hard siege surrendered to General Santa Anna, by whose order he was put to death with the other survivors in 1836.

Two or more Lodges accompanied the American Army during the Mexican War. The chief commanders, Generals Winfield Scott and Zachary Taylor, were not members of the Craft, but the latter always entertained a high opinion of the Institution. Shortly after his inauguration as President of the United States, in 1849, he said that many of his personal friends and officers of the army with whom he had been associated were Masons, and that he should have been one himself had circumstances been more favourable to his joining a Lodge, and he added, " I would do so now, but have got to be too old."

William J. Worth served during the last war with England, and was present at the actions of Chrystler's Farm, Chippewa, and Lundy's Lane. In 1842 he commanded the army which defeated the hostile savages in Florida, and subsequently greatly distinguished himself in the leading battles of the Mexican War. A monument was dedicated to his memory by the Grand Lodge of New York in 1857.

John A. Quitman, Grand Master of Mississippi, commanded a division of General Scott's army, and when the city of Mexico was taken, he was made its Governor until peace was proclaimed.

Field Lodges were freely established on both sides during the late Civil War, but the experience of that great conflict was decidedly unfavourable to their utility. The practice was to issue dispensations, and when the regiments in which they were held were mustered out of the service, or the individuals to whom they were granted returned to civil life, the Lodges ceased to exist. More than a hundred of these dispensations were issued during the war, the largest number granted by any single Grand Lodge being thirty-three, which was the case in the State and Masonic jurisdiction of Indiana. There are no Lodges in the standing army of the United States, and for this a sufficient reason will be found in the fact, that the few regiments of the Regular Army are generally—if not invariably—divided into small fractions, separated at widely different posts.

The brethren holding high military rank during the Civil War were very numerous, as may be imagined from the circumstance that "Miner's Lodge," No. 273, Galena (Illinois), consisting of about fifty members, alone supplied five Generals to the Federal Army. Among them were John A. Rawlings (p. 89), Ely S. Parker, a Seneca Indian, and William R. Rowley (all of whom were on the Staff of General Grant), together with John Corson Smith, who served through all the grades from private soldier to general officer, and has since been Lieutenant-Governor and Grand Master of his State.

The following brethren commanded armies in the field :— George B. McClellan ; Winfield Scott Hancock, whose bayonet charge at Williamsburg won from McClellan the compliment, which became proverbial, that "Hancock was superb"; N. P. Banks ; John A. McClernand ; John A. Logan ; George E. Pickett, who led the famous final assault on the Union lines at Gettysburg in 1863 ; Robert E. Patterson ; and Benjamin F. Butler, against whose life a plot was formed by Confederate prisoners, but given up on their learning that he was a Freemason. .

Among the Masonic veterans of the war, General James A. Garfield was, and Major William McKinley now is, the President of the United States. Generals Robert Anderson, of Fort Sumpter fame, and Albert Pike, scholar, orator, poet, and man-of-letters, were also of the Fraternity. The valuable library of the latter at Little Rock, Arkansas, was about to be destroyed by the Federal troops during the war, but General Thomas H. Benton (Grand Master of Iowa), in command of the Union forces, interposed, and, by making the house his head-quarters, not only preserved the library but also the residence.

General Nelson A. Miles now commands the American army, and another General (and Mason), Russell A. Alger, has just vacated the office of Secretary of War.

Dispensations for the formation of Military Lodges were issued by the Grand Lodges of Kentucky and North Dakota during the late war with Spain. Many prominent officers of the army and navy who took part in that short conflict are Freemasons, and among them General William R. Schafter and Admiral Schley, the former of whom commanded the American land forces before Santiago de Cuba, and the latter the squadron which performed such brilliant service off the coast.

More Masonic Books from Cornerstone

Morgan: The Scandal That Shook Freemasonry
by Stephen Dafoe
Foreword by Arturo de Hoyos
6x9 Softcover 484 pages
ISBN 1-934935-54-9

Haunted Chambers: the Lives of Early Women Freemasons
by Karen Kidd
6x9 Softcover 274 pages
ISBN 1-934935-55-7

The Bonseigneur Rituals
Edited by Gerry L. Prinsen
Foreword by Michael R. Poll
8x10 Softcover 2 volumes 574 pages
ISBN 1-934935-34-4

Outline of the Rise and Progress of Freemasonry in Louisiana
by James B. Scot
Introduction by Alain Bernheim
Afterword by Michael R. Poll
8x10 Softcover 180 pages
ISBN 1-934935-31-X

More Light - Masonic Enlightenment Series
Edited by Michael R. Poll
6 x 9 Softcover 194 pages
ISBN 1-934935-36-0

Of George Washington
Edited by Michael R. Poll
6x9 Softcover 146 pages
ISBN 1-934935-46-8

Cornerstone Book Publishers
www.cornerstonepublishers.com

More Masonic Books from Cornerstone

Masonic Enlightenment
The Philosophy, History and Wisdom of Freemasonry
Edited by Michael R. Poll
6 x 9 Softcover 180 pages
ISBN 1-887560-75-0

God's Soldiers: Roman Catholicism and Freemasonry
by Dudley Wright
6 x 9 Softcover 148 pages
ISBN 1-887560-71-8

Masonic Questions and Answers
by Paul M. Bessel
6 x 9 Softcover 144 pages
ISBN 1-887560-59-9

Our Stations and Places - Masonic Officer's Handbook
by Henry G. Meacham
Revised by Michael R. Poll
6 x 9 Softcover 164 pages
ISBN: 1-887560-63-7

Knights & Freemasons: The Birth of Modern Freemasonry
By Albert Pike & Albert Mackey
Edited by Michael R. Poll
Foreword by S. Brent Morris
6 x 9 Softcover 178 pages
ISBN 1-887560-66-1

Robert's Rules of Order: Masonic Edition
Revised by Michael R. Poll
6 x 9 Softcover 212 pages
ISBN 1-887560-07-6

Cornerstone Book Publishers
www.cornerstonepublishers.com

More Masonic Books from Cornerstone

The Freemasons Key
A Study of Masonic Symbolism
Edited by Michael R. Poll
6 x 9 Softcover 244 pages
ISBN: 1-887560-97-1

Éliphas Lévi and the Kabbalah
by Robert L. Uzzel
6 x 9 Softcover 208 pages
ISBN: 1-887560-76-9

The Teachings of Freemasonry
by H.L. Haywood
Edited by Michael R. Poll
6x9 Softcover 144 pages
ISBN 1-887560-92-0

A.E. Waite: Words From a Masonic Mystic
Edited by Michael R. Poll
Foreword by Joseph Fort Newton
6 x 9 Softcover 168 pages
ISBN: 1-887560-73-4

Freemasons and Rosicrucians - the Enlightened
by Manly P. Hall
Edited by Michael R. Poll
6 x 9 Softcover 152 pages
ISBN: 1-887560-58-0

Masonic Words and Phrases
Edited by Michael R. Poll
6 x 9 Softcover 116 pages
ISBN: 1-887560-11-4

Cornerstone Book Publishers
www.cornerstonepublishers.com

More Masonic Books from Cornerstone

The History of the Shrine for North America
by William B. Melish
6 x 9 Softcover 288 pages
ISBN 1-934935-59-X

The Grand Orient of Louisiana
A Short History and Catechism of a Lost French Rite Masonic Body
Introduction by Michael R. Poll
Softcover 52 pages
ISBN 1-934935-23-9

Lectures of the Ancient and Primitive Rite of Freemasonry
by John Yarker
6x9 Softcover 218 pages
ISBN 1-934935-10-7

The Schism Between the Scotch & York Rites
by Charles Laffon de Ladébat
6x9 Softcover 66 pages
ISBN 1-934935-33-6

The Ceremony of Initiation
by W.L. Wilmshurst
6x9 Softcover 74 pages
ISBN 1-934935-02-6

The Secret Tradition in Freemasonry
by A. E. Waite
2 volumes 6x9 Softcover 926 pages
ISBN 1-934935-13-1

Cornerstone Book Publishers
www.cornerstonepublishers.com

Made in the USA
San Bernardino, CA
14 December 2014